S0-ANR-662

Parallel Programming in ANSI Standard Ada®

George W. Cherry

Thought**Tools
and
George Washington University

Reston Publishing Company, Inc.
A Prentice-Hall Company
Reston, Virginia

Library of Congress Cataloging in Publication Data

Cherry, George William
Parallel programming in ANSI standard Ada.

Includes index.
1. Parallel programming (Computer science) 2. Ada (Computer program language) I. Title. II. Title: Parallel programming in A.N.S.I. standard Ada.
QA76.6.C444 1984 001.64'2 83-26927
ISBN 0-8359-5434-X

George W. Cherry
703-437-4450
P.O. Box 2037
Reston, Virginia 22090

10 9 8 7 6 5 4 3 2 1

Printed in the United States of America

Contents

Preface

WHAT THIS BOOK IS ABOUT

This book is about parallel programming; its notation is ANSI standard Ada. I wrote it with nearly equal interest in parallel programming and Ada. If you're interested in either topic, you'll find this book a useful tool.

WHY A BOOK ON PARALLEL PROGRAMMING WITH ADA?

The two introductory textbooks on Ada that I admire most devote 39 and 54 pages, respectively, to parallel programming (multitasking). Considering the intellectual novelty and challenge of parallel concepts, I believe the topic deserves more detailed and deliberate treatment.

Another reason is that multicomputers and multiprocessors are fully within the state of the art of fourth generation hardware. Ada--a fourth generation high-order language--allows the harnessing of tens--even hundreds--of MIPS (millions of instructions per second) of parallel processing power. Coupled to the appropriate multiprocessing architectures (for example, the iAPX-432) Ada supports software-transparent performance extensibility and failure tolerance. (Another example: the August 1983 issue of the Communications of the ACM reports that MIT is developing multiprocessing computers. One of these will include thirty-two Motorola MC68000 microprocessor chips. Yet another example: the Hewlett-Packard HP 9000 can be purchased with one, two, or three central processing units.) Ada gives us a superior cognitive tool, communication vehicle, and control code for harnessing these exciting and promising architectures.

A final reason is that certain problems (for example, problems with "structure clash") are most easily and elegantly solved by parallel communicating processes (tasks). For these problems, sequential solutions are actually harder to develop and understand than parallel solutions. Therefore, we should employ parallel programming for these problems even when our program will execute on a uniprocessor computer. Furthermore, parallel solutions frequently outperform sequential solutions even on uniprocessors.

THE EMPHASIS OF THIS BOOK

In the preceding section, I did not mention the advantages of Ada for real-time programs, operating systems, process control, and other concurrent applications. My omission of these areas from this book is because it deals with parallel programs, not asynchronous, concurrent programs. I don't, for example, treat low-level IO, interrupt handling, or resource sharing (except in passing). I do treat parallel sorting, searching, root-finding, process pipelining, object (data) flow graphs, exception handling, and so on. Understanding the concepts in this book is a prerequisite for programming real-time systems, writing operating systems, or writing process control programs; but the concepts in this book are also useful in other application domains which have previously been dominated by sequential solutions.

TASK IDIOMS

The teaching of Ada tasking requires special care. The Ada task is a mechanism that can do many things. As the goto is to control structures, as the pointer is to data types, the task is to program units. The goto is awful in the hands of people who don't use it in a few carefully defined idiomatic ways. Used in well-defined idiomatic ways, the goto is certainly capable (though awkwardly) of expressing structured programs.

Tasks can be used to express many programming idioms: pure processes, monitors, buffers, messengers, semaphores, interface units, coroutines, and others (useful or bizarre) that programmers will no doubt invent. The semantics of Ada tasking is very flexible--like the semantics of the goto. Therefore, we must take care to teach much more than just the syntax and semantics of Ada tasking. We must teach the useful idioms that can be expressed by Ada tasks. These idioms will be useful, even if we don't have an Ada compiler and merely wish to employ Ada as a program or process design language (PDL).

This book proposes a disciplined way to think about and use tasks. The discipline is to think of tasks in certain idioms. The most important idiom of all is the process. Indeed, Ada's ability to support the concept of process abstraction is every bit as important as its ability to support the far less intuitive concept of data abstraction. (The Ada literature gives much more emphasis to data abstraction. I have no idea why.)

PROGRAMMING STYLE

I deplore the typographical style used in so many of our Ada textbooks. I refer to the style of using uppercase letters for all the letters of predefined identifiers and user-defined identifiers. Not since the first-grade of elementary school have most of us had to read such text. This style also wastes the distinctions that uppercase/lowercase can telegraph to the reader. To distinguish types from objects typographically, I use uppercase letters for the initial letters of types, sometimes also for the embedded letters starting new words in types. Without resorting to artificially different spellings, this style can distinguish types from objects (by using uppercase letters in the former and underlines in the latter). I also distinguish packages and tasks from subprograms by employing uppercase letters for the initial letters of the former. I use lowercase letters everywhere else. (Does anyone today have a terminal or printer that can't display lowercase letters?)

Composing programs offers us the choice between clarity of intention and efficiency of computation (or at least presumed efficiency of computation). Where I have faced such choices I have endeavored to choose clarity over efficiency.

ACKNOWLEDGMENTS

I owe a large debt of gratitude to the more than a thousand participants in my Ada seminars who performed the valuable service of constructive walkthroughs of my case studies and example programs. This kind of experience does more than any other I can think of to improve the quality of a program which an author already believes is nearly perfect.

Especially, I want to thank BDM, CACI, General Electric, Hazeltine, IBM, Motorola, the National Security Agency, the Naval Underwater Systems Center, the Planning Research Corporation, RCA, Rockwell International, and Westinghouse for opportunities to present many of these concepts in in-plant seminars, and to the Washington Chapter of the Association for Computing Machinery, the U.S. Professional Development Institute, The Institute for Advanced Professional Studies, and Intermetrics for opportunities to present some of these concepts in public seminars.

I warmly acknowledge my gratitude to Dr. Duane W. Small, Division Scientist of SAI Comsystems, Donald R. Clarson of Teledyne-Brown Engineering, and Helmut E. Thiess of the Navy Regional Data Automation Center, Washington and Chairman of the Professional Development Committee of the Washington DC chapter of the Association for Computing Machinery for their careful reviews and numerous heeded suggestions for improvements of early versions of this text.

And, finally, I want to express my appreciation to my wife and editor, Ellen R. Cherry, who gave me freedom, consultation and guidance on this project as often as I needed them.

INVITATION

I welcome all observations concerning the concepts, algorithms, and programming style in this book.

George W. Cherry

703-437-4450
P.O. Box 2037
Reston, VA 22090

Also by George W. Cherry, published by Reston Publishing Company:

Pascal Programming Structures: An Introduction to Systematic Programming

Pascal Programming Structures for Motorola Microprocessors

(with David E. Cortesi)
Personal Pascal: Compiled Pascal for the IBM Personal Computer

Chapter 1
Introduction to Petri Net Graphs

Carl Adam Petri, a German scientist, developed "special nets" (which we call Petri nets) in the early 1960s to study and model communicating parallel automata. Petri nets have a mathematical side and a graphical, intuitive side. We use the graphical, intuitive side to clarify the abstract concepts of parallel programming.

PLACES AND TRANSITIONS

A Petri net is a directed graph containing two kinds of nodes, place nodes and transition nodes. (See Figure 1.1.) We represent places (place nodes) by means of circles. We represent transitions (transition nodes) by means of bars, small black boxes, or sometimes rectangles with statements in them. How many places are there in Figure 1.1? How many transitions are there in Figure 1.1? (The correct answers are 5 places and 4 transitions.)

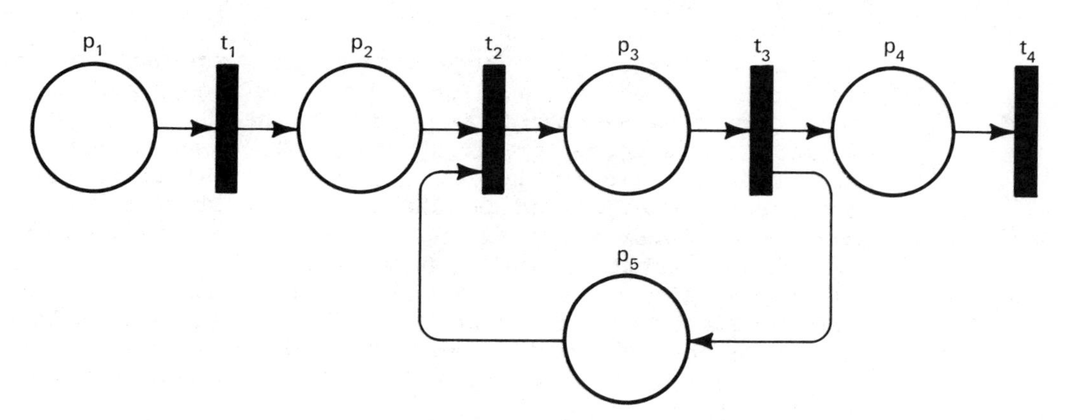

Figure 1.1. A Petri net graph

INPUT PLACES AND OUTPUT PLACES

Directed arcs connect places to transitions and transitions to places, but places cannot be connected directly to places and transitions cannot be connected directly to transitions. As we said, the Petri net in Figure 1.1 has 5 places and 4 transitions. How many directed arcs does it contain? (The correct answer is 9 directed arcs.) Note the alternation of places and transitions on any path through the net.

In general, a transition has input places and output places. A place is an input place of a transition when that place has an arc directed at the transition. For example, place p_5 is one of the input places of transition t_2. In case you haven't already guessed, a place is an output place of a transition when the transition has an arc directed at the place. For example, place p_5 is one of the output places of transition t_3. What are the input places of all of the transitions in Figure 1.1? (The input places of the four transitions in Figure 1.1 are $I(t_1) = \{p_1\}$; $I(t_2) = \{p_2, p_5\}$; $I(t_3) = \{p_3\}$; $I(t_4) = \{p_4\}$.) What are the output places of all of the transitions in Figure 1.1? (The output places of the four transitions in Figure 1.1 are $O(t_1) = \{p_2\}$; $O(t_2) = \{p_3\}$; $O(t_3) = \{p_4, p_5\}$; $O(t_4) = \{ \}$.) Note that the input places and output places of a transition are sets of places. These sets may have zero, one, or more places in them. For example, the output set of t_4 has zero places in it (so it is the empty set, $\{ \}$); the output set of t_2 has one place in it, $\{p_3\}$; and the output set of t_3 has two places in it, $\{p_4, p_5\}$.

MARKING AND EXECUTING A PETRI NET

We can mark a Petri net by placing tokens, represented by small dots, in the net's place nodes. (See Figure 1.2.) In fact, think of places as containers for tokens.

A Petri net executes by firing its enabled transitions. A transition is enabled when every one of its input places contains at least one token. Therefore, the structure and marking of a Petri net determines its execution. In general, firing a transition changes the marking of the Petri net, that is, changes the distribution and number of tokens in its places. The firing of a transition changes the marking by this rule: take one token from each of the enabled transition's input places; deposit one token in each of the transition's output places.

Consider Figure 1.2, which is a marked version of Figure 1.1. Which transitions are enabled in Figure 1.2? (Only t_1 is enabled; t_2 is not enabled because p_2 contains no token.)

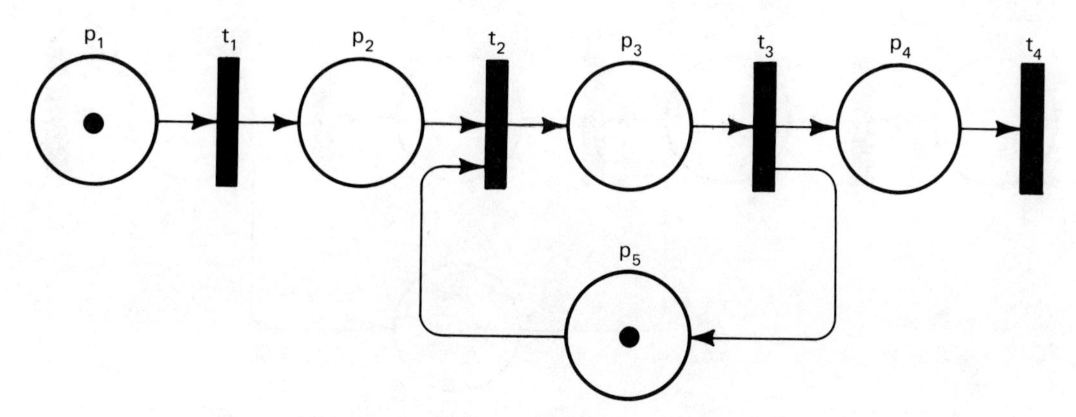

Figure 1.2. A marked Petri net graph

Now assume that enabled transition t_1 in Figure 1.2 fires. What is the new marking that results from this firing? (The new marking has tokens in p_2 and p_5; all other places are empty.) This marking is illustrated in Figure 1.3.

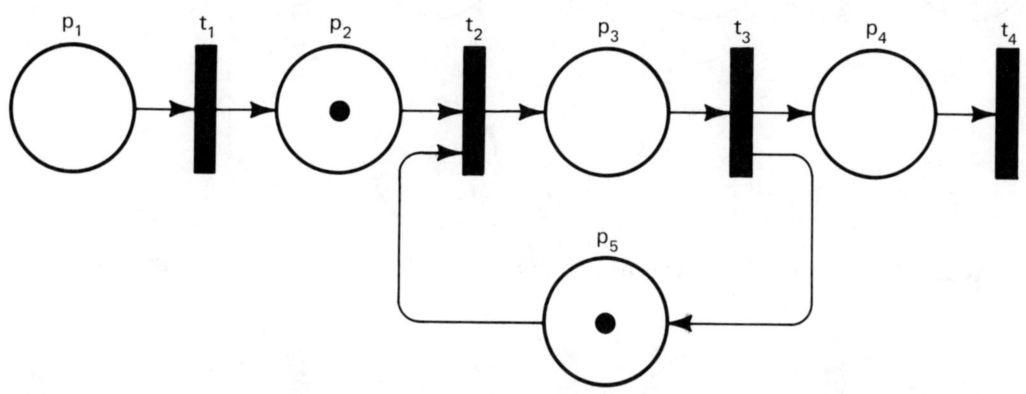

Figure 1.3. A marked Petri net graph (result of firing t_1 in Figure 1.2)

Which transitions are enabled in Figure 1.3? (t_2) Assume that t_2 in Figure 1.3 fires. What is the new marking? (The new marking has a token in place p_3; all other places are empty.) This marking is illustrated in Figure 1.4.

Which transitions are enabled in Figure 1.4? (t_3) Now assume that enabled transition t_3 in Figure 1.4 fires. What is the new marking? (The new marking has tokens in places p_4 and p_5; all other places are empty.) This marking is illustrated in Figure 1.5. In Figure 1.5 only t_4 is enabled. The firing of t_4 removes the token in p_4, resulting in the marking shown in Figure 1.6.

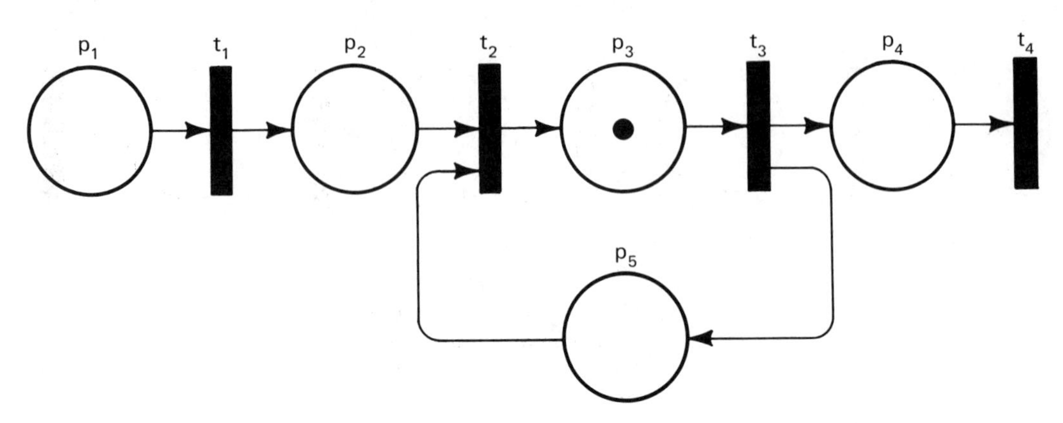

Figure 1.4. A marked Petri net graph (result of firing t_2 in Figure 1.3)

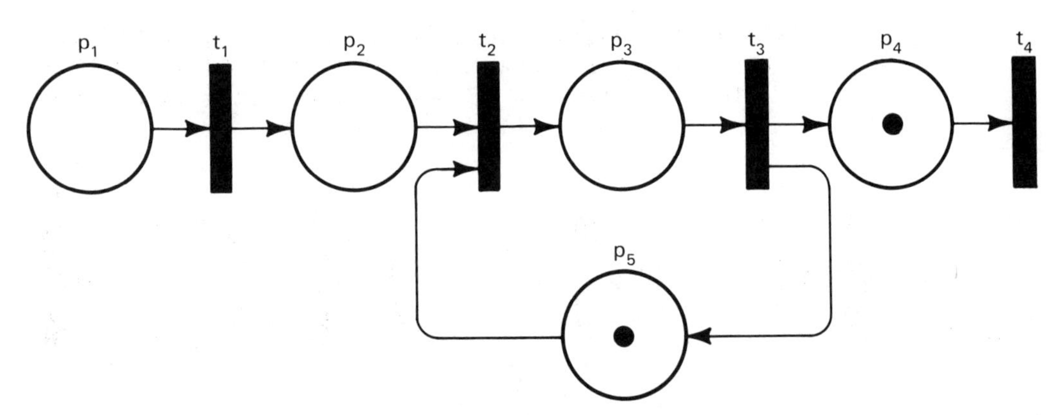

Figure 1.5. A marked Petri net graph (result of firing t_3 in Figure 1.4)

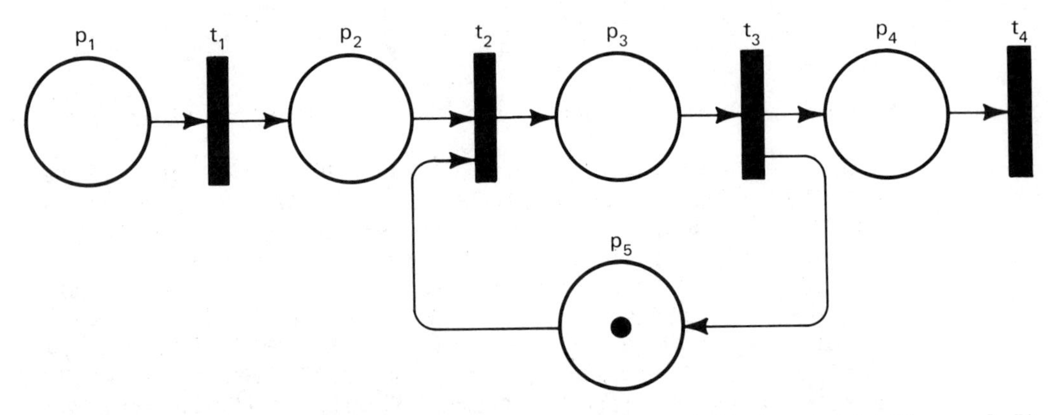

Figure 1.6. A marked Petri net graph (result of firing t_4 in Figure 1.5)

MODELLING COMPUTER PROGRAMS WITH PETRI NETS

We can easily model computer programs with Petri nets. We can represent sequences of statements (actions) by transitions, the points between actions by places, and the value of a program counter by the location of a Petri net token. Thus, the movement of the token from p_1 to p_2 to p_3 to p_4 in Figures 1.2, 1.3, 1.4, and 1.5 represents the sequence of values of the program counter controlling the order of execution of statements t_1 through t_4. Place p_5 represents some condition or resource required for the execution of t_2. The presence of a token in p_5 represents the truth of the condition or the availability of the resource. (Note that the execution of t_3 restores the token to p_5.)

We introduced Petri nets in order to model (later) parallel programs; but we should assure ourselves that we can model sequential programs. Any sequential program can be represented by a sequence of structured statements of the following kinds:

a sequence of statements,

a conditional statement, and

a loop statement.

Figure 1.7 shows how to translate the flowchart representations of these structured statements into corresponding Petri net representations. Particularly note the Petri net representation of the conditional, which has one thread of control entering the construct and, of course, one thread of control leaving the construct. The input place has two labeled output arcs, one going to the then statement and one going to the else statement. We have not seen this configuration before. We postulate a "conditional statement agent" which evaluates the Boolean condition and forces the correct statement to fire.

Consider the following Ada code for dividing the positive number x by the positive number y, yielding both the integer quotient q and the remainder r.

```
q := 0; r := x;
while r >= y
loop
  q := q + 1; r := r - y;
end loop;
```

See Figure 1.8 for a flowchart of this code; see Figure 1.9 for its Petri net graph.

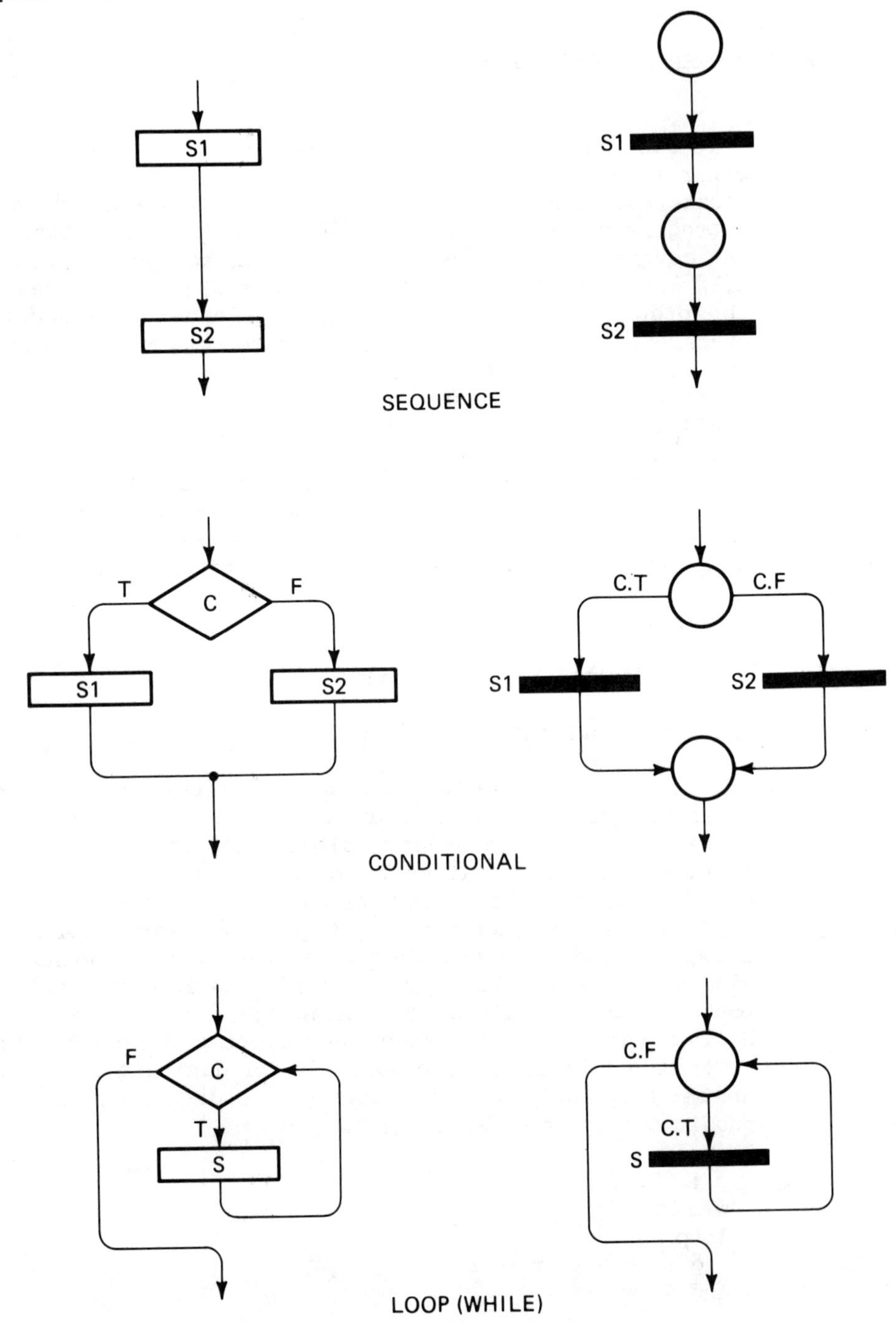

Figure 1.7. Modelling structured elements with flowcharts and Petri nets

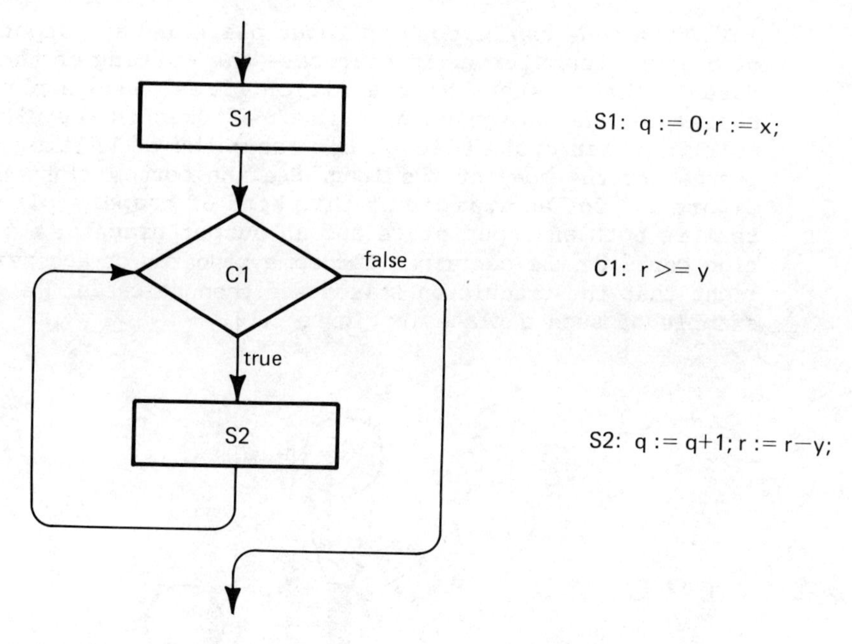

Figure 1.8. Flowchart for division by repeated subtraction

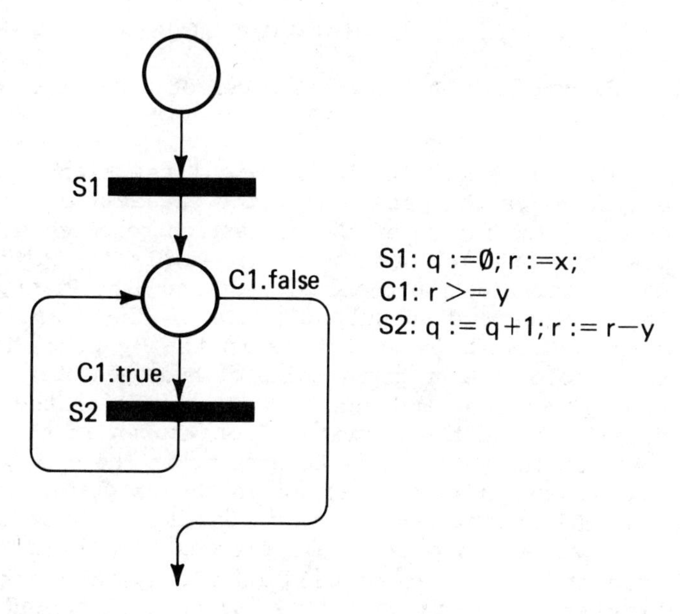

Figure 1.9. Petri net for division by repeated subtraction

A place node can be both an input place and an output place of a given transition. In that case the marking of the place doesn't change when the transition fires. Such a place may represent the beginning of a loop: a token in the place enables another cycle through the loop; the transition itself represents the body of the loop. See the bottom right half of Figure 1.7 for an example of this kind of graph. A place node that is both an input place and an output place of a transition could be the container for some resource or accessibility right that the transition seizes and then releases. We give an example of such a place in Figure 1.10.

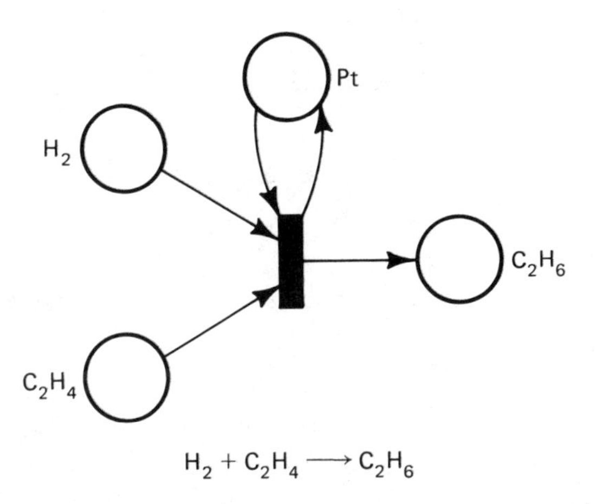

Figure 1.10. A Petri net model of a chemical reaction

Figure 1.10 models the chemical reaction of hydrogen and ethylene (in the presence of the catalyst platinum) to form ethane. The firing of the transition requires the presence of platinum (a token must be in the Pt place); but this token is not consumed by the chemical reaction--the Pt place is both an input place and an output place of the transition. If we start out with three tokens in the H_2 place (representing three molecules or three moles of hydrogen gas), two tokens in the C_2H_4 place, and one or more tokens in the Pt place, we finally reach the marking of one token in the H_2 place, no token in the C_2H_4 place, two tokens in the C_2H_6 place, and, of course, the original token(s) in the Pt place.

At this point I urge you to obtain a set of tokens (about one dozen dried peas, small buttons, small pills, or markers from children's games will do nicely) and make a habit of simulating the execution of our Petri nets and any nets you may draw. Your efforts will do wonders for your understanding.

This Ada code simulates the Petri net in Figure 1.10. It assumes that we start out with some platinum, three moles of hydrogen, two moles of ethylene, and zero moles of ethane.

```
platinum := 1;
hydrogen := 3;
ethylene := 2;
ethane   := 0;
while hydrogen > 0 and ethylene > 0 and platinum > 0
loop
  hydrogen := hydrogen - 1;  -- \
  ethylene := ethylene - 1;  --  > the transition
  ethane   := ethane + 1;    -- /
end loop;
```

What are the final values of the variables after execution of this code (or the corresponding Petri net in figure 1.10)? The answer is the same as the example given a few paragraphs earlier: platinum = 1; hydrogen = 1; ethylene = 0; ethane = 2. The first four assignment statements in the Ada code are isomorphic to the initial marking of the Petri net; the while loop is isomorphic to the structure of the Petri net. Note that the Petri net continues to execute as long as it has an enabled transition. The truth of the condition in the while iteration rule corresponds exactly to the presence of at least one token in each of the three input places to the Petri net's single transition.

MULTIGRAPHS

Petri nets are multigraphs, a feature we have ignored until now. It simply means that Petri nets allow multiple arcs between the two kinds of nodes. Incorporating the multigraph feature requires us to modify slightly the firing rule for transitions: A transition is enabled when each one of its input places contains at least one token for each arc from that place to the transition. The firing of a transition changes the marking by this rule: remove from each of the transition's input places one token for each arc from that input place to the transition (these are called the enabling tokens); deposit into each of the transition's output places one token for each arc from the transition to the given output place. Figures 1.11 and 1.12 give examples of multigraphs.

The example in Figure 1.11 models the reaction of sodium with water to form the chemical products sodium hydroxide and hydrogen. For this reaction to occur, there must be at least two molecules of sodium and two molecules of water. The Ada code for the reaction is shown preceding the figure.

```
while sodium >= 2 and water >= 2
loop
  sodium := sodium - 2;
  water  := water  - 2;
  sodium_hydroxide := sodium_hydroxide + 2;
  hydrogen_gas     := hydrogen_gas + 1;
end loop;
```

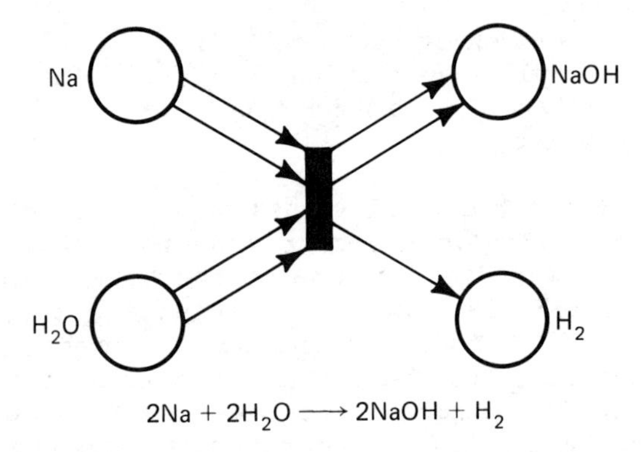

Figure 1.11. A Petri net multigraph

Drawing many arcs (say three or more) between two nodes would be messy. When there are a large number of arcs directed from one node to another we can adopt the labelled bundle notation illustrated in Figure 1.12. The labels give the number of arcs in each bundle. There must be at least 17 parts of oxygen and two parts of gasoline for the transition (reaction) to fire.

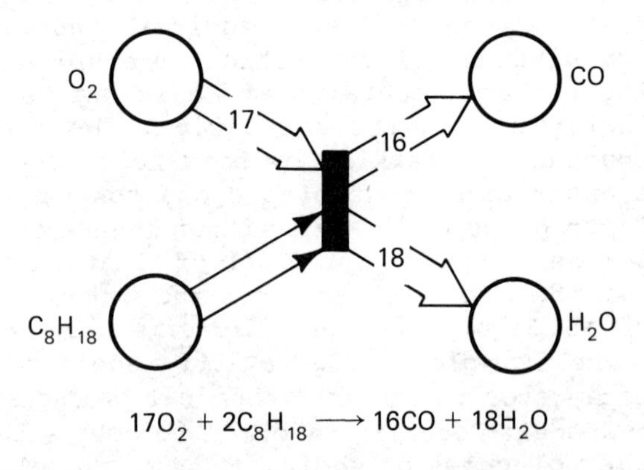

Figure 1.12. A Petri net illustrating bundles of arcs

A USEFUL EXTENSION TO PETRI NETS

So far we have described classical Petri nets. We now extend our classical Petri nets with a mechanism for "zero testing" a place: this mechanism is the <u>inhibitor arc</u>. An inhibitor arc from a place p_j to a transition t_k terminates with a small circle (borrowed from the "not" of switching theory) rather than an arrowhead. See Figure 1.13, where transition t_k has a normal input from p_i and an inhibitor input from p_j. For t_k to fire there must be at least one token in p_i and zero tokens in p_j. Thus, the transition t_k "tests" place p_j for zero. The general rule for firing becomes: A transition is enabled when every one of its normal input places contains at least as many tokens as the number of arcs from the place to the transition and every one of its inhibitor input places is empty. As before, the firing of a transition removes the enabling tokens from each of the transition's normal input places and deposits into the transition's output places one token for each arc from the transition to the given output place.

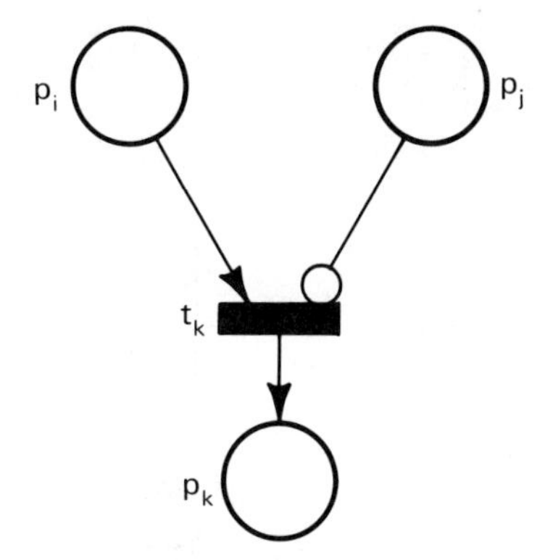

Figure 1.13. The inhibitor arc extension

The Petri net in Figure 1.14 uses an inhibitor arc to grant priority to one set of requests over another set of requests. The problem to be solved is this: Suppose that there is one group of processes that periodically request the execution of t1 and another group of processes that periodically request the execution of t2. Suppose, furthermore, that all requests (for t1 or t2) should be honored in a strictly mutually exclusive fashion. The requirement for strict mutual exclusion may be due to both t1's and t2's execution depending on the same resource, shared channel, or shared variable. Suppose, finally, that the processes that request the execution of t1 should be given priority (with respect to executing this particular request) over the processes that request the execution of t2.

The Petri net in Figure 1.14 implements these specifications. The place pc (initialized with one token) enforces mutual exclusion in responding to all requests: as soon as the system accepts a request (for t1 or t2), the token in pc is removed from that place, not to be returned until the completion of the request. This guarantees the required mutual exclusion.

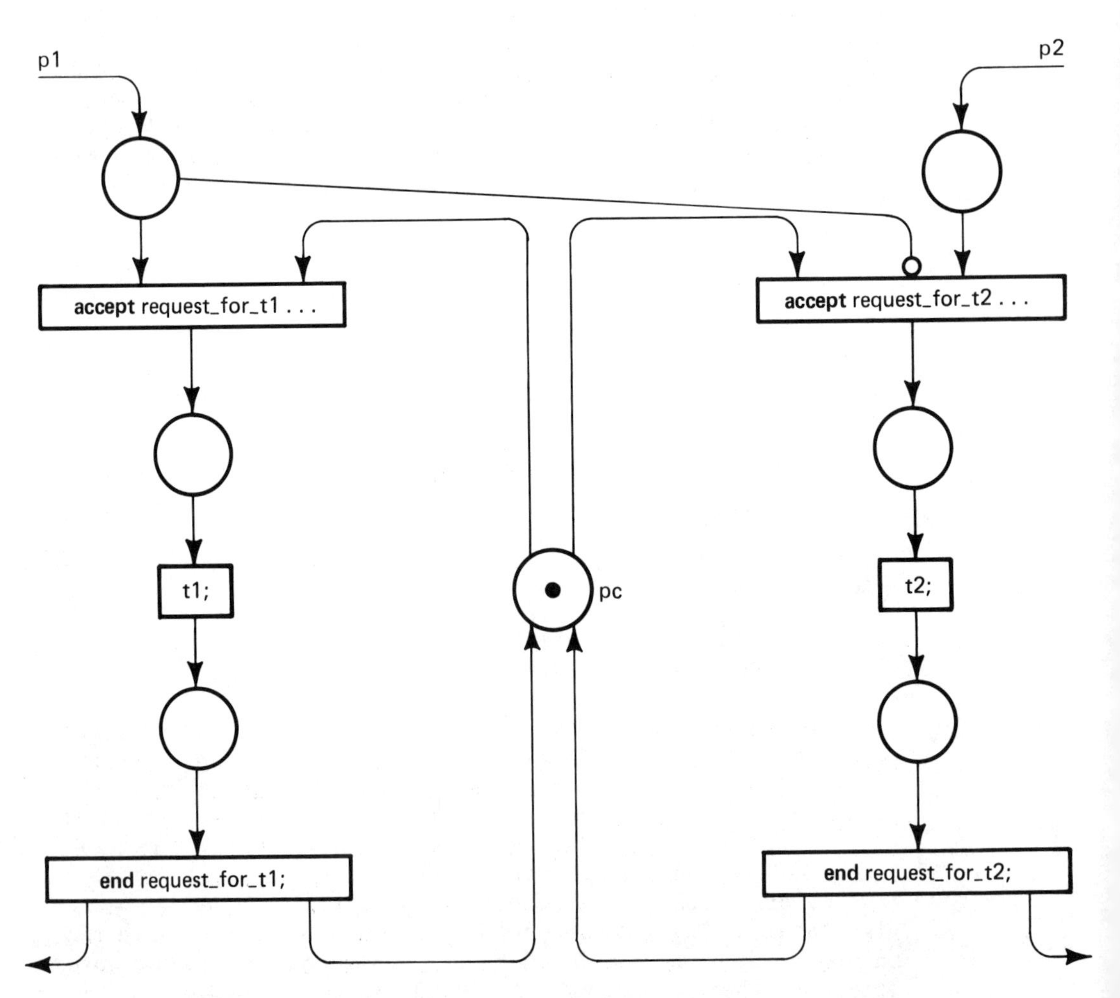

Figure 1.14. Using the inhibitor arc to grant priority

The processes that desire the execution of t1 make known their requests by placing a token in p1. The system signals the completion of servicing a request by returning a token to the served task. This returned token is transmitted on the second arc issuing from "**end** request_for_t1."

The mechanism for processes desiring the execution of t2 is similar: these processes make known their requests by placing a token in p2. However, the system will never accept a request for t2 while a request for t1 is waiting--because of the inhibitor arc from p1 to "**accept** request_for_t2."

Using Ada, we can implement Figure 1.14 with the select statement. Although I have not laid the groundwork for your thorough understanding of this statement, I want to take this opportunity to illustrate the isomorphism between Figure 1.14 and Ada's select statement. (The select statement is syntactically similar to Ada's case statement--especially in respect to the syntax of the when clause.) The when clause in the following code preconditions the possibility of the select statement's accepting a "request_for_t2." The condition in the when clause is true when the attribute count'request_for_t1 equals zero; this is equivalent to testing place p1 for zero in the Petri net. The attribute count'request_for_t1 gives the number of calls of request_for_t1 that have been issued but not yet discharged.

```
loop
  select
    accept request_for_t1 do
      t1;                                 -- execute t1
    end request_for_t1;
  or
    when count'request_for_t1 = 0 =>   -- zero test for p1
    accept request_for_t2 do
      t2;                                 -- execute t2
    end request_for_t2;
  end select;
end loop;
```

The key concept in Figure 1.14 is that place p1 contains a token for every undischarged call of request_for_t1. In the Ada scheme for process communication, place p1 represents a queue for processes waiting for acceptance of request_for_t1; similarly, place p2 represents a queue for processes waiting for acceptance of request_for_t2. The inhibitor arc from p1 to the transition "**accept** request_for_t2" gives all the requests for t1 priority over all the requests for t2.

Finally, I hope the syntax of the Petri net and the syntax of the select statement suggest to you that executions of t1 and t2 are carried out in strict mutual exclusion.

CONCURRENCY IN PETRI NETS

At last we come to our main reason for introducing Petri nets. In our programs so far, we have moved a single token around a Petri net to designate the next point of execution of the program. This corresponds to the single thread of control in a sequential program. But we want to build programs with potentially many threads of control, because we may have multiple processors or we may want to structure our programs with conceptually parallel activities.

It's odd that many programmers regard concurrent programming as exotic. Many if not most human projects are conducted concurrently. To get projects done fast enough and to use all the resources at our disposal, we usually schedule activities concurrently. Of course, a single processor cannot execute two tasks at exactly the same time. But a single processor can be time-shared among many tasks. And multiple processors (like the many human members of a project team) can indeed execute multiple tasks concurrently.

We do not have to introduce any new Petri net mechanisms to represent concurrent activities. The mechanisms we've already introduced will do the job. To spawn new paths of control, we shall use the fork (or cobegin), shown in Figure 1.15 (a). Be sure to distinguish the fork (cobegin) from the binary conditional, illustrated in Figure 1.15 (b). It is a consequence of the Petri net execution rules that a binary fork spawns two threads of control; on the other hand, the binary conditional selects only one thread of control.

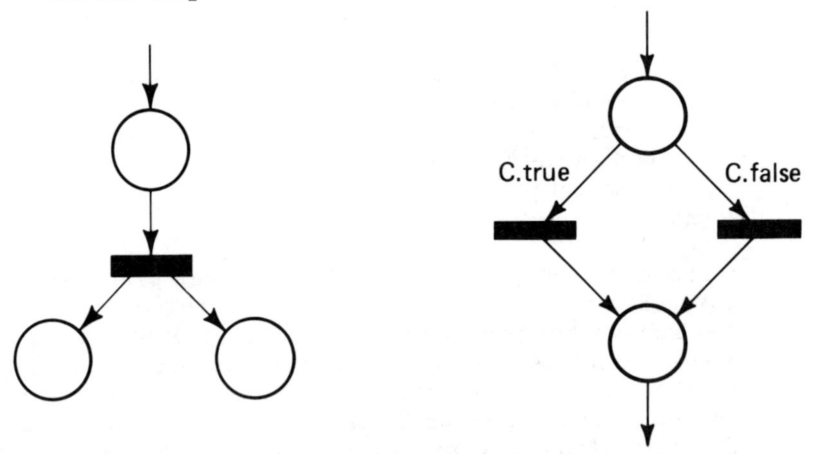

(a) FORK (one path in, two paths out)   (b) CONDITIONAL (one path in, one path out)

Figure 1.15. The binary fork (cobegin) and binary conditional contrasted

Figure 1.16 uses the cobegin (fork) to illustrate precedence and parallelism on a project. As soon as the project starts, the (co)begin starts two teams working in parallel, one team executing task t_1, the other team executing task t_2. As soon as the team working on t_1 finishes its task, there is another cobegin and two teams can tackle t_3 and t_4 in parallel. Thus, t_2, t_3, and t_4 may be undergoing execution concurrently. The project cannot begin t_5 until the teams working on t_3 and t_4 have finished these tasks. (Task t_5 could be the integration and testing of two software components built in development tasks t_3 and t_4.) Note that the firing of t_5 constitutes a coend (or join), a kind of inverse of a cobegin (or fork). Finally, for the project to (co)end, the teams working on t_5 and t_2 must both finish their tasks. The graph clearly shows precedence relationships; for example, the completion of tasks t_1, t_3, and t_4 must precede the start of task t_5.

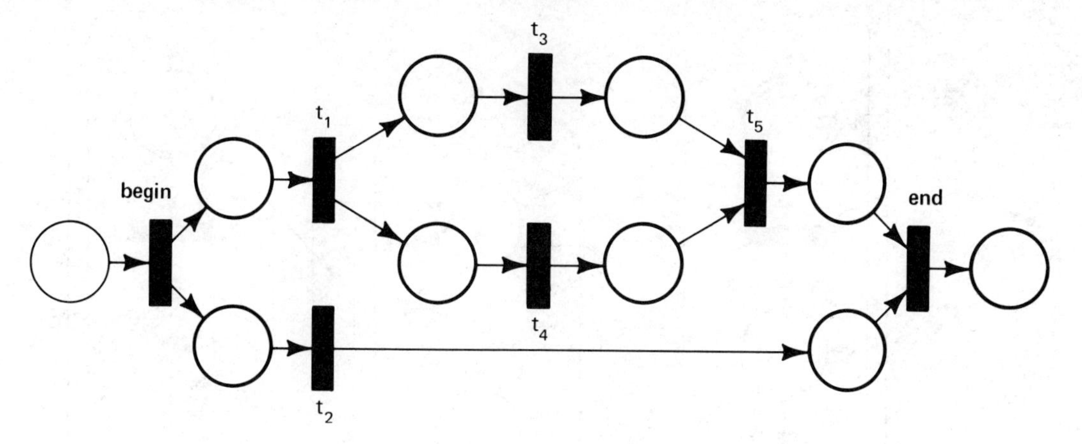

Figure 1.16. Precedence and parallelism on a project

SHARED RESOURCES AND CONFLICTS

We come again to the problem of allocating shared resources among concurrently executing tasks. (We touched upon this problem in our discussion of Figure 1.14.) If the allocation is ill-considered, the system can deadlock, a situation where each member of some set of tasks waits forever for its critical set of resources.

For example, suppose we want to hold two sandlot baseball contests. Suppose further that we have two baseball diamonds but only one bat and only one ball. A poor allocation scheme would have the two groups toss a coin to determine who gets the bat and then toss the coin again to see who gets the ball. Assuming fair tosses, the probability is 0.5 that this allocation scheme will lead to deadlock. If the first group wins the toss for the bat and the second group wins the toss for the ball (or vice versa), then the allocation prevents either group from playing.

Figure 1.17 illustrates a Petri net that can lead to deadlock. In order to execute A.t_3, Task A must have acquired both of the resources represented by tokens in places R.p_1 and R.p_2. In competition for these resources, task B needs both of

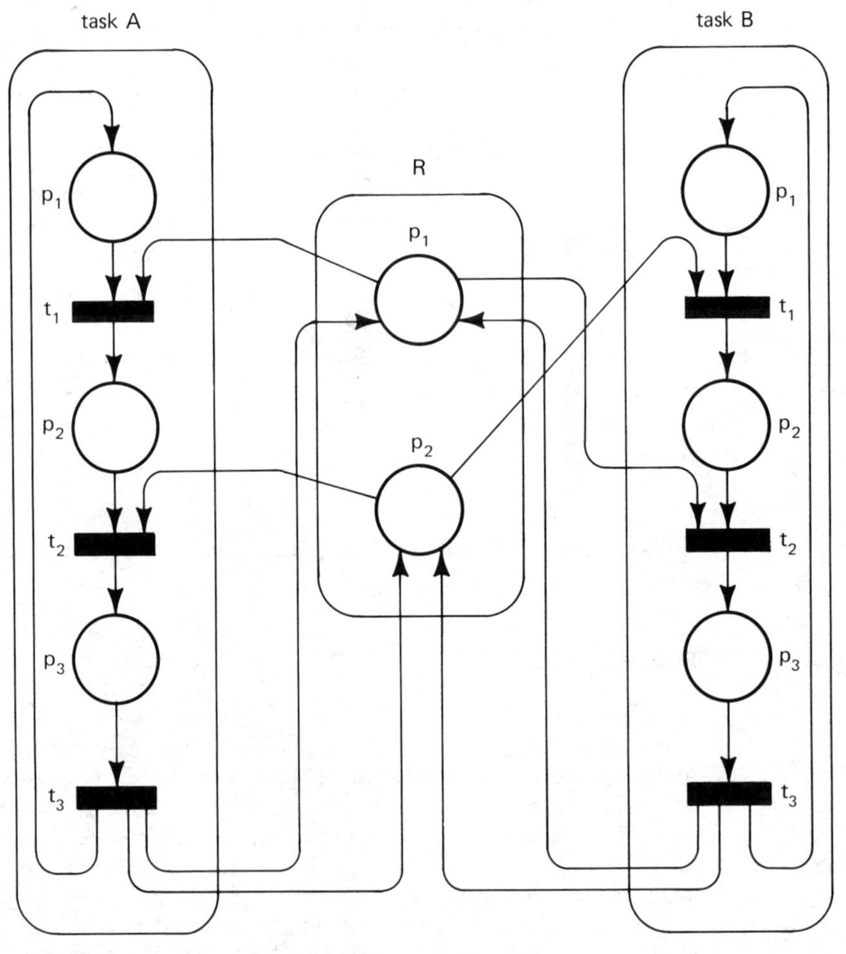

Figure 1.17. A resource allocation scheme leading to deadlock

them in order to execute B.t_3. In the strategy illustrated in Figure 1.17, task A asks for the resource in R.p_1 and then asks for the resource in R.p_2 whereas task B asks for the resource in R.p_2 and then asks for the resource in R.p_1. Sometimes this strategy will work: for example, the following sequences avoid deadlock

A.t_1, A.t_2, A.t_3, B.t_1, B.t_2, B.t_3 or

B.t_1, B.t_2, B.t_3, A.t_1, A.t_2, A.t_3

but either of these sequences deadlock

A.t_1, B.t_1 or B.t_1, A.t_1

because neither A nor B will ever be able to fire its t_2 transition. At the end of the first deadlocking sequence, task A has the resource that was in R.p_1 and needs the resource that was in R.p_2; task B has the resource that was in R.p_2 and needs the resource that was in R.p_1. Consequently, both tasks are blocked forever.

AVOIDING DEADLOCK

One strategy used to prevent deadlock is to require every task to request simultaneously all the resources it needs for its next transition. When a task tries to acquire resources piecemeal, it may succeed in blocking other tasks while still failing to accumulate its own critical set of resources. Figure 1.18 illustrates an "all or nothing at all" acquisition scheme. Before task A tries to execute its transition t_3, it acquires (through transition t_2) all of the resources it needs. If it can't get both resources, it waits in place p_2. Task B behaves similarly. This strategy clearly prevents deadlock. (Compare this situation to the one in Figure 1.17.) Each task releases in transition t_3 the resources it acquired in transition t_2.

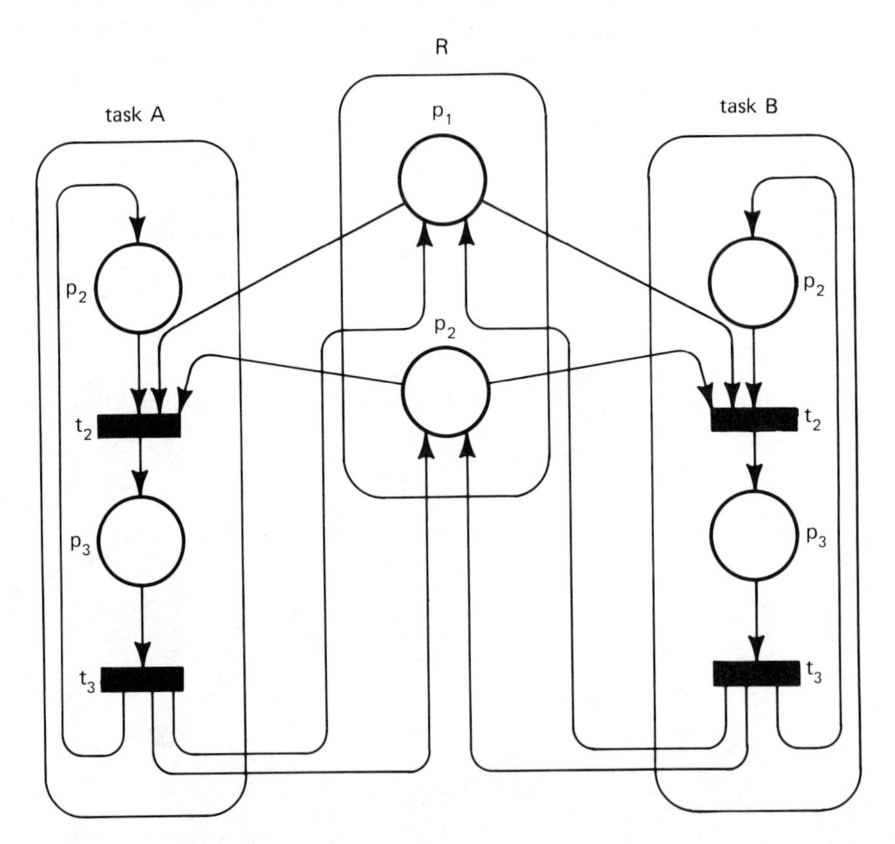

Figure 1.18. A resource allocation scheme that avoids deadlock

Notice that there is a _conflict_ in Figure 1.18. With tokens in A.p_2, B.p_2, R.p_1, and R.p_2, both transitions A.t_2 and B.t_2 are enabled. But whichever transition fires first immediately disables the other transition by removing both resources from R. Clearly, if task A arrives at its p_2 slightly before task B arrives at its p_2, then A.t_2 fires first; and task B will have to wait until task A has finished with both resources.

But, you may ask, what happens if task A arrives at A.p_2 and task B arrives at B.p_2 _simultaneously_? There are two ways of dealing with simultaneity in abstract Petri nets. One way is to rule out simultaneity by arguing that time is a continuous real variable: the probability of two events occurring at exactly the same point on the time continuum is zero. If you don't like this solution to the problem of simultaneity, then you may want to postulate a Petri net demon who monitors all conflicts and arbitrarily chooses which transition should fire. In social life, problems of simultaneity are solved by agents or servers. For example, if two customers approach a ticket agent shoulder-to-shoulder, the agent will neither be paralyzed nor try to serve both of them at the same time. Instead, the agent will select (perhaps arbitrarily) one of the customers to serve first.

COMMUNICATION AND SYNCHRONIZATION BETWEEN CONCURRENT TASKS

Two concurrent tasks may need to synchronize or communicate with each other. We can represent synchronization and communication with Petri nets. However, we prefer to delay the discussion of intertask communication until we introduce the details of Ada's rendezvous mechanism. In Ada, both synchronization and communication between tasks are accomplished by means of the rendezvous.

Figure 1.19 shows how synchronization can be achieved by rendezvous. Suppose that for good reasons task B does not want to fire its t_1 until task A has fired its t_1 and that task A does not want to fire its t_2 until task B has fired its t_2. The Petri net in Figure 1.19 provides the required synchronization. If task B reaches $B.p_1$ before task A has fired $A.t_1$, task B will wait in $B.p_1$ for task A. Task B detects that task A has fired $A.t_1$ by the presence of a token in $B.p_3$. After task A fires its t_1, it waits in its p_2 until task B has finished firing both $B.t_1$ and $B.t_2$. Task A detects that task B has fired $B.t_2$ by the presence of a token in $A.p_3$.

Suppose that task B is a server task; it provides some service to client tasks like task A. Under this interpretation the transitions have the following meanings:

$A.t_1$: A requests service from B (A's operation is suspended)

$B.t_1$: B accepts A's request for service (the rendezvous begins)

$B.t_2$: B finishes performing the service for A (the rendezvous ends)

$A.t_2$: A resumes operation after its rendezvous with B

The transitions in Figure 1.19 always fire in the following order

$A.t_1$, $B.t_1$, $B.t_2$, $A.t_2$

no matter which task, A or B, reaches its p_1 first. It should be obvious that if A reaches its p_1 first, A will fire its t_1 and then wait in its p_2 for the completion of the rendezvous. On the other hand, if B reaches its p_1 first, B will wait in p_1 until A fires $A.t_1$ and sends a token to $B.p_3$.

If B is a server task, it may have many clients, not just task A. In other words there may be a many-to-one relationship between the tasks that request B's service and B. (This is analogous to the many-to-one relationship between the callers of a procedure and the procedure.) This implies several things about the nature of $B.p_3$ and the meaning of the tokens

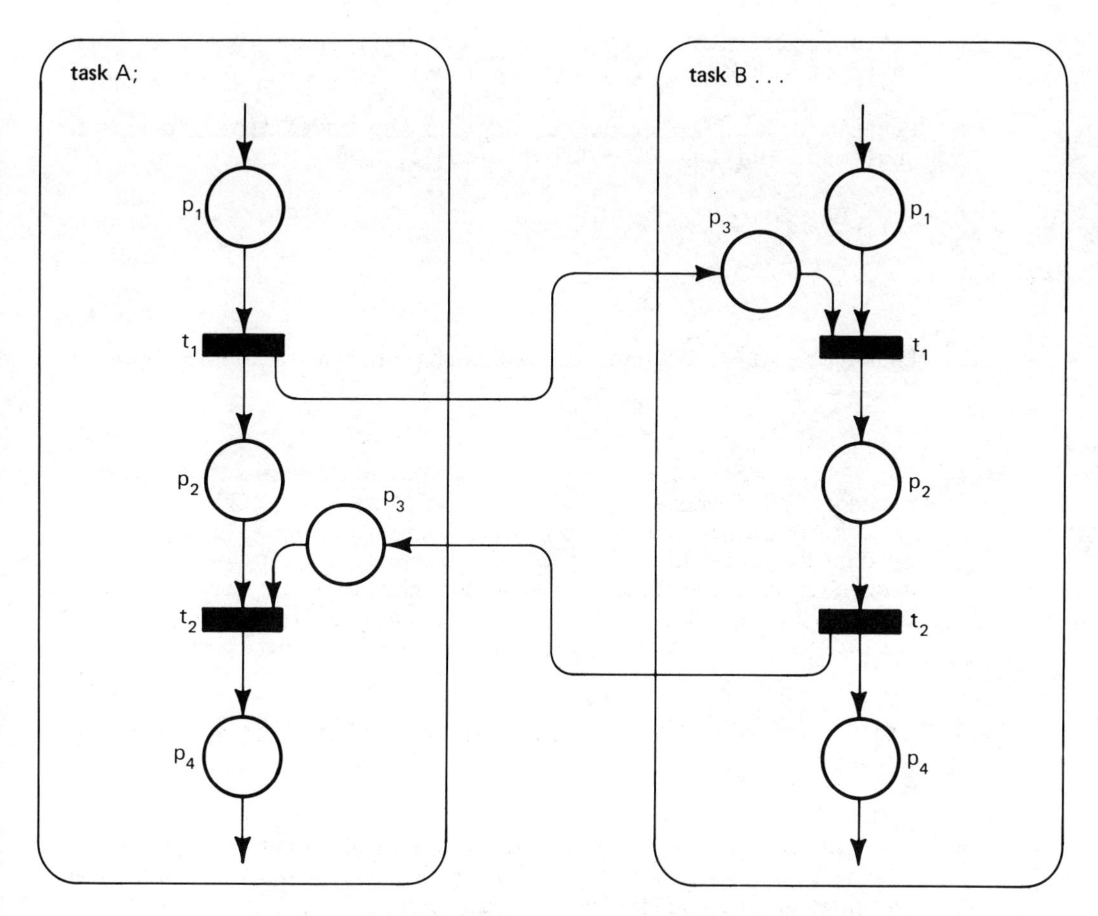

Figure 1.19. Synchronization of two tasks

in that place. First, we probably should implement B.p_3 as a queue to give first-in/first-out service to the clients of B. Second, the tokens sent to B.p_3 will have to contain information about the clients who sent the tokens--at least enough information for the server task to send an enabling token back to the client so that the client can resume its operation after the rendezvous ends. Finally, the clients may send data to the server task--therefore, the tokens sent to B.p_3 may include this data. (Similarly, the token sent back to the client by the firing of B.t_2 may contain data provided by B to the client; this data may be the service provided by B.)

REFERENCE AND ACKNOWLEDGEMENT

I am particularly indebted to Jim Peterson's excellent book on Petri net theory and applications:

Peterson, J. L. Petri net theory and the modelling of systems. Englewood Cliffs, N.J.: Prentice-Hall, 1981.

EXERCISES

1.1. Enumerate all the possible sequences of transition firings in Figure 1.16.

1.2. The Petri net in Figure 1.20 computes the product of the nonnegative numbers m and n (supplied as the initial numbers of tokens in places p_m and p_n). The net computes the product by depositing m*n tokens in the output place p_{m*n}. List the sequence of transition firings for the initial marking (p_m = 2, p_n = 3, p_1 = 1). (The net must always be initialized with one token in p_1, which plays the role of a control token.)

1.3. Write a detailed explanation of the multiplier's operation (Figure 1.20).

1.4. The inhibitor arc from place p_n to transition t_2 gives the firing of transition t_3 priority over the firing of transition t_2. What would the net do if this inhibitor arc were removed?

1.5. Why (for a given marking) does the Petri net in Figure 1.16 support many sequences of transition firings while the Petri net in Figure 1.20 determines only one?

1.6. Draw a Petri net that represents the concurrent execution of n statements, S1, S2, ... , Sn. The program notation for such an execution might be

cobegin S1; **also** S2; **also** ...; **also** Sn; **coend**

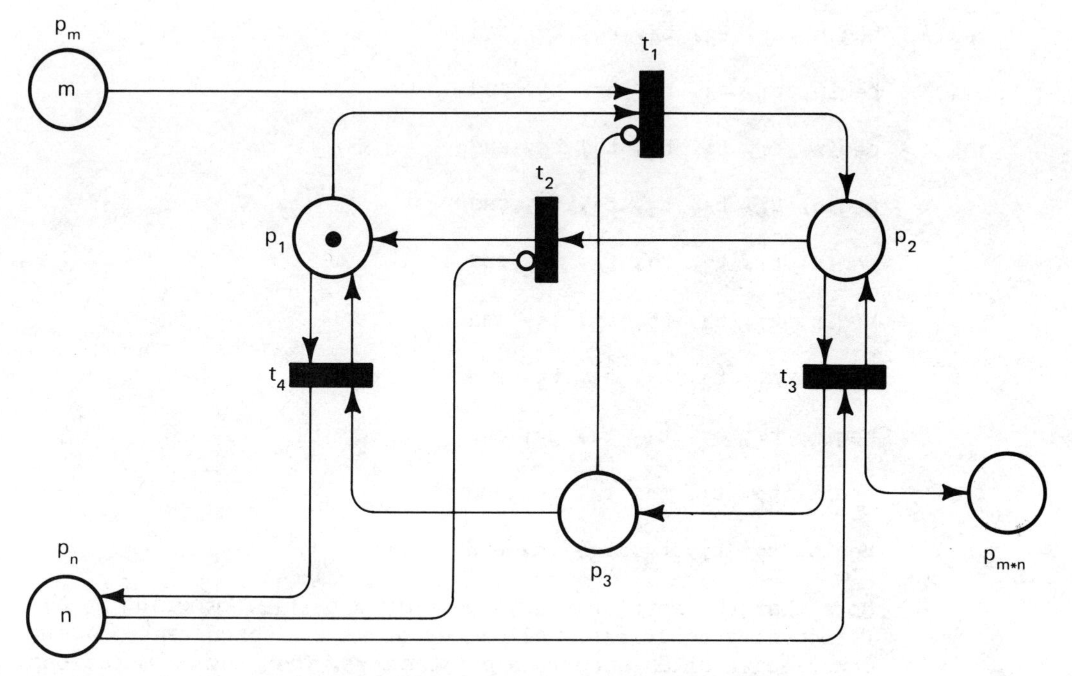

Figure 1.20. A Petri net multiplier

ANSWERS TO EXERCISES

1.1. begin, t_1, t_3, t_4, t_5, t_2, end

begin, t_1, t_4, t_3, t_5, t_2, end

begin, t_1, t_3, t_4, t_2, t_5, end

begin, t_1, t_4, t_3, t_2, t_5, end

begin, t_1, t_3, t_2, t_4, t_5, end

begin, t_1, t_4, t_2, t_3, t_5, end

begin, t_1, t_2, t_3, t_4, t_5, end

begin, t_1, t_2, t_4, t_3, t_5, end

begin, t_2, t_1, t_3, t_4, t_5, end

begin, t_2, t_1, t_4, t_3, t_5, end

Note that the Petri net implies only a _partial_ ordering in the firing of transitions. The number of ways a concurrent program can execute often surprises programmers. The many permutations constitute a combinatorial explosion; but the Petri net graph "masters" the explosion by permitting only those execution sequences that meet the precedence constraints.

1.2. t_1, t_3, t_3, t_3, t_2, t_4, t_4, t_4, t_1, t_3, t_3, t_3, t_2, t_4, t_4, t_4

Note that t_3 fired six times in order to deposit the correct number of tokens (the product 2*3) in the output place.

1.3. The net computes the product by first firing transition t_1, which removes one token from place p_m and moves the "control" token from place p_1 to place p_2. The token in place p_2 enables as many firings of t_3 as there are tokens in place p_n. These firings remove the n tokens from place p_n and deposit n tokens in the output place p_{m*n} as well as place p_3. After p_n is empty, t_2 can fire, moving the control token from p_2 back to p_1. The token in pl enables firings of t_4; these firings have the effect of moving the n tokens in p_3 back to p_n.

The entire process we have just described is repeated m times, once for each token originally in p_m. Since the cycle repeats m times, and since each cycle deposits n tokens in the output place, the correct result, m*n tokens, is deposited in the output place. The net's execution terminates by moving n tokens from p_3 back into p_n, an irrelevant but harmless sequence of transitions.

Note that places p_1 and p_2 play the role of holding the program counter token (or, as we called it, the "control" token) whereas the other places play the role of holding data tokens. Finally, we note that this multiplier works with only the primitive operations of testing a place for the presence of a token, testing a place for zero tokens, and incrementing or decrementing (by one) the number of tokens in a place.

1.4. With the inhibitor arc removed, the net would _weakly_ compute the product of m and n. "Weakly compute" means that the net's output will not exceed m*n. In fact, the net could output any integer between Ø and m*n! The reason is that--without the inhibitor arc--the run token's presence in p_2 enables (assuming a token in p_n) both transition t_2 and t_3. (Perhaps you recall that we called this kind of situation a _conflict_.) If the Petri net demon always selects t_2 in the case of conflict, the net will output zero tokens. If the demon always selects t_3 in the case of conflict, the net will behave just as we want it to. If the demon likes nondeterminacy and flips a coin to select one of the transitions, the net will output some number of tokens between Ø and m*n. Because we don't like nondeterminacy in the output of a multiplier, we used the inhibitor arc to take away the demon's role.

1.5. The Petri net in Figure 1.16 supports many sequences of transition firings because it is a concurrent Petri net: these nets only partially order the firing of their transitions. A concurrent Petri net cannot determine--and in real systems we cannot determine--which one of the tokens racing down a parallel thread of control will reach a given point first (unless we explicitly provide synchronization, as in Figure 1.19). The Petri net in Figure 1.2Ø determines only one sequence of firing (per initial marking) because its structure contains neither concurrency nor conflict. (In other words, the latter net could be programmed as an ordinary sequential program.)

1.6. A Petri net graph that represents the concurrent execution of n statements (or processes), S1, S2, ..., Sn, is given in Figure 1.21, page 26.

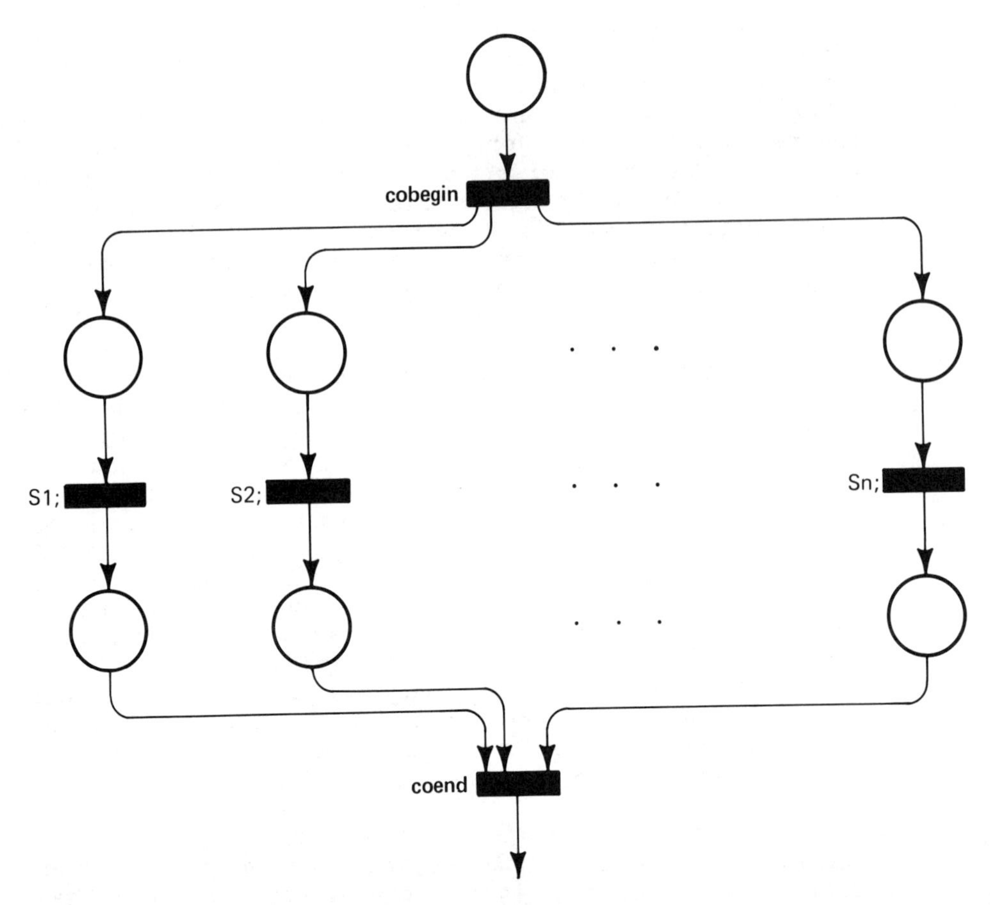

Figure 1.21. A Petri net modeling **cobegin** S1; **also** S2; ... **also** Sn; **coend**

Chapter 2
Parallel Independent Processes

We are all familiar with the concept of parallel processes operating independently of each other but nevertheless contributing to a common goal: ten typists independently typing the same book (each typist types a different chapter); a half dozen detectives checking a list of two dozen suspects (each detective independently interviews four of the suspects).

Similar to these social examples, the simplest multitasking programs employ parallel independent tasks to accomplish a common goal. By "independent", I mean the tasks do not have to synchronize or communicate with each other in order to contribute to the common goal. The tasks can operate completely independently of each other because each possesses its own set of objects, resources, or part of a common data structure.

PARALLEL, INDEPENDENT, NONIDENTICAL PROCESSES

Figure 1.21 is a Petri net representation of n parallel independent, nonidentical processes. Each process executes a sequence of statements. Process 1 executes the sequence of statements S1; process 2 executes the sequence of statements S2; and so on.

How can we implement Figure 1.21 in Ada? The Ada procedure on the next page, spawn_n_independent_processes, creates n-1 different tasks. Notice that we have arranged matters so that the master procedure (a process itself) executes the sequence of statements S1, task T2 executes S2, task T3 executes S3, and so on. Compare the procedure (look at its comments!) to Figure 1.21. The main **begin** in spawn_n_independent_processes plays the role of the cobegin in Figure 1.21; and the final **end** of spawn_n_independent_processes plays the role of the figure's coend.

```
procedure spawn_n_independent_processes is
  .
  .                      -- global declarations can go here
  .
  task T2;               --\
                         -- \
  task T3;               --  \
  .                      --   > n-1 distinct task specifications
  .                      --  /
  .                      -- /
  task Tn;               --/

  task body T2 is        --\
    declarative-part     -- \
  begin                  --  \
    S2;                  --   \
  end T2;                --    \
                         --     \
  task body T3 is        --      \
    declarative-part     --       \
  begin                  --        \
    S3;                  --         > and n-1 distinct task bodies
  end T3;                --        /
  .                      --       /
  .                      --      /
  .                      --     /
  task body Tn is        --    /
    declarative-part     --   /
  begin                  --  /
    Sn;                  -- /
  end Tn;                --/
begin
  --                     -- Parallel activation of tasks occurs here, between
  S1;                    -- the main begin and the sequence of statements, S1.
  --                     -- Wait here for termination of all the n-1 tasks.
end spawn_n_independent_processes;
```

The procedure spawn_n_independent_processes declares n-1 nonidentical tasks. (Later we'll see a convenient way to declare a set of identical tasks.)

Other declarations could, of course, appear in the declarative part of spawn_n_independent_processes. For example, we sometimes allow each task to update a disjoint part of a global data structure.

Notice that each task body has its own declarative part. This facilitates making the parallel processes (implemented as tasks) independent and disjoint. Figure 2.1 is the Petri net graph of spawn_n_independent_processes.

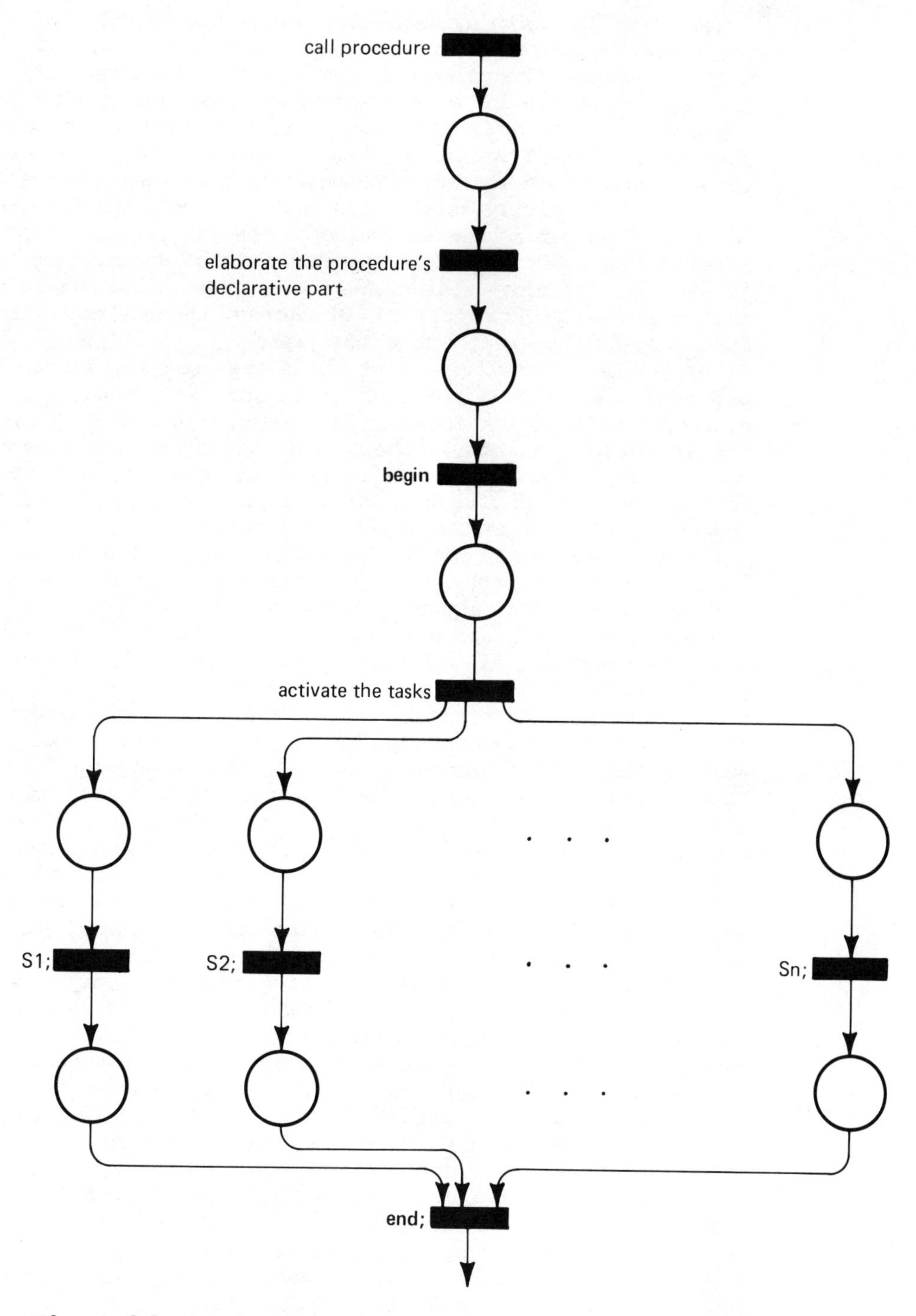

Figure 2.1. Petri net graph of spawn_n_independent_processes

The tasks in spawn_n_independent_processes function as pure processes; they are rather like implicitly invoked, parameterless procedures. The principal way in which these tasks differ from procedures is in the way they are elaborated and invoked.

Elaboration of a declaration is the process by which the declaration has its effect; for example, elaboration of an object declaration includes the object's creation; elaboration of a task body simply establishes that this body can from then on be used to define the execution of the task. Elaboration of a task's body must precede elaboration of the declarative part (if any) of its body (violation of this order of events raises the exception program_error). Of course, these elaborations must precede the execution of the task.

Figure 2.1 depicts the execution of the program: first, the procedure call; then, the elaboration of the procedure's declarative part (which includes the elaboration of each task's specification and body); then, the passing of the reserved word **begin**; then, the parallel activation of the n-1 tasks (the activation of a task consists of the elaboration of its body's declarative part); then, the parallel execution of the n-1 tasks and the procedure's own sequence of statements; finally, after the termination of its n-1 tasks and the completion of its own sequence of statements, return from the procedure. (Each of the n-1 tasks terminates when it reaches its final end and all of its dependent tasks (if any) have terminated.)

Each task depends directly on the procedure whose execution creates the task. In our example the tasks depend directly on spawn_n_independent_processes. We call this procedure a taskmaster or simply a master. The execution of a master creates its directly dependent tasks. (Note that the tasks are completely independent of one another but existentially dependent on the master.) We emphasize the rule for leaving a master: after the master creates some dependent tasks, it cannot be left until all those dependent tasks are terminated **and** the master has completed its own sequence of statements.

We also emphasize that the master executes its sequence of statements in parallel with its dependent tasks. If the master delegates the entire computational burden to its dependent tasks, the master's sequence of statements may be vacuous (the null statement). However, the master may shoulder part of the computational burden along with (in parallel with) its tasks.

The task's bodies define their execution. What can appear in these bodies? In our example the tasks do not have entries (if they had entries, their specifications would have declared them). Because the tasks don't have to accept entry calls, their bodies resemble procedure bodies. In form, therefore, our tasks resemble independent, **concurrent**, parameterless procedures (which the master calls implicitly). (In this example and most of this chapter the tasks closely resemble procedures. In later chapters we'll see forms of tasks, containing entries, that encapsulate data; tasks of this kind resemble packages that provide their clients mutually exclusive access to the encapsulated data.)

Consider the following program. All the Sk in this program are identical to the corresponding Sk in the previous program. This program--except for its time to execute--has exactly the same effect as spawn_n_independent_processes. Because the processes are independent, the order in which the program executes them is irrelevant. Any permutation of the statements in execute_n_sequential_processes' sequence of statements would produce the same final effect. Whether the first program executes the processes in partial or full concurrency is also irrelevant. Except for the execution time, the effect of executing and completing all the processes is the same for all orders of execution and all degrees of concurrency. These claims hold because the effects of executing the sequences of statements S1, S2, ..., Sn are independent of one another. Note that the first program invokes all the processes (tasks) implicitly and executes them concurrently, while the second program invokes all the processes (procedures) explicitly and executes them sequentially.

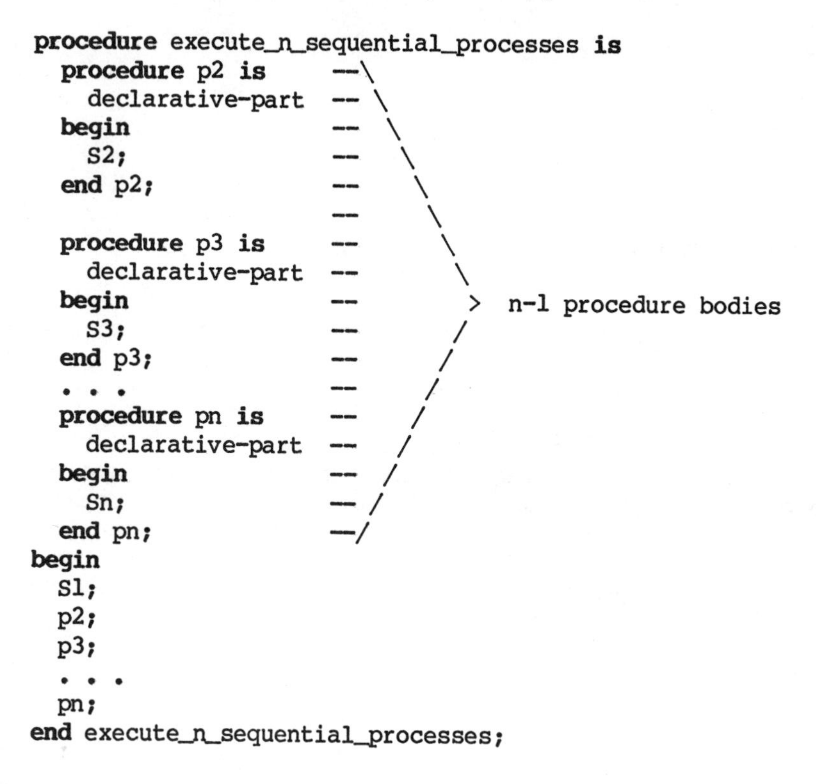

```
procedure execute_n_sequential_processes is
  procedure p2 is        --\
    declarative-part     -- \
  begin                  --  \
    S2;                  --   \
  end p2;                --    \
                         --     \
  procedure p3 is        --      \
    declarative-part     --       \
  begin                  --        >  n-1 procedure bodies
    S3;                  --       /
  end p3;                --      /
  . . .                  --     /
  procedure pn is        --    /
    declarative-part     --   /
  begin                  --  /
    Sn;                  -- /
  end pn;                --/
begin
  S1;
  p2;
  p3;
  . . .
  pn;
end execute_n_sequential_processes;
```

A variation on the syntax in spawn_n_independent_processes is to group each task specification and task body (or task body stub) together. A task unit consists of a task specification and a task body. The following program is semantically identical to the first version.

```
procedure spawn_n_independent_processes is
  . . .
  task T2;                          -- \
  task body T2 is separate;         --  \
                                    --   \
  task T3;                          --    \
  task body T3 is separate;         --     > n distinct task units
  . . .                             --    /
  . . .                             --   /
  task Tn;                          --  /
  task body Tn is separate;         -- /
  . . .
begin
  S1;
end spawn_n_independent_processes;

separate (spawn_n_independent_processes)
task body T2 is
  declarative-part
begin
  S2;
end T2;
  .
  .
  .
separate (spawn_n_independent_processes)
task body Tn is
  declarative-part
begin
  Sn;
end Tn;
```

As a whimsical instance of our first paradigm, we offer prepare_dinner. This program prepares dinner with the assistance of three cooks (processors). Since the cooks prepare dinner without sharing resources (each has its own resources) or directly cooperating, they can execute their recipes concurrently and independently.

```
procedure prepare_dinner(salad, entree, vegetables : out Food) is
   task PrepareSalad;
   task PrepareEntree;
   task PrepareVegetables;

   task body PrepareSalad is
      -- the declarations for PrepareSalad's local entities go here
   begin
      -- the instructions for preparing the salad go here
   end PrepareSalad;

   task body PrepareEntree is
      -- the declarations for PrepareEntree's local entities go here
   begin
      -- the instructions for preparing the entree go here
   end PrepareEntree;

   task body PrepareVegetables is
      -- the declarations for PrepareVegetable's local entities go here
   begin
      -- the instructions for preparing the vegetables go here
   end PrepareVegetables;
begin
   -- All three tasks are activated before the following statement.
   null;
   -- Wait here for all three tasks to terminate.
end prepare_dinner;
```

The procedure prepare_dinner declares three subordinate tasks: PrepareSalad, PrepareEntree, and PrepareVegetables. The procedure has delegated the substance of preparing dinner to these subordinates. When called, prepare_dinner elaborates the declarations of the tasks, activates the tasks, executes the null statement, and then waits for all three subordinates to finish their contributions.

Before we discuss the execution of prepare_dinner, look at the declaration of the task unit, PrepareSalad.

```
task PrepareSalad;           -- this is a task-specification

task body PrepareSalad is    -- this is the corresponding task-body
   -- the declarations of PrepareSalad's local entities go here
begin
   -- the instructions for preparing the salad go here
end PrepareSalad;
```

The declaration

```
task PrepareSalad;
```

declares a single task object; its body defines its execution. Later we will see that this form--the declaration of a single task object--is a special case. (In the more general case we can declare a task type and then declare as many objects of the task type as we desire.) Here we are preparing dinner for a small group, not an army; therefore we don't require a whole array of salad preparers.

In prepare_dinner we grouped the three task specifications together at the beginning of the declarative part in order to give an overview of the entities in the procedure.

Note that we used lowercase letters throughout the name of the procedure prepare_dinner but we mixed uppercase and lowercase letters in the names of the tasks (PrepareSalad, and so on). We use this convention throughout this book to help distinguish tasks from procedures.

When a caller invokes prepare_dinner, its three dependent tasks are activated <u>after</u> the elaboration of its declarative part (this elaboration includes, of course, the elaboration of the tasks' bodies but it does not include the elaboration of the declarative parts of the tasks' bodies) and <u>before</u> execution of the first statement in its sequence of statements. In other words, the dependent tasks are activated right after the main **begin** which separates the declarative part of prepare_dinner from its sequence of statements. The activation of a task elaborates the task body's declarative part (thereby creating the task's local entities, if any) and then invokes the execution of the task's body. We can compare this with a procedure call. A procedure call elaborates the procedure's declarative part (if any) and then executes the procedure's sequence of statements. The invocation of a task is automatic, rather like the automatic creation and initialization of a data object in the declarative part. Tasks have this dual nature, they are both program units and objects (which have anonymous or named types).

After their activation, the three tasks execute in parallel with the master's sequence of statements. The main **begin** in the procedure is like a multiple fork (or multiple cobegin) because it establishes three additional threads of control.

We wrote prepare_dinner so that it delegated the substance of its assignment to its three dependent tasks. In another approach, the master could delegate the preparation of the salad and the vegetables to dependent tasks while the master retained the responsibility to prepare the entree. Pursuing this approach, we could write:

```
procedure prepare_dinner(salad, entree, vegetables : out Food) is
   -- The declaration of the entities required
   -- to prepare theentree could go here.

  task PrepareSalad;
  task PrepareVegetables;

  task body PrepareSalad is
    -- the declarations for PrepareSalad's local entities go here
  begin
    -- the instructions for preparing the salad here
  end PrepareSalad;

  task body PrepareVegetables is
    -- the declarations for PrepareVegetable's local entities go here
  begin
    -- the instructions for preparing the vegetables go here
  end PrepareVegetables;
begin
  -- both tasks start
  -- the instructions for preparing the entree go here
end prepare_dinner; --
```

This implementation isn't as satisfactory as the first one--the two subordinate tasks have access to the (global) entities required by the process (the main procedure in this case) that prepares the entree. Remember that the processes should be completely independent: they should limit themselves to operating on disjoint objects and use disjoint resources (because we haven't provided for synchronization and communication among the processes). We can hide the entities needed by the entree process from the other two processes by coding a block in prepare_dinner's sequence of statements.

```
procedure prepare_dinner(salad, entree, vegetables : out Food) is
  task PrepareSalad;
  task PrepareVegetables;

  task body PrepareSalad is
    -- the declarations for PrepareSalad's local entities go here
  begin
    -- the instructions for preparing the salad here
  end PrepareSalad;

  task body PrepareVegetables is
    -- the declarations for PrepareVegetable's local entities go here
  begin
    -- the instructions for preparing the vegetables go here
  end PrepareVegetables;
begin
  declare
    -- The declaration of the entities
    -- required to prepare the entree go here.
  begin
    -- The instructions for
    -- preparing the entree go here.
  end;
end prepare_dinner;
```

Interestingly, in this implementation the two tasks obtain their local entities before the master obtains its local entities. This is because the processor completes the activation of the master's dependent tasks before it executes the first statement following the master's declarative part. (Recall that the activation of a task object consists of the elaboration of the declarative part of the task's body; and this elaboration creates the task's local entities.) Since the processor activates both of the tasks before it executes the master's block statement (which elaborates the declarative part of the block statement), the dependent tasks obtain their local entities before the master obtains its local entities.

Still another way to hide the entities required to prepare the entree is to declare a subordinate procedure that the main procedure invokes. This solution is

```
procedure prepare_dinner(salad, entree, vegetables : out Food) is
  procedure prepare_entree is
    -- the declarations for prepare_entree's local entities go here
  begin
    -- the instructions for preparing the entree go here
  end prepare_entree;

  task PrepareSalad;
  task body PrepareSalad is
    -- the declarations for PrepareSalad's local entities go here
  begin
    -- the instructions for preparing the salad here
  end PrepareSalad;

  task PrepareVegetables;
  task body PrepareVegetables is
    -- the declarations for PrepareVegetable's local entities go here
  begin
    -- the instructions for preparing the vegetables go here
  end PrepareVegetables;
begin
  -- The master implicitly "invokes" PrepareSalad & PrepareVegetables here.
  prepare_entree;    -- The master explicitly invokes prepare_entree.
end prepare_dinner; -- To return, all invoked program units must finish.
```

This solution is interesting because it illustrates the differences between a subordinate task and a subordinate procedure. First, note the syntactic differences: there are, of course, the obvious syntactic differences of the reserved word **procedure** and the reserved words **task** and **task body**; in addition, note that the task unit declaration always requires a separate task specification whereas the procedure declaration doesn't always require a separate procedure specification. The semantic differences (which the syntactic differences bring to our attention!) are more significant. The executions of the task bodies are invoked automatically; but execution of the procedure body must be invoked by an explicit procedure-call-statement.

We have been considering the task unit as a programming construct for implementing processes. We have noted the many similarities between task units so employed and the procedure program unit. In fact, at this stage of what we have learned about tasks, it may seem unnecessary to distinguish tasks syntactically from procedures. (Of course, if one tried to eliminate Ada's task construct and use procedures for parallel processes, one would have to provide an explicit coinitiate or cobegin statement.) For example, Per Brinch Hansen's language Edison does not have separate syntactic forms for sequential and concurrent program units. In Edison, our program for preparing dinner might take this form

```
proc prepare_dinner(var salad, entree, vegetables : Food)
  proc prepare_salad
    -- the declarations for prepare_salad's local entities go here
  begin
    -- the instructions for preparing the salad go here
  end

  proc prepare_entree
    -- the declarations for prepare_entree's local entities go here
  begin
    -- the instructions for preparing the entree go here
  end

  proc prepare_vegetables
    -- the declarations for prepare_vegetable's local entities go here
  begin
    -- the instructions for preparing the vegetables go here
  end
begin
  cobegin 1 do
    prepare_salad
  also 2 do
    prepare_entree
  also 3 do
    prepare_vegatables
  end
end
```

Though syntactically different from (and considerably less inky than!) our Ada programs, this Edison program is semantically identical to our Ada solutions. Nevertheless, Ada has good reasons to make a syntactic distinction between task program units and procedure program units (as we shall see).

AN EXAMPLE OF PARALLEL INDEPENDENT PROCESSES: READING, PROCESSING, WRITING

In the typical computing system, input and output operations are very slow compared to cpu operations; but input devices, output devices, and the cpu itself are disjoint entities. Therefore, in order to increase system throughput, we will overlap input, processing, and output. To achieve this overlap safely, the master will have to manage synchronized, switched buffers which its dependent tasks employ disjointly.

Here is a sequential procedure for the reading, processing, writing problem.

```
with Sequential_IO;
procedure sequential_read_transform_write is
  x : X_Type;     -- the type of the elements on the input file
  y : Y_Type;     -- the type of the elements on the output file

  package X_IO is new Sequential_IO(Element_Type => X_Type);
    -- This package has been instantiated to provide
    -- open, read, and close procedures for files of type X_Type.
  file_of_x : X_IO.File_Type;
  use X_IO;

  package Y_IO is new Sequential_IO(Element_Type => Y_Type);
    -- This package has been instantiated to provide
    -- create, write, and close procedures for files of type Y_Type.
  file_of_y : Y_IO.File_Type;
  use Y_IO;

  procedure transform(x : in X_Type; y : out Y_Type) is separate;
begin
  open(file_of_x, mode => in_file, name => "----------");
  create(file_of_y, mode => out_file, name => "**********");

  while not end_of_file(file_of_x) loop
    read(file_of_x, x);
    transform(x, y);
    write(file_of_y, y);
  end loop;

  close(file_of_x);
  close(file_of_y);
end sequential_read_transform_write;
```

Notice the iterative sequential role of the "boss" (main) procedure: it calls each procedure (read, transform, and write) in sequence and passes the necessary data from one procedure to the next.

The following program introduces parallelism (but not as much parallelism as possible) into the reading, transforming, writing processes. It illustrates that a block statement can be the direct master of tasks. (Control cannot leave a block statement until all its dependent tasks are terminated.) The role of the direct master in the parallel program is somewhat different from the role of the boss module in the sequential program. This master creates, activates, and invokes its three dependent tasks in parallel and then waits for them to terminate; but it doesn't manage the exchange of data among them.

The all-important reponsibility of managing the exchange of data among the three tasks falls to their indirect master. The indirect master in this case is the main program, which has the critical assignment of creating the buffers as well as managing the transfer of data from Read_x to Transform_x_to_y and from Transform_x_to_y to Write_y. (Tasks also depend upon their indirect masters.)

Note that this program delegates no productive computational burden to the direct master. The activation of a task involves some overhead. Therefore, this program's allocation of every process to a subtask of the master may not be efficient. Instead of merely executing the null statement, the block statement could execute, for example, the transform procedure and thereby reduce the number of task activations. An optimizing compiler might even make this optimization for us. In an exercise (2.4) at the end of this chapter we suggest and illustrate the more efficient approach.

Notice that our tasks are ignorant of one another. The program relies upon a knowledgeable master to manage the tasks' "communication" with one another. (In the next chapter we will introduce Ada's rendezvous facility which allows tasks to communicate directly with one another (as well as with their masters). The rendezvous allows tasks to behave much more intelligently than our parallel independent tasks. The thrust of this chapter is to illustrate what we can accomplish without invoking Ada's rendezvous mechanism. But note the relative complexity of the buffer management. Direct task communcation will be simpler as well as more efficient.)

```
with Sequential_IO;
procedure parallel_read_transform_write_1 is
  x_buffer_1, x_buffer_2 : X_Type;
  y_buffer_1, y_buffer_2 : Y_Type;

  package X_IO is new Sequential_IO(Element_Type => X_Type);
  file_of_x : X_IO.File_Type;
  use X_IO;

  package Y_IO is new Sequential_IO(Element_Type => Y_Type);
  file_of_y : Y_IO.File_Type;
  use Y_IO;

  procedure transform(x : in X_Type; y : out Y_Type) is separate;
begin
  open(file_of_x, mode => in_file, name => "----------");
  create(file_of_y, mode => out_file, name => "**********");

  read(file_of_x, x_buffer_1);          -- May raise end_error; but that's okay.
  transform(x_buffer_1, y_buffer_1); -- y_buffer_1 is ready for writing.
```

```
if end_of_file(file_of_x) then       -- write the single value and quit
  write(file_of_y, y_buffer_1);
else
  read(file_of_x, x_buffer_2);       -- the buffers are initialized for tasks
  while not end_of_file(file_of_x)
  loop
    declare                          -- a direct master for three tasks
      task Read_x;
      task body Read_x is
      begin
        read(file_of_x, x_buffer_1);
      end Read_x;

      task Transform_x_to_y;
      task body Transform_x_to_y is
      begin
        transform(x_buffer_2, y_buffer_2);
      end Transform_x_to_y;

      task Write_y;
      task body Write_y is
      begin
        write(file_of_y, y_buffer_1);
      end Write_y;
    begin                            -- the tasks are activated in parallel
      null;
    end;

    x_buffer_2 := x_buffer_1; -- Move data from Read_x to Transform_x_to_y.
    y_buffer_1 := y_buffer_2; -- Move data from Transform_x_to_y to Write_y.
  end loop;

  write(file_of_y, y_buffer_1);          -- \  Clean up the
  transform(x_buffer_2, y_buffer_2);     --  > unfinished business
  write(file_of_y, y_buffer_2);          -- /  left by the direct master.
end if;

close(file_of_x);
close(file_of_y);
end parallel_read_transform_write_1;
```

It is easy to reason about the correctness of this program because the buffers accessed by the three parallel processes are disjoint and because the indirect master transfers data between the buffers while the program is sequential (that is, after the three dependent tasks have terminated). The program is sequential before the execution of the block statement, concurrent during the execution of the block statement, and sequential again after the execution of the block statement.

CASE STUDY: A CONCURRENT PROCEDURE FOR COPYING TEXT

This case study deliberately recapitulates a great deal of the previous sections. The reader who feels confident of the concepts of these sections may want to read the programs presented here and skip most of the rest of the section.

Consider the problem of copying a text file from one medium to another medium. (A text file is a sequence of characters, which may be organized into lines.) To simplify our problem, we assume the text file is organized into lines that contain exactly 80 characters. Here is a sequential procedure that solves this problem.

```
with Text_IO; use Text_IO;
procedure copy_text_sequentially is
  buffer : String(1..80);
begin
  while not end_of_file loop
    get(buffer); -- read 80 characters and store them in buffer
    skip_line;   -- scan past line terminator to beginning of next line

    put(buffer); -- write the contents of the buffer on the output file
    new_line;    -- write a line terminator on the output file
  end loop;
end copy_text_sequentially;
```

The preceding program is slower than necessary because it executes its input and output processes sequentially. We can increase copying speed by introducing parallel independent processes.

The following program executes (usually) its read and write statements concurrently. It writes the first line while it reads the second; it writes the second line while it reads the third; it writes the third line while it reads the fourth; and so on. The only time it isn't concurrently reading and writing is when it reads the first line and when it writes the last.

Incidentally, this program is somewhat more efficient than the concurrent program in the previous section because it avoids copying the contents of one buffer into another. It avoids copying buffers by swapping the indexes of an array of two buffers.

```
0  with Text_IO; use Text_IO;
1  procedure copy_text_concurrently is
2    buffer      : array(1..2) of String(1..80); -- 2 buffers indexed
3    for_reading : Integer range 1..2 := 1;      -- by for_reading
4    for_writing : Integer range 1..2 := 2;      -- and for_writing
5
6    procedure switch_buffers is                 -- which are switched
7      tmp_reading : Integer range 1..2;         -- between Input and
8    begin                                       -- and Output by this
9      tmp_reading := for_reading;               -- procedure
10     for_reading := for_writing;
11     for_writing := tmp_reading;
12   end switch_buffers;
13   pragma inline(switch_buffers);
14 begin
15   if end_of_file then
16     raise end_error;
17   end if;
18
19   get(buffer(for_reading));          -- Read the first line
20   skip_line;                         -- while still sequential.
21   switch_buffers;
22
23   while not end_of_file loop
24     declare                          -- a block that declares two tasks
25       task Output;                   -- declaration of first task
26       task body Output is            -- the first task's body
27       begin
28         put(buffer(for_writing));    -- These are the actions
29         new_line;                    -- performed by the Output task.
30       end Output;
31
32       task Input;                    -- declaration of a second task
33       task body Input is             -- the second task's body
34       begin
35         get(buffer(for_reading));    -- These are the actions
36         skip_line;                   -- performed by the Input task.
37       end Input;
38     begin
39       -- Input and Output are activated and run in parallel
40       null;
41       -- Advance beyond here when both tasks have terminated.
42     end;
43
44     switch_buffers; -- switch buffer roles for next pass thru loop
45   end loop;
46   put(buffer(for_writing));       -- write the last line and then
47   new_line;                       -- write line terminator for last line
48 end copy_text_concurrently;
```

The procedure initially executes as a single, sequential process that (line 19) reads the first line from the input file and stores it in buffer(1). Then the procedure switches (line 21) the roles of the buffers. (The procedure will later write the contents of buffer(1) on the output file.)

The program then executes the loop statement (line 23) while end_of_file is not true. The first statement in the loop's sequence of statements is the block statement (line 24) which elaborates and activates two parallel tasks, Input and Output. (Figure 2.2 is a Petri net graph of the block statement.) The Output task writes the previously read line onto the output file while the Input task reads the next line from the input file. The block statement's execution is completed when both of its dependent tasks have terminated. Execution then continues as a single thread of control which invokes the procedure switch_buffers to switch the roles of buffer(1) and buffer(2). Execution of the while loop is completed when the test for end_of_file yields true. The last line can then be found in the buffer selected by for_writing. The put statement (line 46) writes this last line.

Figure 2.3 illustrates the "ganged switching" of buffer(1) and buffer(2) between the tasks Input and Output. Subprogram switch_buffers implements the "ganged switch". For_reading takes the sequence of values 1, 2, 1, 2, ... while for_writing takes the sequence of values 2, 1, 2, 1, ... The correctness of the program depends upon guaranteeing that for_writing and for_reading contain opposite values at all times and that the values stored in the indexes are swapped after the completion of every copy cycle. In a larger program, we could consider enforcing this necessary invariant condition by encapsulating the buffers and their indexes in a package which helps ensure that the Input and Output tasks always use opposite, correct buffers.

The block statement (lines 24 to 42) introduces the desired parallelism in copy_text_concurrently. The Petri net graph of the block statement depicts the three parallel threads of control that exist during the execution of the block. Note that the block's null statement is executed in parallel with its tasks. The block's sequence of statements is trivial in our example, but we could have programmed nontrivial statements for the block's sequence of statements. Indeed, we could have eliminated one of the tasks and let the block itself execute the eliminated task's statements. This would have made the text of our program somewhat shorter; but it would have obscured the parallelism of the reading and writing processes. Note that the block statement cannot end until all three threads of control have finished executing their statements. This is well depicted in the Petri net graph.

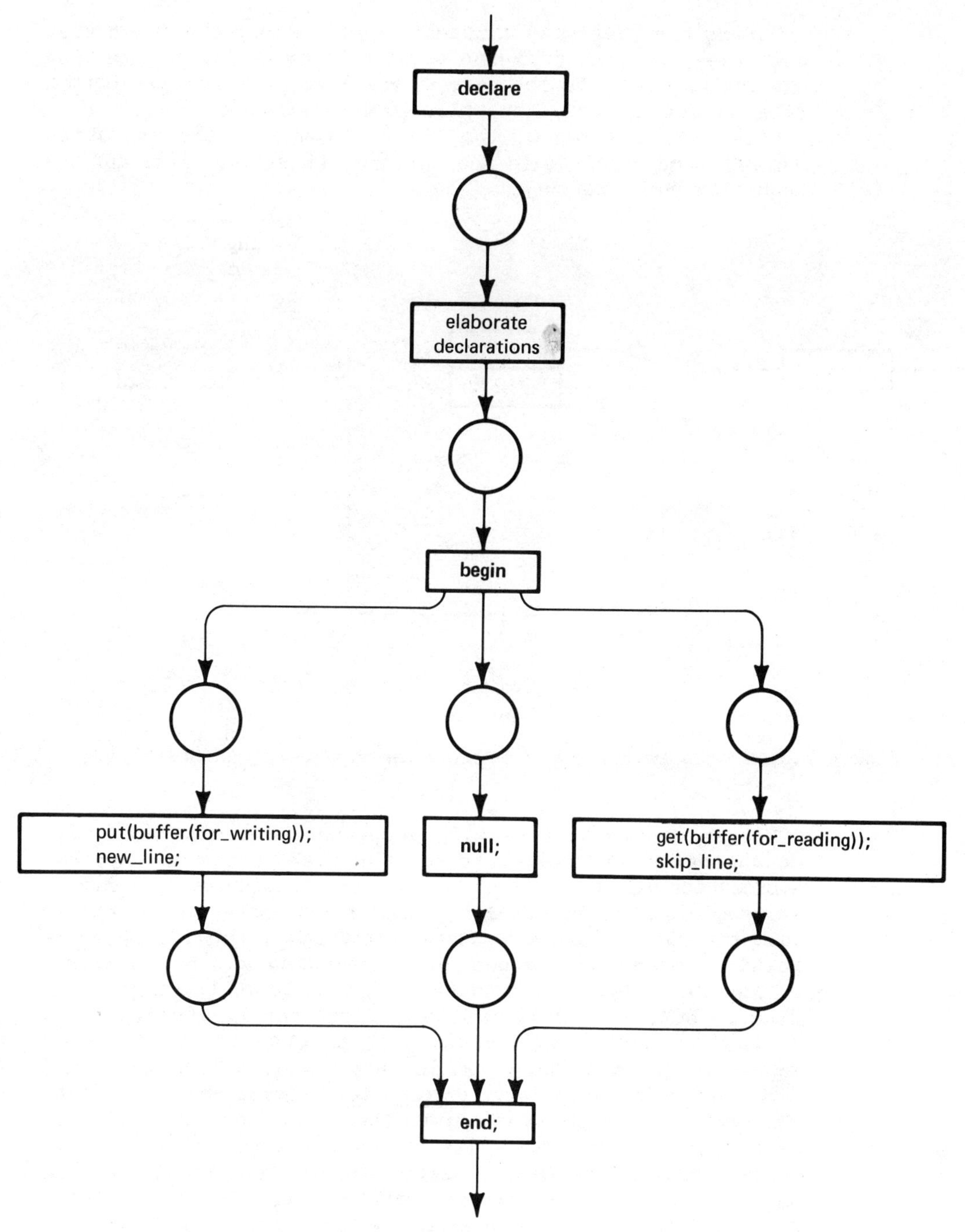

Figure 2.2. The block statement in copy_text_concurrently

During the last pass through the while loop the Input task gets the last line from the input file at the same time that the Output task puts the next to the last line onto the output file. Following this, the while loop terminates.

After termination of the while statement, the execution becomes sequential again and the program writes (line 46) the last line onto the output file.

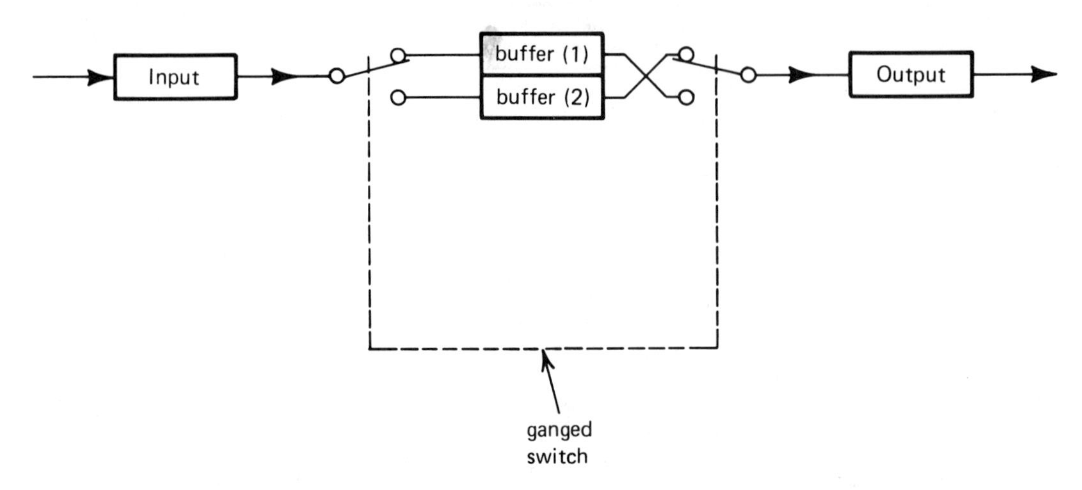

Figure 2.3. Ganged switching of buffers in copy_text_concurrently

We can reason quite easily about the correctness of this concurrent program because the two tasks share neither resources nor variables: they operate on disjoint peripherals as well as disjoint variables, buffer(1) and buffer(2). We ensure that the two tasks access these variables disjointly by maintaining "opposite" values in for_reading and for_writing. During the first pass through the while loop, Input stores a line in buffer(2) while Output writes the line which is in buffer(1); during the second pass through the while loop, Input stores in buffer(1) while Output writes from buffer(2).

The appealing simplicity of copy_text_concurrently is due to the fact that the program spawns the tasks Input and Output on each cycle through the while loop after setting the correct buffer indexes. No synchronization of the concurrent tasks is necessary because we swap the buffer indexes when the execution is strictly sequential--before elaborating and activating the tasks. It might seem to the reader that the overhead of spawning two tasks for the transfer of each line would be impractical or unrealistic. But the reader would be mistaken: the overhead of multitasking in Ada is comparable to the overhead of procedure calls.

This program could nearly halve the time it takes to copy a text file from one file to another--assuming that the transfer rates of the input device and the output device are about equal. If the transfer rates of the two devices are quite incomparable (for example, copying from a disk to a printer), then the throughput of the program should approach the top speed of the slower device. Of course, there is some overhead due to the spawning of the tasks. Considering this overhead, our prediction is that the concurrent program will copy at better than 90 per cent of the top speed of the slower device.

A typical structure of an Ada multitasking program is the definition of several tasks that jointly and concurrently perform the required actions. These tasks are usually declared as co-workers in a common master. Our example typifies this structure.

FAST COMPUTATIONS AND OPERATIONS

In this section we describe a strategy for writing concurrent programs that are potentially faster than functionally equivalent sequential programs. Why did I write "potentially" in the above sentence? Because multitasking Ada programs may or may not execute in genuine concurrency. Whether they do depends on the computing system on which they execute. We can distinguish three kinds of computing systems:

1. The computing system contains multiple general purpose processors--at least one for each task ready to run. These programs can be executed with genuine task concurrency.

2. The computing system contains fewer general purpose processors than the number of tasks ready to run. (An important example of this kind of system is the computer that contains one general purpose processor.) For this kind of system the processor(s) must be time-shared among the ready to run tasks, and ready to run tasks have to wait their turn on a processor. These programs are executed with partial or quasi concurrency.

3. The computing system contains several processors; but some of them are limited to executing certain specialized tasks. An important example of this kind of system is a computer with one general purpose processor and several special purpose processors for input/output devices. For this kind of system some programs (like our text copying program) may be executed in genuine concurrency; but other programs (like the ones below) may be executed in quasi concurrency.

Ada provides an abstract model of concurrency which discounts the details of the three kinds of systems. According to this model, tasks execute in parallel in the following sense: "Each task can be considered to be executed by a logical processor of its own." In actuality, n parallel tasks (parallel logical processors) may be implemented on n physical processors or with interleaved execution on fewer than n physical processors. The programmer, however, can take the abstract view that a logical processor executes each one of his tasks. As he writes his program, he may ignore the issue of how many physical processors the target machine actually contains. The actual number of processors is totally hidden from the programmer and his program.

An advantage of this model is that no software changes are required in order to move an Ada multitasking program from a uniprocessor system to a multiprocessor system or vice versa. Programs written to take advantage of potential concurrency can tap performance extensibility. Ada target machines can offer ranges of performance by the simple measure of adding or removing physical processors from their configurations. System designers may be unshackled from choosing a single, inflexible cost/performance tradeoff.

In order to illustrate concurrent computations, we develop a subprogram that computes the product of a matrix and vector. Assuming these declarations

```
subtype Index is Integer range 1..3;
type Vector is array(Index) of Float;
type Matrix is array(Index, Index) of Float;
u, v : Vector;
m    : Matrix;
```

we will develop a "fast" function for forming the following product

```
u := m*v; -- matrix times vector
```

This product can be written as three (scalar) assignment statements

```
u(1) := m(1, 1)*v(1) + m(1, 2)*v(2) + m(1, 3)*v(3);

u(2) := m(2, 1)*v(1) + m(2, 2)*v(2) + m(2, 3)*v(3);

u(3) := m(3, 1)*v(1) + m(3, 2)*v(2) + m(3, 3)*v(3);
```

The following sequentially coded function computes the product of an object of type Matrix and an object of type Vector:

```
function "*"(m : Matrix; v : Vector) return Vector is
  u : Vector;
begin
  for j in 1..3 loop
      u(j) := m(j, 1)*v(1) + m(j, 2)*v(2) + m(j, 3)*v(3);
  end loop;
  return u;
end "*";
```

This function is far more sequential than necessary: for example, it performs nine sequential multiplications. The function could do all these multiplications concurrently. We won't go so far as declaring nine tasks to perform the nine multiplications; instead, we'll be contented to write a function declaring three independent tasks, one to compute each component of the result. Thus, we'll introduce concurrency--but not maximum possible concurrency--into the solution.

```
function "*"(m : Matrix; v : Vector) return Vector is
  u : Vector;
begin
  Master:
  declare
    task FirstComponent;
    task SecondComponent;
    task ThirdComponent;

    task body FirstComponent is
    begin
      u(1) := m(1, 1)*v(1) + m(1, 2)*v(2) + m(1, 3)*v(3);
    end FirstComponent;

    task body SecondComponent is
    begin
      u(2) := m(2, 1)*v(1) + m(2, 2)*v(2) + m(2, 3)*v(3);
    end SecondComponent;

    task body ThirdComponent is
    begin
      u(3) := m(3, 1)*v(1) + m(3, 2)*v(2) + m(3, 3)*v(3);
    end ThirdComponent;
  begin
    --    activate all three tasks
    null;
    --    wait here for all three tasks to terminate
  end Master;

  return u;
end "*";
```

This program works without task synchronization because the tasks refer to the shared variables <u>without conflict</u>. All the tasks refer to every component of the vector v; but they only read v's components (v is a local constant). On the other hand, all the tasks write (change) the vector u; but--and this is essential--they write disjoint components of u. If any of these tasks wrote objects that other tasks wrote or read, the result would be chaotic.

PARALLEL ARRAY SORT

Our next example is the development of a fast sort program. Here is a sequential sort program which uses the Straight Selection method. This method is moderately efficient.

```
with Everypersons_IO; use Everypersons_IO;
procedure sequential_sort_program is
  type FloatArray is array(Integer range <>) of Float;
  ub : Positive; -- upper bound on number of floating point numbers

  procedure sort_array_sequentially(a : in out FloatArray) is
    k : Integer range a'range;           -- index of smallest value so far
    x : Float;                           -- smallest value so far
  begin
    for i in a'first..a'last - 1 loop    -- Selection Sort
      k := i;                            -- To begin, guess that the ith
      x := a(i);                         -- component is the smallest.
      for j in i + 1..a'last loop        -- Find the smallest component
        if a(j) < x then                 -- in the slice a(i..a'last);
          k := j;                        -- save this component's index;
          x := a(j);                     -- and save its value.
        end if;
      end loop;
      a(k) := a(i);                      -- Swap the smallest component
      a(i) := x;                         -- with the ith component.
    end loop;
  end sort_array_sequentially;
begin
  put("Enter an upper bound on the number of floating point numbers: ");
  get(ub);

  declare
    a : FloatArray(1..ub);             -- big enough to hold all the floats
    n : Natural := 0;                  -- will be the index of last input
  begin
    while not end_of_file and n < ub loop
      n := n + 1;
      get(a(n));
    end loop;

    sort_array_sequentially(a(1..n)); -- n is the actual number of floats

    for j in 1..n loop
      put(a(j));
    end loop;
  end;
end sequential_sort_program;
```

To develop a faster sort program, we could consider a faster algorithm such as Heapsort or Quicksort. Or we could employ parallel processes to conduct the sort. Of course, we select the latter in keeping with the objectives of this book. (We could, of course, combine a better sorting algorithm with parallel sorting and achieve even faster performance than we could with either technique alone. I have chosen not to do this in order that the reader may concentrate on the parallel aspects of the program. Additionally, our approach dramatizes that functionality or performance that is difficult to achieve in a sequential program may be very easy to achieve in a parallel program.)

Our approach to improving this program is straightforward: We divide the array into two strictly disjoint parts: a first half and a second half. Then we set one task to sorting the first half while we set another task to sorting the second half. After each task has finished sorting its half, we merge the two sorted halves on the output file.

For example, if the array to be sorted were

    80 68 30 67 70 21 62 01 79 75 18 53 29 65 18 85 68

then the task Sort_First_Half would sort

    80 68 30 67 70 21 62 01 79

while the task Sort_Second_Half concurrently sorted

    75 18 53 29 65 18 85 68

Each task calls the procedure sort_array_sequentially to sort its *disjoint* slice of the original array. (Note that we depend upon sort_array_sequentially's reentrancy for our strategy to work.) After both tasks have terminated, the new value of the array would be

    01 21 30 62 67 68 70 79 80 18 18 29 53 65 68 75 85

The final operation merges the two sorted slices, A(1..9) and a(10..17), onto the output file.

```
with Everypersons_IO; use Everypersons_IO;
procedure concurrent_sort_program is
  type FloatArray is array(Integer range <>) of Float;
  ub : Positive; -- upper bound on number of floating point numbers

  procedure sort_array_sequentially(a : in out FloatArray) is separate;
    -- the body of this procedure is exactly the same as before

  procedure merge_arrays_on_output_file(x, y : in FloatArray) is separate;
begin
  put("Enter an upper bound on the number of floating point numbers: ");
  get(ub);

  declare
    a : FloatArray(1..ub);     -- an array big enough to hold all the floats
    n : Natural := 0;          -- eventually, the index of the last float
    m : Positive;              -- the middle index of the slice a(1..n)
  begin
    while not end_of_file and n < ub loop
      n := n + 1;
      get(a(n));
    end loop;
    m := (1 + n)/2; -- the middle index of the slice a(1..n)

    declare                                  -- This
      task Sort_First_Half;                  -- block
      task body Sort_First_Half is           -- which
      begin                                  -- spawns
        sort_array_sequentially(a(1..m));    -- two
      end Sort_First_Half;                   -- concurrent
                                             -- tasks
      task Sort_Second_Half;                 -- replaces
      task body Sort_Second_Half is          -- the
      begin                                  -- previous
        sort_array_sequentially(a(m+1..n)); -- single
      end Sort_Second_Half;                  -- invocation
    begin                                    -- of
      null;                                  -- procedure
    end;                                     -- sort_array_sequentially.

    merge_arrays_on_output_file(a(1..m), a(m+1..n));
  end;
end concurrent_sort_program;
```

```
separate (concurrent_sort_program)
  -- This procedure merges the arrays x and y onto the output file
procedure merge_arrays_on_output_file(x, y : in FloatArray) is
  index_x : Integer := x'first;
  index_y : Integer := y'first;
begin
  loop
    if x(index_x) < y(index_y) then
      put(x(index_x));
      index_x := index_x + 1;
      if index_x > x'last then      -- all of x has been output
        for j in index_y..y'last    -- so output the rest of y
        loop
          put(y(j));
        end loop;
        return;
      end if;
    else                            -- y(index_y) <= x(index_x)
      put(y(index_y));
      index_y := index_y + 1;
      if index_y > y'last then      -- all of y has been output
        for j in index_x..x'last    -- so output the rest of x
        loop
          put(x(j));
        end loop;
        return;
      end if;
    end if;
  end loop;
end merge_arrays_on_output_file;
```

The procedure concurrent_sort_program is indeed more efficient than sequential_sort_program. If we compute the number of comparisons required to sort a large array, we find that the concurrent program requires a little more than half the number of comparisons that the sequential program requires. If most of these comparisons can be done concurrently, than the concurrent program can be executed in just a little more than one-fourth the time of the sequential program.

We must admit that we did not completely sort the array _in situ_. The final phase of our algorithm merged the two disjoint sorted slices onto the output file. If our objective had been to sort the array _in situ_ (i.e., without an auxiliary array or file storage) our program would not have been so lucid and easy to derive. See the exercises for a parallel program that sorts an array _in situ_.

PARALLEL LINEAR SEARCH

In this section we will illustrate how parallel processors can speed up linear search.

Linear search is very simple--and very inefficient. The reader might question whether we should take any interest in such an inefficient search technique. The answer is, linear search is sometimes appropriate--or even unavoidable. We give two examples.

For the first example, consider an array of records sorted on some particular component (the component on which the records are sorted is usually called the key). To find a record that contains a particular key value, efficient search procedures can be invoked (for example, binary search). But suppose a client of the data base wants to retrieve a record that contains some particular nonkey value. To avoid resorting the array or maintaining the data sorted on several components, we can find the desired record by a linear search based on the nonkey value.

For the second example, consider an array that is organized by "hashing": the insertion procedure proceeds by computing the index of the new record from a hash function operating on the new record's key. Unfortunately, hash functions frequently map different keys into the same index. Since two records cannot be stored at the same index, the insertion procedure may have to search linearly from the computed index until it comes to an empty component of the array. Similarly, a find procedure looking for a record with a certain key will use the hash function to compute the index where the desired record may be located. If the desired record is not at at that index (because of hash collisions during insertions), the find procedure may have to conduct a linear search starting at the hashed index.

We choose the first example for the context of a parallel linear search algorithm. We assume that the database is composed of a sequence of objects of the type Rekord.

```
subtype KeyType is String(1..24); -- Any scalar type definition will do.
subtype ValType is ...;           -- This type may be any nonlimited type.

type Rekord is
  record
    key : KeyType; -- the data base is sorted on the key component
    val : ValType; -- any value of this type occurs uniquely in the table
    . . .          -- other components may be included, of course
  end record;
```

We assume that the database is sorted on KeyType; but there are occasional inquiries based on a ValType value. We furthermore assume that any given value of ValType can occur at most one time in the database. For example, the key could be a person's name and the val component could be a person's social security number or automobile license number. A reasonable but not necessarily complete specification for our database is

```
package DataBase is
  size : constant := 30_000;          -- the size of the encapsulated table
  subtype KeyType is String(1..24);   -- the type on which the table is sorted
  subtype ValType is ...;             -- may be any nonlimited type
  type Rekord is
    record
      key : KeyType; -- the data base is sorted on the key component
      val : ValType; -- any value occurs uniquely in the table
      . . .          -- other components may be included, of course
    end record;

  procedure read_table;         -- reads table of Rekords from disk

  procedure write_table;        -- writes table on disk

  procedure insert_item(item : Rekord);
    -- inserts item into table sorted on the key field
  table_overflow : exception;
    -- insert_item may raise this exception

  function find_key(key : KeyType) return Rekord;
  function find_val(val : ValType) return Rekord;
  not_in_table : exception;     -- may be raised by either find_key or find_val
end DataBase;
```

Our goal is to program find_val using parallel linear search. We assume two processes in our solution. How shall we proceed, assuming that the data structure, named table, is an array? One approach would be to start one process at the right end of the array working toward the middle while the other process started at the left end of the array, also working toward the middle. The trouble with this approach and others like it is that the processes would have to check the index (e.g., for the middle value) as well as check the val component. A more desirable solution is to provide sentinels to stop a fruitless search (remember that one search will always be fruitless). Our strategy is to declare table with two extra components and store the desired value of ValType in two dummy records at the high end of table. We can start two processes at the low end of table, one searching table's odd components and the other searching table's even components.

```
package body DataBase is
  type Index is Integer range 1..size + 2; -- make room for search sentinels
  table : array (Index) of Rekord;

  -- Other subprogram bodies go here.

  function find_val(val : ValType) return Rekord is
    j : Index := size + 1;          -- Make j point at a dummy record.
  begin
    table(size + 1).val := val; -- Insert sentinel into first dummy record.
    table(size + 2).val := val; -- Insert sentinel into second dummy record.
    declare
      task Searcher_1;              -- searches odd records
      task Searcher_2;              -- searches even records

      task body Searcher_1 is
        j : Index := 1;             -- hides direct visibility of global j
      begin
        while table(j).val /= val loop  -- scan the 1st, 3rd, 5th, 7th, etc.
          j := j + 2;
        end loop;
        if j <= size then
          find_val.j := j;
          abort Searcher_2;         -- Abort the fruitless searcher so that the
        end if;                     -- master block can complete its execution.
      end Searcher_1;

      task body Searcher_2 is
        j : Index := 2;             -- hides direct visibility of global j
      begin
        while table(j).val /= val loop  -- scan the 2nd, 4th, 6th, 8th, etc.
          j := j + 2;
        end loop;
        if j <= size then
          find_val.j := j;
          abort Searcher_1;         -- Abort the fruitless searcher so that the
        end if;                     -- master block can complete its execution.
      end Searcher_2;
    begin
      -- both tasks are activated here
      null;
      -- wait here for both tasks to terminate
    end;
    if j > size then
      raise not_in_table;
    end if;
    return table(j);
  end find_val;
end DataBase;
```

PARALLEL, INDEPENDENT, IDENTICAL PROCESSES

In our examples so far all the tasks declared in a given master have been dissimilar. But frequently we need many identical tasks. It would be burdensome to have to write the same task declaration over and over to create several identical instances of a given task. If we needed 1000 instances of a task, it would be downright outrageous to have to write 1000 identical task declarations.

We would like to be able to define a task template and then declare instances of the task template--much as as we define a data type and then declare objects of the data type. In fact, Ada uses its data type mechanism to declare templates for task objects. The extension of the data type mechanism to tasks integrates multitasking with the rest of Ada and gives the programmer facilities for declaring and creating task objects as well as composite structures of task objects.

For example, suppose that we have to prepare lunch for a small army, and that we require 16 hamburger chefs and 10 french fry chefs.

```
procedure prepare_large_lunch(hamburgers, french_fries : out Food) is
  task type HamburgerChef;
  task type FrenchfryChef;

  hamburger_chef : array(1..16) of HamburgerChef; -- 16 hamburger chefs
  frenchfry_chef : array(1..10) of FrenchfryChef; -- 10 frenchfry chefs

  task body HamburgerChef is
    declaration of a hamburger chef's local entities
  begin
    instructions for preparing the hamburgers
  end HamburgerChef;

  task body FrenchfryChef is
    declaration of a french fry chef's local entities
  begin
    instructions for preparing the french fries
  end FrenchfryChef;
begin
  -- all 26 chefs are activated here
  null;
  -- wait for all 26 chefs to complete their instructions and terminate
end prepare_large_lunch;
```

The 26 chefs do not interact or communicate with one another. They do not share entities: each chef has all the entities it requires to prepare its contribution to lunch.

We see now that our earlier declaration of a single salad chef,

```
task PrepareSalad;
```

was equivalent to

```
task type AnonymousCook;
PrepareSalad : AnonymousCook;
```

CONCURRENT PROGRAMS FOR ROOT SEARCHING

In this section we will develop several programs for root searching. First, for comparison and orientation, we will exhibit an efficient sequential program; then we will develop a very efficient concurrent program--written for a three-processor computer; finally, we will develop a very efficient concurrent program written for an n-processor computer. Our final program will dramatize that the master must sometimes communicate with its dependent tasks after it creates them.

Let us write a function that attempts to find a root of an equation, say

```
f(x) = 0
```

first by strictly sequential processing and then by concurrent processing.

We assume the following global entities:

```
function f(x : Float) return Float; -- the function whose root we want
epsilon : constant Float :=  ;      -- desired tolerance of the root
no_root : exception;                -- in case there is no root
```

Further, we assume that the function f(x) is continuous--that is, that we can draw it without lifting our pen from the paper. Thus, we desire to implement

```
function root_of_f(a, b : Float) return Float;
```

where a..b is the closed interval in which we must try to find the value of x for which

```
f(x) = 0.
```

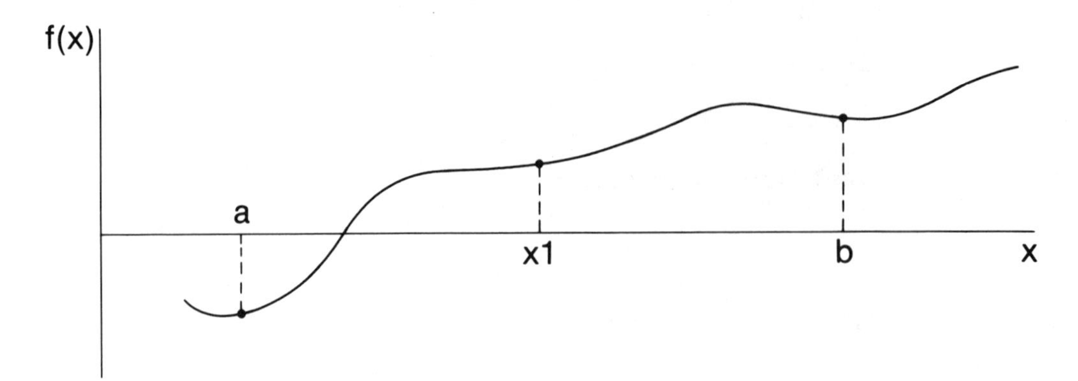

Figure 2.4. The bisection method of root searching

An efficient sequential method of finding a root of a continuous function is the bisection method. In this method we repetitively halve the interval containing the root until the length of the search interval is equal to or less than epsilon. Consider Figure 2.4 where x1 is the midpoint of the interval a..b. If

```
f(a)*f(x1) < 0.0
```

then the interval a..x1 surely contains a zero crossing (a root) of f(x)—because f(a) and f(x1) have different signs and therefore the continuous function f(x) must cross zero somewhere between a and x1. If

```
f(a)*f(x1) = 0.0
```

then the interval a..x1 also contains a root—it happens to be either the point a or the point x1. On the other hand if

```
f(x1)*f(b) < 0.0
```

or

```
f(x1)*f(b) = 0.0
```

then the closed interval x1..b surely contains a root of f(x)--for the same kind of arguments that we gave for the a..x1 subinterval.

Here is an Ada program using the bisection method:

```
function root_of_f(a, b : Float) return Float is
  -- This function uses the bisection method of root searching.
  xØ, xl, x2, fxØ, fxl, fx2, : Float;
begin
  xØ := a;                    -- left end-point of the search interval
  x2 := b;                    -- right end-point of the search interval
  fxØ := f(xØ);
  fx2 := f(x2);

  if x2 - xØ <= epsilon and fxØ*fx2 > Ø.Ø then
    raise no_root;
  end if;

  while x2 - xØ > epsilon loop
    xl := (xØ + x2)/2.Ø;          -- Find middle of search interval.
    fxl := f(xl);                 -- Evaluate f(x) at the mid-point.
    if fxØ*fxl <= Ø.Ø then        -- Shrink search interval to xØ..xl.
      x2 := xl;
      fx2 := fxl;
    elsif fxl*fx2 <= Ø.Ø then     -- Shrink search interval to xl..x2.
      xØ := xl;
      fxØ := fxl;
    else
      raise no_root;
    end if;
  end loop;
  return (xØ + x2)/2.Ø;
end root_of_f;
```

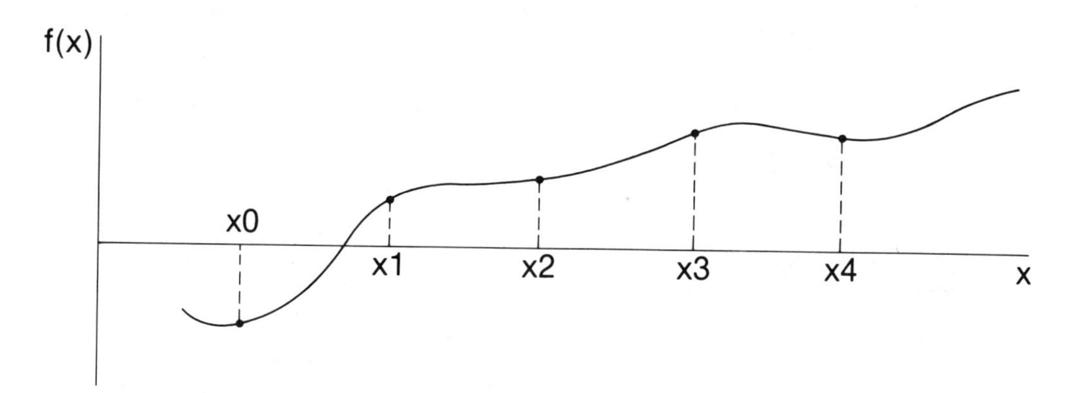

Figure 2.5. A parallel method of root searching

In the bisection root-searching program, the while loop repeatedly evaluates f(x); and, of course, the loop performs these evaluations sequentially. The evaluation of f(x) may be very time-consuming--in fact, it may dominate the execution time of root_of_f.

Could we use multiple physical processors to evaluate f(x1), f(x2), f(x3), and so on <u>concurrently</u>--and thereby speed up the operation of the function root_of_f? We will illustrate that we can. See Figure 2.5. Let us assume that we have three processors. We set one to work evaluating f(x1), one to work evaluating f(x2), and one to work evaluating f(x3). When all three concurrent processes have finished, we can apply our sign tests: f(xØ)*f(x1) <= Ø.Ø, f(x1)*f(x2) <= Ø.Ø, and so on to determine which of the intervals xØ..x1, x1..x2, ..., contain a root. Here is the Ada solution.

```
function root_of_f(a, b : Float) return Float is
  xØ, x1, x2, x3, x4, fxØ, fx1, fx2, fx3, fx4 : Float;
begin
  xØ := a; x4 := b; fxØ := f(xØ); fx4 := f(x4);

  if x4 - xØ <= epsilon and fxØ*fx4 > Ø.Ø then raise no_root; end if;

  while x4 - xØ > epsilon loop
    x1 := xØ + Ø.25*(x4 - xØ); -- \  Partition the search interval
    x2 := xØ + Ø.5Ø*(x4 - xØ); --  > into four equal quarters.
    x3 := xØ + Ø.75*(x4 - xØ); -- /

    declare                    -- Elaborate a block (task master) to
      task Compute_fx1;        -- concurrently compute f(x1), f(x2),
      task Compute_fx2;        -- and f(x3);
      task Compute_fx3;

      task body Compute_fx1 is
      begin
        fx1 := f(x1);
      end;

      task body Compute_fx2 is
      begin
        fx2 := f(x2);
      end;

      task body Compute_fx3 is
      begin
        fx3 := f(x3);
      end;
    begin
      null;
    end;
```

```
    if fxØ*fxl <= Ø.Ø then          -- Shrink search interval to xØ..xl.
      x4 := xl;
      fx4 := fxl;
    elsif fxl*fx2 <= Ø.Ø then       -- Shrink search interval to xl..x2.
      xØ := xl;
      x4 := x2;
      fxØ := fxl;
      fx4 := fx2;
    elsif fx2*fx3 <= Ø.Ø then       -- Shrink search interval to x2..x3.
      xØ := x2;
      x4 := x3;
      fxØ := fx2;
      fx4 := fx3;
    elsif fx3*fx4 <= Ø.Ø then       -- Shrink search interval to x3..x4.
      xØ := x3;
      fxØ := fx3;
    else
      raise no_root;
    end if;
  end loop;
  return (xØ + x4)/2.Ø;
end root_of_f;
```

How efficient is this program? It is very efficient--in fact, it is optimum--if the computer on which it executes has three processors to devote to the program's execution. The sequential bisection algorithm halves the search interval on each cycle; but--with three processors--our concurrent algorithm quarters the search interval on each cycle. This makes a huge difference in convergence of the interval to the desired tolerance.

(The claims for optimality in the previous paragraph are true if the time to evaluate f(x) is the same for all values of x. To see why this is so, just assume that the time to evaluate f(xl) is very small compared to the time to evaluate f(x2). In this case our synchronous algorithm makes the processor that evaluated f(xl) wait until the processor that is evaluating f(x2) is finished. We are not only wasting the first processor, we may also be wasting the second processor--because we may already be able to determine that the root lies in the interval xØ..xl. If the time required to evaluate f(x) is quite different for different values of x, then no synchronous concurrent algorithm can be optimum among all the possible concurrent algorithms. However, the optimum asynchronous concurrent algorithm may be very hard to synthesize.)

How does our synchronous concurrent algorithm perform on a uniprocessor? Not well at all. In fact, it is less efficient than the sequential bisection algorithm. Consider why this is so: The evaluations of f(xl), f(x2), and f(x3) take place in *quasi* concurrency--that is, they take place in the same amount of time as they would if executed sequentially. But this wastes processor time: because at least one and possibly two evaluations of the function f(x) are for values of x falling outside the subinterval containing the root. Look at the problem this way: if we run our three-process "concurrent" program on a uniprocessor, then three sequential computations of f(x) (namely, f(x1), f(x2), and f(x3)) will narrow the search interval to one-fourth of the original search interval; but if we run the sequential bisection program on a uniprocessor, then three sequential computations of f(x) (namely, f(x_middle), f(x_middle), f(x_middle)) will narrow the search interval to *one-eighth* of the original search interval.

On the other hand, how does our three-processor algorithm perform on a computer that could dedicate more than three processors to the program? Just as well as on a computer that has only three processors (which is to say a great deal better than the sequential bisection method), but less efficiently than an algorithm that takes advantage of all the available processors.

Clearly, we should try to write our root-searching algorithm to work optimumly for any number of processors. In order to do this we must devise a strategy for n processors.

Our general strategy for parallelism is simple: if we have n processors, divide the search interval into n + 1 equal intervals and determine which one of these subintervals contains a zero crossing; then divide this subinterval into n + 1 subsubintervals and determine which one of these contains a zero crossing; continue this shrinking of the subintervals containing the zero crossing until the length of some subsub...subinterval is equal to or less than epsilon, the desired root accuracy.

How shall we implement our n-processor strategy in Ada? Our program for three processors declared a **distinct** task object to compute each of the values f(x1), f(x2), and f(x3). This approach (declaring a distinct task object for each process) will be tedious for a large number of processors. Even worse, this approach will not work at all if we try to write a generic subprogram or make a run-time determination of the number of processors.

Therefore, we are tempted to declare a task *type* and create an array of tasks. How many tasks? Why n, of course, one for each processor. Therefore, the length of the array should be n, the number of available processors. Yielding to this temptation, we write the following program. (Verify that this program reduces to the bisection program when n = 1 and that it reduces to our three-process program when n = 3.)

```
function root_of_f(a, b : Float; n : Positive := 1) return Float is
  -- n is the number of tasks and hopefully the number of processors
  subtype ProcessNumber is Integer range 1..n; -- n tasks/processes
  x  : array(0..n + 1) of Float; -- \ x(0) and x(n + 1) are the end-points
  fx : array(0..n + 1) of Float; -- / of the interval under investigation.
  zero_crossing_detected : Boolean;
begin
  x(0) := a; x(n + 1) := b; fx(0) := f(a); fx(n + 1) := f(b);

  if b - a <= epsilon and fx(0)*fx(n + 1) > 0.0 then -- no zero crossing
    raise no_root;
  end if;

  while x(n + 1) - x(0) > epsilon loop -- Continue to look for zero crossing.
    declare                            -- a block that is a task master
      task type Compute_fx_j;

      Compute_fx : array(1..n) of Compute_fx_j; -- n tasks

      task body Compute_fx_j is
        j : ProcessNumber;             -- process number of the jth task
      begin
        x(j)  := x(0) + (Float(j)/Float(n + 1))*(x(n + 1) - x(0));
        fx(j) := f(x(j));
      end Compute_fx_j;
    begin
      -- all n tasks are invoked here
      null;
      -- wait here for all n tasks to terminate
    end;

    zero_crossing_detected:= false;
    for j in 0..n loop
      if fx(j)*fx(j + 1) <= 0.0 then
        zero_crossing_detected := true;
        x(0) := x(j);                  -- \  Shrink the search
        x(n + 1) : = x(j + 1);         --  \ interval to
        fx(0) := fx(j);                --  / x(j)..x(j + 1).
        fx(n + 1) := fx(j + 1);        -- /
        exit;
      end if;
    end loop;
    if zero_crossing_detected = false then
      raise no_root;
    end if;
  end loop;
  return (x(0) + x(n + 1))/2.0;
end root_of_f;
```

Our temptation was reasonable; but our implementation won't work. Study the implementation carefully: there is much about it that is quite sound--but there is one fatal problem. Can you can spot the problem?

The problem is that all n tasks share the same task body; all n tasks are identical. The local variable j in each task _could_ distinguish the tasks; but the program doesn't initialize these local variables. In other words, the individual tasks do not know who they are! We might hope that there is an attribute of each component of the array of tasks that each task can query to determine its respective identity (position in the array). We're not used to hoping for some facility in Ada and not finding it! But in this case our hopes are vain.

Notice that the master can easily access any component of the array of tasks. For example, Compute_fx(j) identifies a task that could execute

```
x(j)  := x(Ø) + (Float(j)/Float(n + 1))*(x(n + 1) - x(Ø));
fx(j) := f(x(j));
```

But, as we said, there is no built-in Ada attribute or function that Compute_fx(j) itself can use to discover its index and hence its assignment. Nor can tasks have parameters (as procedures do) which their invoker can use to communicate with them.

This problem shouldn't surprise us. The components of data structures are usually passive objects--operands. Operators require knowledge of operands; but operands don't require knowledge of themselves.

There are several techniques for sequentially informing every task of its identity so that each task can work on the appropriate f(x(j)). One technique is to have the master rendezvous with every task in turn: during each rendezvous the master gives each task its assignment (informs each task of its identity). In the next chapter, we show how the master can conduct a rendezvous with each of its dependent tasks.

REFERENCE

Yemini, S. On the suitability of Ada multitasking for expressing parallel algorithms. Proceedings of the AdaTEC Conference on Ada, 1982, 91-97.

EXERCISES

2.1. Write an Ada procedure for the Petri net in Figure 2.6.

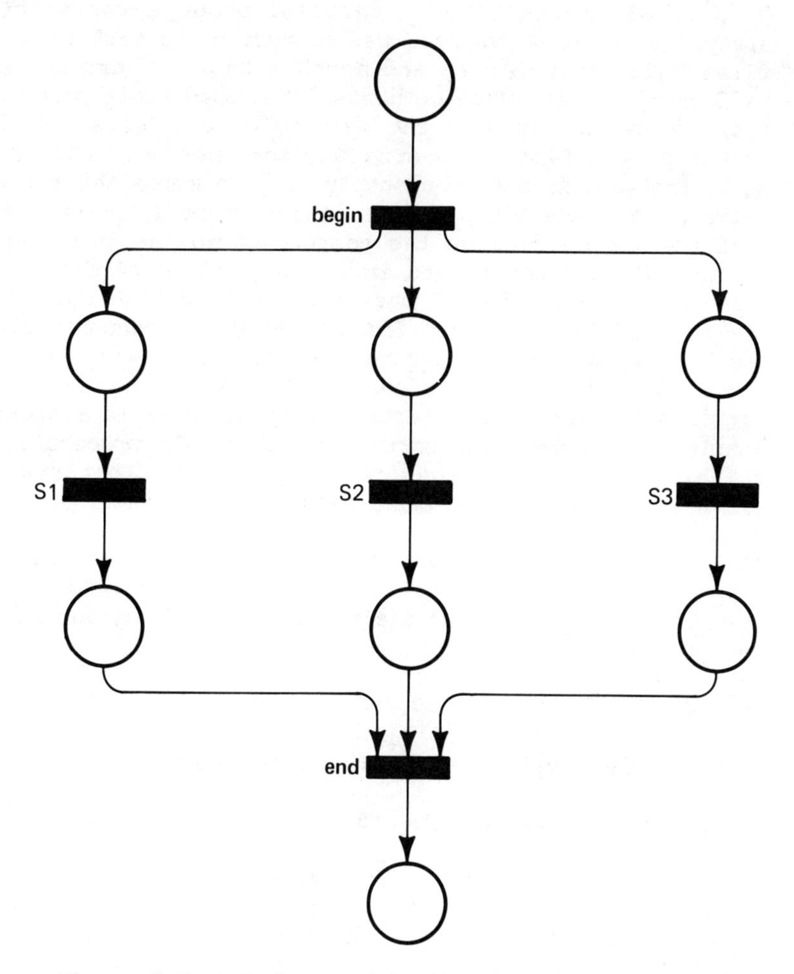

Figure 2.6. Petri net with three parallel processes

2.2. Write a skeleton procedure that executes the project depicted in the Petri net in Figure 1.16 on page 15.

2.3 Draw a Petri net for the prepare_dinner procedure on page 37.

2.4 Rewrite the procedure on page 40 so that it reads a file of real numbers, converts each real number to an integer, and writes each integer onto another file. Reduce the number of tasks by programming the master to perform the conversion.

2.5. Write a parallel program which reads a text file, capitalizes all the lower-case letters, and writes this transformed text onto the output file.

2.6. On page 53 we exhibited a parallel program for sorting an array. The strategy we used was to assign one task to sort the first half of the array and another task to sort the second half of the array. When both tasks finished their parts of the job, the master invoked the merging of the two sorted halves on the output file. This strategy does not sort the array *in situ*: instead, it uses the output file to merge the two sorted halves. For some applications, this may be inappropriate.

If we could rearrange the components in the incoming array so that all the components in the left slice of the array are less than or equal to all the components in the right slice of the array, then we could independently and concurrently sort the left slice and the right slice, with the happy result that the whole array would be sorted. This rearranging is called *partitioning* the array. Partitioning an array is a great deal simpler and faster than sorting an array. The procedure on the following page partitions an array of type FloatArray. For example, assume the initial arrangement of a is

```
80  68  30  67  70  21  62  79  01  75  18  53  29  65  18  85  68
```

then the initial sort of a(a'first), a(middle), and a(a'last) results in

```
01  68  30  67  70  21  62  79  68  75  18  53  29  65  18  85  80
```

and the pivot value is 68. The partitioning results in

```
01  18  30  67  65  21  62  29  53  18||75  68  79  70  68  85  80
```

where the right slice is (75, 68, 79, 70, 68, 85, 80) and the left slice is (01, 18, 30, 67, 65, 21, 62, 29, 53, 18). (The partition has fallen between 18 and 75--note the vertical bars). This partition is fortunate; but a perfect partition would result in two slices of equal length.

```
-- The following  procedure partitions the array a so that:
-- the values in a(a'first..a1_last) are less than or equal to pivot_value;
-- the values in a(a1_last + 1..a2_first - 1) (if any) equal pivot_value;
-- the values in a(a2_first..a'last) are greater than or equal to pivot_value.
procedure partition_the_array(a        : in out FloatArray;
                              a1_last  : out    Integer;
                              a2_first : out    Integer) is
  i, j, m     : Integer range a'range;
  pivot_value : Float;

  procedure swap(x, y : in out Float) is
    t : Float := x;
  begin
    x := y;
    y := t;
  end swap; pragma inline(swap);
begin
  i := a'first;
  j := a'last;
  m := (i + j)/2;               --        the middle component of the array

  if a(i) > a(m) then           -- \      Sort the array components
    swap(a(i), a(m));           --  \     a(a'first), a(middle), and a(a'last).
  end if;                       --   \    The purpose of this preliminary sort
  if a(m) > a(j) then           --    \   is to obtain an estimate of the med-
    swap(a(m), a(j));           --     >  ian value of the array's values. If
  end if;                       --    /   a(m) happens to be the median value
  if a(i) > a(m) then           --   /    then we are very fortunate--because
    swap(a(i), a(m));           --  /     about half the values will precede
  end if;                       -- /      a(m) and half the values will follow.

  pivot_value := a(m);          --        Hopefully, it's close to the median.

  loop                          --        Partition the array about pivot_value.
    while a(i) < pivot_value loop     -- Scan from the left end toward the
      i := i + 1;                     -- right end, searching for the next
    end loop;                         -- value >= pivot_value.
    while a(j) > pivot_value loop     -- Scan from the right end toward the
      j := j - 1;                     -- left end, searching for the next
    end loop;                         -- value <= pivot_value.
    if i <= j then                    -- If the scans haven't passed each other
      swap(a(i), a(j));               -- swap the out-of-place components
      i := i + 1;                     -- and then advance the left scan
      j := j - 1;                     -- and advance the right scan.
    end if;
    exit when i > j;                  -- Exit when the scans pass each other.
  end loop;
  a1_last  := j;
  a2_first := i;
end partition_the_array;
```

2.7. Rewrite the parallel sort program on page 53 so that the tasks are created in a procedure rather than a block statement.

2.8. Rewrite the partitioning procedure partition_the_array (page 69) as a parallel program. (Hint: execute the two scans in parallel rather than serially.)

2.9. Rewrite the parallel linear search function find_val (page 57) for a three-processor computer. Assume that the table data structure is long enough to hold the sentinels.

2.10. Rewrite the root-searching program on pages 62-63 in order to make it "more parallel".

ANSWERS TO EXERCISES

2.1. Either of the following (and several others) will suffice. (Since the null statement does nothing, we may omit it from the Petri net.)

```
procedure do_figure_2.7 is
   task For_S1;
   task For_S2;
   task For_S3;

   task body For_S1 is
   begin
     S1;
   end For_S1;

   task body For_S2 is
   begin
     S2;
   end For_S2;

   task body For_S3 is
   begin
     S3;
   end For_S3;
begin
  null;
end do_figure_2.7;
```

```
procedure do_figure_2.7 is
  task For_S1;
  task For_S2;

  task body For_S1 is
  begin
    S1;
  end For_S1;

  task body For_S2 is
  begin
    S2;
  end For_S2;
begin
  S3;
end do_figure_2.7;
```

2.2 Here is one solution.

```
procedure execute_project is
  task For_t1_and_successors;
  task For_t2;

  task body For_t1_and_successors is
  begin
    t1;

    block_for_t3_and_t4:
    declare
      task For_t3;
      task For_t4;

      task body For_t3 is
      begin
        t3;
      end For_t3;

      task body For_t4 is
      begin
        t4;
      end For_t4;
    begin
      -- Activate Both For_t3 and For_t4 here.
      null;
      -- Wait here for both For_t3 and For_t4 to terminate.
    end block_for_t3_and_t4;

    t5;
  end For_t1_and_successors;

  task body For_t2 is
  begin
    t2;
  end For_t2;
begin
  -- Activate both For_t1_and_successors and For_t2 here.
  null;
  -- Wait here for both For_t1_and_successors and For_t2 to terminate.
end execute_project;
```

2.2. Here is another solution.

```
procedure execute_project is
  task For_tl_and_successors;
  task For_t2;

  task body For_tl_and_successors is
    procedure t3_also_t4 is
      task For_t3;
      task For_t4;

      task body For_t3 is
      begin
        t3;
      end For_t3;

      task body For_t4 is
      begin
        t4;
      end For_t4;
    begin
      -- Activate both For_t3 and For_t4 here.
      null;
      -- Wait here for both For_t3 and For_t4 to terminate.
    end t3_also_t4;
  begin
    tl;
    t3_also_t4;
    t5;
  end For_tl_and_successors;

  task body For_t2 is
  begin
    t2;
  end For_t2;
begin
  -- Activate both For_tl_and_successors and For_t2 here.
  null;
  -- Wait here for both For_tl_and_successors and For_t2 to terminate.
end execute_project;
```

2.3.

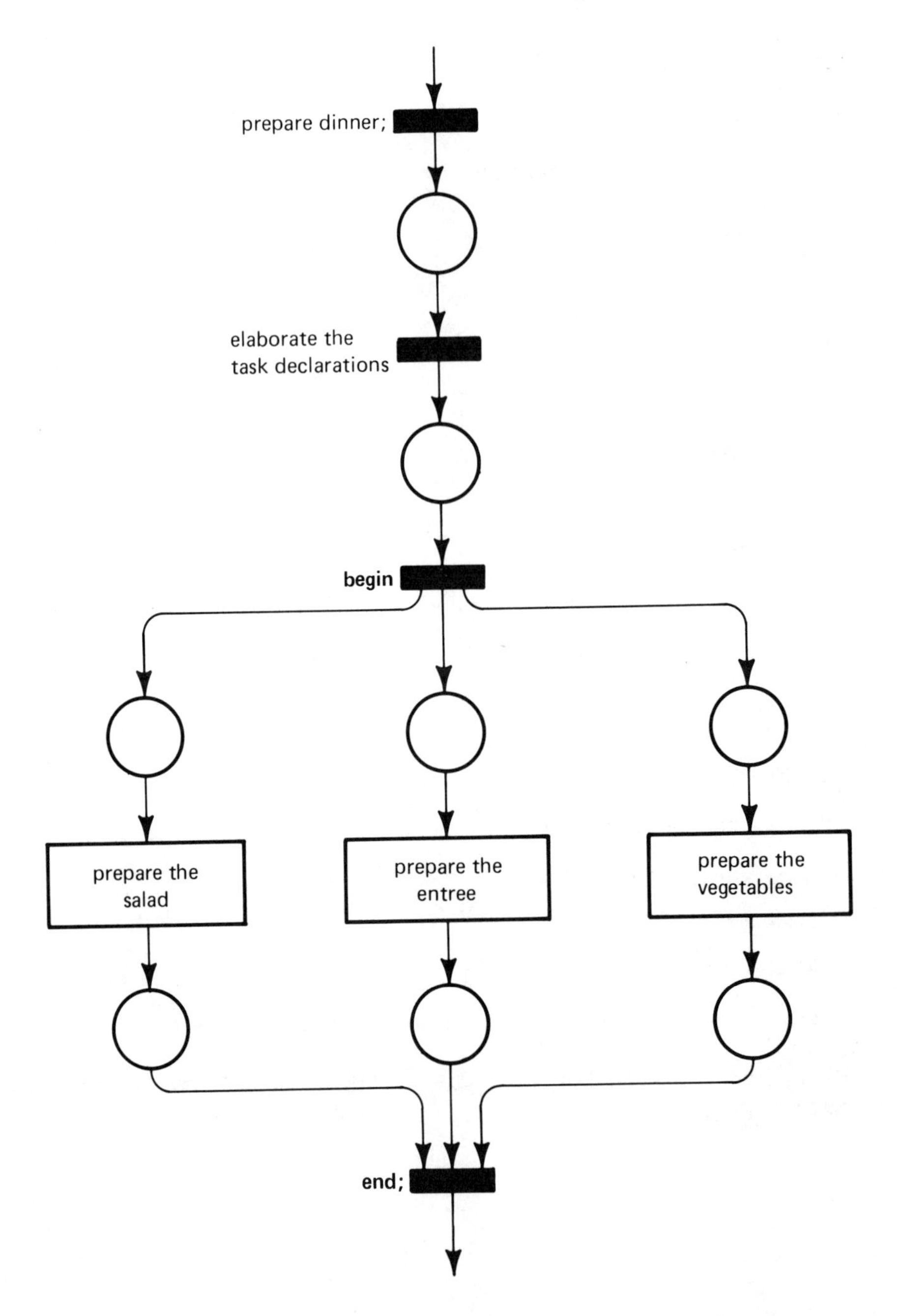

Figure 2.7. Petri net for prepare_dinner procedure, page 37

2.4.

```
with Sequential_IO;
procedure parallel_read_convert_write_2 is
  real_buffer_1, real_buffer_2 : Float;
  integer_buffer_1, integer_buffer_2 : Integer;

  package Float_IO is new Sequential_IO(Float); use Float_IO;
  file_of_real : Float_IO.File_Type;

  package Integer_IO is new Sequential_IO(Integer); use Integer_IO;
  file_of_integer : Integer_IO.File_Type;
begin
  open(file_of_real, mode => in_file, name => "----------");
  create(file_of_integer, mode => out_file, name => "**********");

  read(file_of_real, real_buffer_1);
  integer_buffer_1 := Integer(real_buffer_1);
  if end_of_file(file_of_real) then
    write(file_of_integer, integer_buffer_1);
  else
    read(file_of_real, real_buffer_2);
    while not end_of_file(file_of_real) loop
      declare  -- a master for two tasks
        task Read_real;
        task body Read_real is
        begin
          read(file_of_real, real_buffer_1);
        end Read_real;

        task Write_integer;
        task body Write_integer is
        begin
          write(file_of_integer, integer_buffer_1);
        end Write_integer;
      begin
        integer_buffer_2 := Integer(real_buffer_2);
      end;

      real_buffer_2    := real_buffer_1;
      integer_buffer_1 := integer_buffer_2;
    end loop;
    write(file_of_integer, integer_buffer_1);
    integer_buffer_2 := Integer(real_buffer_2);
    write(file_of_integer, integer_buffer_2);
  end if;
  close(file_of_real);
  close(file_of_integer);
end parallel_read_transform_write_2;
```

2.5.

```
with Text_IO; use Text_IO;
procedure get_capitalize_put is
  buffer1, buffer2, buffer3 : Character;

  procedure capitalize(ch : in out Character) is
  begin
    if ch in 'a'..'z' then
      ch := Character'val(Character'pos(ch) - 32); -- ASCII
    end if;
  end capitalize;
  pragma inline(capitalize);
begin
  get(buffer3);                    -- \
  capitalize(buffer3);             --  > initialize buffers
  get(buffer2);                    -- /

  while not end_of_file loop
    declare
      task Input;
      task Output;

      task body Input is
      begin
        get(buffer1);
      end Input;

      task body Output is
      begin
        put(buffer3);
      end Output;
    begin
      capitalize(buffer2);
    end;

    buffer3 := buffer2; -- move data from capitalize's buffer to Output's
    buffer2 := buffer1; -- move data from Input's buffer to capitalize's
  end loop;

  put(buffer3);                    -- \
  capitalize(buffer2);             --  > process data left in buffers
  put(buffer2);                    -- /
end get_capitalize_put;
```

2.6

```
with partition_the_array, sort_array_sequentially;
procedure sort_array_concurrently(a : in out FloatArray) is
  procedure sort_slices_concurrently(x, y : in out FloatArray) is
    -- It is the caller's duty to ensure that x and y are disjoint.
    task Sort_x;
    task body Sort_x is
    begin
      sort_array_sequentially(x);
    end Sort_x;

    task Sort_y;
    task body Sort_y is
    begin
      sort_array_sequentially(y);
    end Sort_y;
  begin
    null;
  end sort_slices_concurrently;
begin
  declare
    a1_last, a2_first : Integer range a'range;
  begin
    partition_the_array(a, a1_last, a2_first);   -- a1_last < a2_first
    sort_slices_concurrently(a(a'first..a1_last), a(a2_first..a'last));
  end;
end sort_array_concurrently;
```

2.7.

```
with Everypersons_IO; use Everypersons_IO;
procedure concurrent_sort_program is
  type FloatArray is array(Integer range <>) of Float;
  ub : Positive; -- upper bound on number of floating point numbers

  procedure sort_arrays_concurrently(x, y : in out FloatArray) is separate;

  procedure merge_arrays_on_output_file(x, y in FloatArray) is separate;
begin
  put("Enter an upper bound on the number of floating point numbers: ");
  get(ub);

  declare
    a : FloatArray(1..ub);     -- an array big enough to hold all the floats
    n : Natural := 0;          -- eventually, the index of the last float
    m : Positive;              -- the middle index of the slice a(1..n)
  begin
    while not end_of_file and n < ub
    loop
      n := n + 1;
      get(a(n));
    end loop;
    m := (1 + n)/2; -- the middle index of the slice a(1..n)

    sort_arrays_concurrently(a(1..m), a(m+1..n));
    merge_arrays_on_output_file(a(1..m), a(m+1..n));
  end;
end concurrent_sort_program;


with sort_array_sequentially;
separate (concurrent_sort_program)
procedure sort_arrays_concurrently(x, y : in out FloatArray) is
  -- It is the caller's duty to ensure that x and y are disjoint.
  task Sort_X;
  task body Sort_X is
  begin
    sort_array_sequentially(x);
  end Sort_X;

  task Sort_Y;
  task body Sort_Y is
  begin
    sort_array_sequentially(y);
  end Sort_Y;
begin
  null;
end sort_arrays_concurrently;
```

2.7. (continued from preceding page)

```
separate (concurrent_sort_program)
  -- This procedure merges the arrays x and y onto the output file
procedure merge_arrays_on_output_file(x, y in FloatArray) is
  index_x : Integer := x'first;
  index_y : Integer := y'first;
begin
  loop
    if x(index_x) < y(index_y) then
      put(x(index_x));
      index_x := index_x + 1;
      if index_x > x'last then      -- all of x has been output
        for j in index_y..y'last    -- so output the rest of y
        loop
          put(y(j));
        end loop;
        return;
      end if;
    else                            -- y(index_y) <= x(index_x)
      put(y(index_y));
      index_y := index_y + 1;
      if index_y > y'last then      -- all of y has been output
        for j in index_x..x'last    -- so output the rest of x
        loop
          put(x(j));
        end loop;
        return;
      end if;
    end if;
  end loop;
end merge_arrays_on_output_file;
```

2.8. The basic loop in the version of partition_the_array on page 69 can be replaced with the following loop, which uses two tasks to perform the two scans. Note that this version could be appallingly inefficient. For example, if the initial array is sorted in the wrong direction, the block statement will perform a'length task activations (!) just to partition the array (assuming that the pivot_value is the median value of the component values). On the other hand, if the array is already nearly sorted, the two-process approach would be quite useful. Of course, we could--and should--reduce the number of task activations by programming the master to perform one of the scans itself. On the other hand, I suppose that a fairly smart compiler could detect that the master (the block statement in this case) should perform one of the task's chores itself.

Note that two scans can be executed in parallel because they are completely independent of each other; therefore, they can be performed in any order (or in parallel).

```
loop                                      -- Partition array about pivot_value.
  declare
    task Scan_from_left_end;
    task Scan_from_right_end;

    task Scan_from_left_end is
    begin
      while a(i) < pivot_value loop       -- Scan from the left end toward the
        i := i + 1;                       -- right end, searching for the next
      end loop;                           -- value >= pivot_value.
    end;

    task Scan_from_right_end is
    begin
      while a(j) > pivot_value loop       -- Scan from the right end toward the
        j := j - 1;                       -- left end, searching for the next
      end loop;                           -- value <= pivot_value.
    end;
  begin
    null;
  end;

  if i <= j then                        -- If the scans haven't passed each other
    swap(a(i), a(j));                   -- swap the out-of-place components
    i := i + 1;                         -- and then advance the left scan
    j := j - 1;                         -- and advance the right scan.
  end if;
  exit when i > j;                      -- Exit when scans pass each other.
end loop;
```

2.9.

```
function find_val(val : ValType) return Rekord is
  i : Index := size + 1;
begin
  table(size + 1).val := val; -- \
  table(size + 2).val := val; --  >  sentinels
  table(size + 3).val := val; -- /
  declare
    task Searcher_1;
    task Searcher_2;
    task Searcher_3;

    task body Searcher_1 is
      j : Index := 1;
    begin
      while table(j).val /= val loop  -- scan the 1st, 4th, 7th, 10th, etc.
        j := j + 3;
      end loop;
      if j <= size then
        i := j;
        abort Searcher_2, Searcher_3;
      end if;
    end Searcher_1;

    task body Searcher_2 is
      j : Index := 2;
    begin
      while table(j).val /= val loop  -- scan the 2nd, 5th, 8th, 11th, etc.
        j := j + 3;
      end loop;
      if j <= size then
        i := j;
        abort Searcher_1, Searcher_3;
      end if;
    end Searcher_2;

    task body Searcher_3 is
      j : Index := 3;
    begin
      while table(j).val /= val loop  -- scan the 3rd, 6th, 9th, 12th, etc.
        j := j + 3;
      end loop;
      if j <= size then
        i := j;
        abort Searcher_1, Searcher_2;
      end if;
    end Searcher_3;
  begin
    null;
  end;  -- program continued on next page
```

2.9. (continued)

```
  if i > size then
    raise not_in_table;
  end if;
  return table(i);
end find_val;
```

2.10. This is a "more parallel" version of the root-searching program on pages 62-63.

```
function root_of_f(a, b : Float) return Float is
  x0, x1, x2, x3, x4, fx0, fx1, fx2, fx3, fx4      : Float;
  root_is_in_1st_interval, root_is_in_4th_interval : Boolean;
begin
  x0 := a; x4 := b; fx0 := f(x0); fx4 := f(x4);

  if x4 - x0 <= epsilon and fx0*fx4 > 0.0 then raise no_root; end if;

  while x4 - x0 > epsilon loop
    declare
      task Compute_fx1;
      task Compute_fx2;
      task Compute_fx3;

      task body Compute_fx1 is
      begin
        x1  := x0 + 0.25*(x4 - x0);
        fx1 := f(x1);
        root_is_in_1st_interval := fx0*fx1 <= 0.0;
      end;

      task body Compute_fx2 is
      begin
        x2  := x0 + 0.50*(x4 - x0);
        fx2 := f(x2);
      end;

      task body Compute_fx3 is
      begin
        x3  := x0 + 0.75*(x4 - x0);
        fx3 := f(x3);
        root_is_in_4th_interval := fx3*fx4 <= 0.0;
      end;
    begin
      null;
    end; -- program continued on next page
```

2.10. (continued)

```
    if root_is_in_1st_interval then     -- Shrink search interval to x0..x1.
      x4 := x1;
      fx4 := fx1;
    elsif fx1*fx2 <= 0.0 then           -- Shrink search interval to x1..x2.
      x0 := x1;
      x4 := x2;
      fx0 := fx1;
      fx4 := fx2;
    elsif fx2*fx3 <= 0.0 then           -- Shrink search interval to x2..x3.
      x0 := x2;
      x4 := x3;
      fx0 := fx2;
      fx4 := fx3;
    elsif root_is_in_4th_interval then -- Shrink search interval to x3..x4.
      x0 := x3;
      fx0 := fx3;
    else
      raise no_root;
    end if;
  end loop;
  return (x0 + x4)/2.0;
end root_of_f;
```

Chapter 3
Introduction to the Ada Rendezvous

In the last section we discovered a requirement for a master to communicate with its dependent tasks: we wanted the master to give each task its assignment. The need to communicate with tasks is much broader than a master's need to tell a task what to do, but this example clearly indicates the requirement for some mechanism for communicating with tasks.

Ada provides the rendezvous mechanism for communication between a program unit (a task, a procedure, or a package) and a task. A rendezvous is the interaction that occurs between a program unit P and a task T when P has called an entry in T and T is executing an accept statement in response to P's entry call.

Entries exist for synchronizing and communicating with tasks. Entries are owned by tasks; they must be declared in their owning tasks' specifications. With the exception that the reserved word **entry** is used instead of the reserved word **procedure**, an entry declaration has the form of a procedure specification. Furthermore, a program unit issues a call to a task's entry with a syntax similar to a procedure call. When a called task accepts an entry call, a rendezvous transpires. The specific events that will occur during a rendezvous with a task's entry are specified in one or more accept statements that must appear in the body of the task owning the entry. Accept statements are rather like synchronized subroutines.

In the preceding section we developed a concurrent root-searching program which required a mechanism for informing each worker task of its assignment. To provide this mechanism, we declare an entry in the specification of the task type that the master can call to give each task object its assignment.

```
task type Compute_fx_j is
  entry you_are(process_number : in ProcessNumber);
end;
```

We must also add to the task type's body the accept statement which specifies what each task does during its rendezvous.

```
task body Compute_fx_j is
  j : ProcessNumber; -- The master must initialize this value
begin
  accept you_are(process_number : in ProcessNumber) do
    j := process_number;
  end you_are;
  x(j) := x(Ø) + (Float(j)/Float(n + 1))*(x(n + 1) - x(Ø));
  fx(j) := f(x(j));
end Compute_fx_j;
```

During its rendezvous with the master, each task copies the incoming value of process_number into its local variable j. This copying is necessary because the scope of the formal parameter process_number is the region of text between the accept statement's "**do**" and "**end** you_are". Notice that the accept statement must repeat the entry declaration's formal part. This repetition allows the compiler (and human reader!) to match an accept statement with its corresponding entry declaration and serves to emphasize the scope of its formal parameters.

We stress that synchronization (rendezvous) must precede direct communication. The master cannot directly transmit a datum to a task until the task is ready to receive it; and the task cannot directly receive a datum from its master until the master is ready to send it.

Therefore the master must issue an entry call to each task and rendezvous with it in order to pass it its assignment. Remembering that our array of tasks is declared this way

```
Compute_fx : array(1..n) of Compute_fx_j; -- n tasks
```

the following for statement (to be placed in the master) issues all the required entry calls.

```
for j in 1..n loop              -- \ The task master gives
  Compute_fx(j).you_are(j);     --  > each task its process
end loop;                       -- / number (assignment).
```

Before we discuss rendezvous further, let's see all the pieces assembled in the correct procedure:

```
function root_of_f(a, b : Float; n : Positive := 1) return Float is
  subtype ProcessNumber is Integer range 1..n; -- n tasks/processes
  x  : array(Ø..n + 1) of Float; -- x(Ø) and x(n + 1) are the end-points
  fx : array(Ø..n + 1) of Float; -- of the interval under investigation.
  zero_crossing_detected : Boolean;
```

```
begin
  x(0) := a; x(n + 1) := b; fx(0) := f(a); fx(n + 1) := f(b);
  if b - a <= epsilon and fx(0)*fx(n + 1) > 0.0 then -- no zero crossing
    raise no_root;
  end if;

  while x(n + 1) - x(0) > epsilon loop -- Continue to look for zero crossing.
    declare                            -- a block that is a task master
      task type Compute_fx_j is
        entry you_are(process_number : in ProcessNumber);
      end;

      Compute_fx : array(1..n) of Compute_fx_j; -- n tasks

      task body Compute_fx_j is
        j : ProcessNumber; -- The master must initialize each j.
      begin
        accept you_are(process_number : in ProcessNumber) do
          j := process_number;
        end you_are;
        x(j) := x(0) + (Float(j)/Float(n + 1))*(x(n + 1) - x(0));
        fx(j) := f(x(j));
      end Compute_fx_j;
    begin                       -- All tasks are activated here and then
      for j in 1..n loop        -- the task master gives each task its assignment.
        Compute_fx(j).you_are(j);
      end loop;
    end;

    zero_crossing_detected:= false;
    for j in 0..n loop
      if fx(j)*fx(j + 1) <= 0.0 then
        zero_crossing_detected := true;
        x(0) := x(j);                  -- \  Shrink the search
        x(n + 1) := x(j + 1);          --  \ interval to
        fx(0) := fx(j);                --  / x(j)..x(j + 1).
        fx(n + 1) := fx(j + 1);        -- /
        exit;
      end if;
    end loop;
    if zero_crossing_detected = false then
      raise no_root;
    end if;
  end loop;
  return (x(0) + x(n + 1))/2.0;
end root_of_f;
```

Immediately after its activation each task tries to execute its accept statement--in order to receive its process number (its assignment); at the same time the master begins executing its for statement. It should be obvious that the tasks higher in the array may reach their accept statements before the master can call their entries; these tasks will be suspended until the master calls them. As soon as the master finishes a rendezvous with a task, that task can begin its assignment (evaluating its x(j) and fx(j)) in parallel with the master's issuing another entry call (to initialize the next task).

Figure 3.1 depicts the state where the master has already conducted a rendezvous with some of the tasks (tasks 1..j-1), has just started a rendezvous with one task (task j), and has yet to issue an entry call to the remaining (suspended) tasks (tasks j+1..n). Notice that the earlier tasks have begun their computations (some may have finished).

It is worth remarking here on a profound difference between Ada tasks and Ada procedures: the action of activating (or invoking) a task and the action of passing a parameter to a task are two separate actions. The master must perform all the task activations first (which it can carry out concurrently) and then it must conduct a series of rendezvous in order to pass parameters to each task. This separation of the actions of invoking and passing parameters to a task is in contrast to the simultaneous actions of invoking and passing parameters to a procedure.

What is perhaps unfortunate is that the Ada master must pass initializing parameters to its dependent tasks _sequentially_. I do not know of any way for Ada to initialize all its identical tasks concurrently. (For a lucid discussion of the delay due to the sequential initialization of identical tasks, see an article by Shaula Yemini (1982).)

In respect to our root-searching program, the delay in initializing the tasks will detract very little from the performance of the program. The time to conduct a rendezvous should be very short compared to the time required to compute f(x)--after all, our assumption from the outset was that the computation of each f(x) dominated all the other operations of an algorithm.

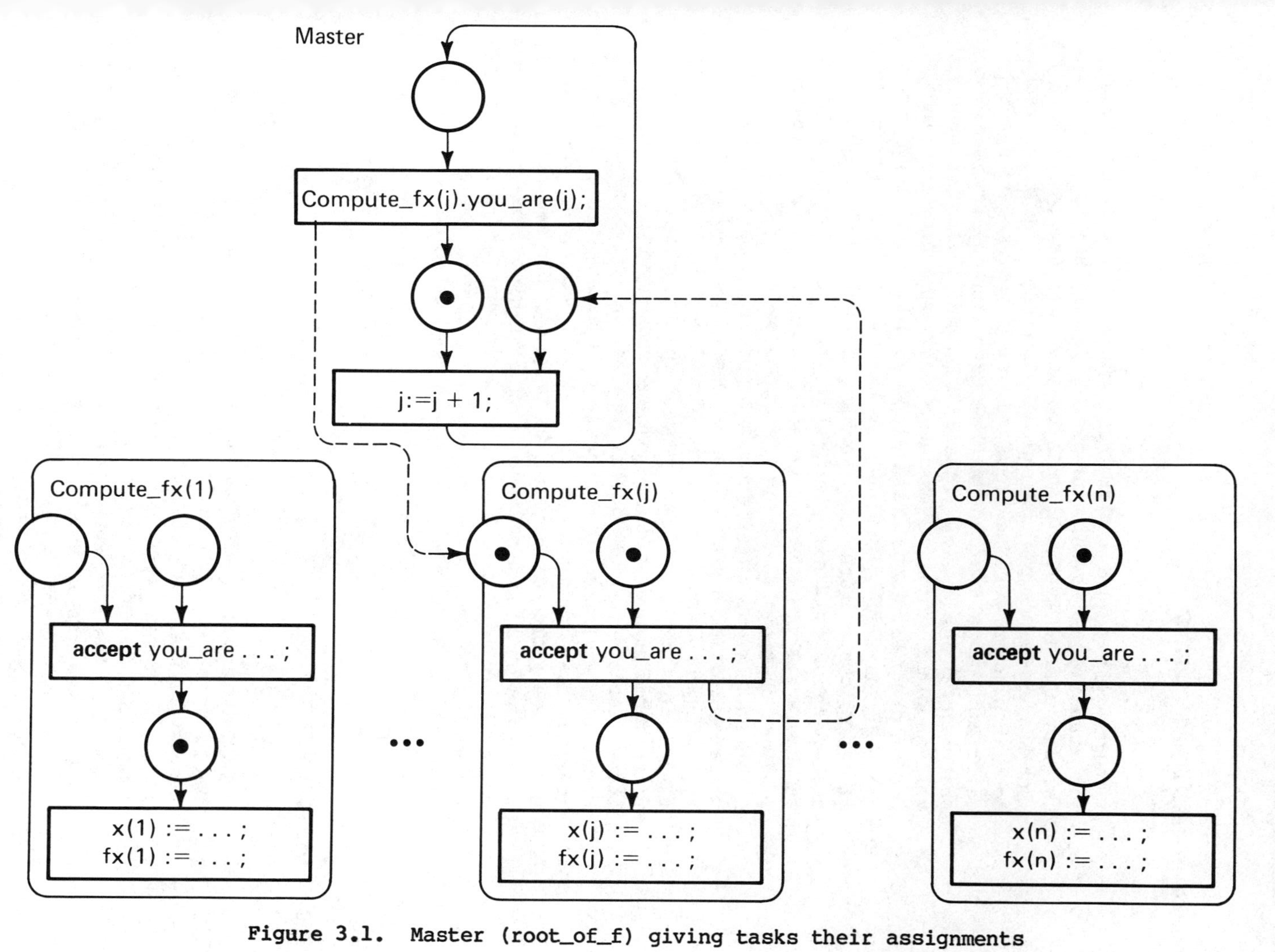

Figure 3.1. Master (root_of_f) giving tasks their assignments

MASTER-TO-TASK COMMUNICATION

There are two ways a master can communicate with its dependent tasks: one is through global variables; the other is through a rendezvous. Our three-process (see pages 62-63) root-searching program used global variables. The three tasks in that program were nonidentical: we programmed each one to refer to its part of the global data. Our n-process root-searching program (see pages 86-87) used the rendezvous as well as global data for master-to-task communication. In the second program, global data alone would not suffice because the individual identical tasks wouldn't know what part of the global data structure they should operate on. In this program, a rendezvous told each task which part of the global data structure was its operand. Carefully compare the two programs (the one on pages 62-63 and the one on pages 86-87).

You should not infer from our specialized examples that global variables are as useful or secure as the Ada rendezvous for interprocess communication. Global variables will not work at all for communication between distributed processes--the distributed processes don't have any shared memory in which to store global variables. Global (shared) variables may not work because of serious interference or synchronization problems (see the next section). Finally, global variables potentially couple every program unit in the program. Suppose that during debugging we find a strange value in a global variable. Who put it there? Anyone! Structured design has been particularly concerned to explicate the evils of global variables. Our programs use global variables in a restricted and disciplined fashion. Be sure yours do too!

TASK-TO-TASK COMMUNICATION

Communication by rendezvous is not limited to interactions between masters and their dependent tasks. Tasks may also rendezvous with each other. (In fact, we should think of every master as a main task; and therefore every rendezvous between master and dependent task is a rendezvous between two tasks.)

Consider the root-searching program on pages 86-87. In that program the master itself gave each task its assignment (i.e, its process number). The master could delegate that job to a dependent task called Assigner that passes a process number to each task. For variation, we have written task Assigner so that each Compute_fx(i) calls Assigner in order to obtain its process number.

```
task Assigner is
  entry give_me_an_assignment(process_number : out ProcessNumber);
end;

task body Assigner is
begin
  for assignment in 1..n loop
    accept give_me_an_assignment(process_number : out ProcessNumber) do
      process_number := assignment;
    end give_me_an_assignment;
  end loop;
end Assigner;
```

We have rewritten below the program on pages 86-87 so that Assigner takes over the assignment task. Do you think that Compute_fx(j) in the new program will invariably receive j for its assignment? (The answer to this question is given in the following paragraphs.)

Let's understand how the n Compute_fx(j) tasks interact with Assigner. Since the first action every Compute_fx(j) takes is to call the give_me_an_assignment entry in Assigner, it should be obvious that many of these calls will "pile up" before Assigner gets around to responding to all of them. How do the calls "pile up"? Where is the "pile"? The calls pile up in such a manner that Assigner can respond to them _fairly_. An obvious method for _fair_ treatment of callers is a FIFO queue. Indeed, Ada provides a FIFO queue for every task entry. Thus the "pile" is the give_me_an_assignment entry queue.

When a process calls an entry in a task and the called task can't immediately respond, the call is placed at the rear of the queue. Every time a task reaches an accept statement for one of its entries, it holds a rendezvous with the call at the front of that entry's queue. (If the entry queue is empty when the called task reaches one of its accept statements, the called task is suspended until some process calls that entry.)

All n Compute_fx tasks are activated in parallel. We can't predict the order in which Assigner.give_me_an_assignment(j) entry calls will be added to the queue for that entry. Therefore, Compute_fx(j) will not in general be given process number j. However, we can be certain--because of the for loop in Assigner--that the tasks will be assigned process numbers in the very same order in which they appear on the entry queue, that each task will be assigned a unique process number, and that all n process numbers will be assigned.

```
function root_of_f(a, b : Float; n : Positive := 1) return Float is
  subtype ProcessNumber is Integer range 1..n; -- n tasks/processes
  x  : array(0..n + 1) of Float; -- x(0) and x(n + 1) are the end-points
  fx : array(0..n + 1) of Float; -- of the interval under investigation.
  zero_crossing_detected : Boolean;
begin
  x(0) := a; x(n + 1) := b; fx(0) := f(a); fx(n + 1) := f(b);

  if b - a <= epsilon and fx(0)*fx(n + 1) > 0.0 then -- no zero crossing
    raise no_root;
  end if;

  while x(n + 1) - x(0) > epsilon loop -- Continue to look for zero crossing.
    declare                            -- a block that is a task master
      task Assigner is
        entry give_me_an_assignment(process_number : out ProcessNumber);
      end;

      task type Compute_fx_j;

      Compute_fx : array(1..n) of Compute_fx_j; -- n tasks

      task body Assigner is
      begin
        for assignment in 1..n loop
          accept give_me_an_assignment(process_number : out ProcessNumber) do
            process_number := assignment;
          end give_me_an_assignment;
        end loop;
      end Assigner;

      task body Compute_fx_j is
        j : ProcessNumber; -- Assigner must initialize each j.
      begin
        Assigner.give_me_an_assignment(j);
        x(j) := x(0) + (Float(j)/Float(n + 1))*(x(n + 1) - x(0));
        fx(j) := f(x(j));
      end Compute_fx_j;
    begin
      -- All tasks, including Assigner, are activated here.
      null;
      -- Wait here for all tasks to terminate.
    end;
```

```
    zero_crossing_detected := false;
    for j in 0..n loop
      if fx(j)*fx(j + 1) <= 0.0 then
        zero_crossing_detected := true;
        x(0)  :=  x(j);  x(n + 1) :=  x(j + 1); --  \ Shrink the interval
        fx(0) := fx(j); fx(n + 1) := fx(j + 1); --  / to x(j)..x(j + 1).
        exit;
      end if;
    end loop;
    if zero_crossing_detected = false then
      raise no_root;
    end if;
  end loop;
  return (x(0) + x(n + 1))/2.0;
end root_of_f;
```

THE HAZARDS OF SHARED VARIABLES

In a previous section we warned against the hazards of shared (global) variables for interprocess communication. In this section we illustrate and analyze these hazards and show how the rendezvous mechanism avoids them.

Suppose we want to simplify the copy program on page 43. In that program we repeatedly spawned the two tasks Input and Output, once for each execution of the while loop's sequence of statements. Can we avoid that overhead, as small as it might be? Can we avoid the complicated buffer switching? Perhaps we might be tempted to write the following, letting the tasks Input and Output communicate through the global variable named shared_variable. (We have deferred solving, for the time being, the problem of how to terminate the tasks.)

```
with Text_IO; use Text_IO;
procedure incorrect_copy_program is
  shared_buffer : String(1..80);      -- a hazardous shared variable

  task Input;
  task body Input is
    local_buffer : String(1..80);
  begin
    loop
      get(local_buffer);              -- get a string from the input file
      skip_line;
      shared_buffer := local_buffer; -- move the string to the shared buffer
    end loop;
  end Input;
```

```
  task Output;
  task body Output is
    local_buffer : String(1..80);
  begin
    loop
      local_buffer := shared_buffer; -- fetch string from the shared buffer
      put(local_buffer);             -- put string on the output file
      new_line;
    end loop;
  end Output;
begin
  null;
end incorrect_copy_program;
```

The new program certainly has an appealing simplicity. But, of course, it won't work--for two reasons. First, the updating of shared_buffer by the Input task can interfere disastrously with the reading of this variable by the Output task. Second, unless the two tasks happen to run at exactly the same speed, the overall effect of the program will be to copy some values from the input file onto the output file several times and copy other values from the input file not at all.

The first problem (interference) is caused by the absence of mutual exclusion in the two tasks' access to shared_buffer. The second problem (repeating or missing values on the input) is caused by the absence of synchronization in the execution of the two tasks.

Let's consider the issue of mutual exclusion first. The Input task may assign a new value to shared_buffer at the same time that Output tries to read it. Since shared_buffer is a composite variable requiring several memory cycles for reading or updating, interference of updating with reading is a high probability event. The symptom of interference would be the "copy" program's printing out strings that don't even occur on the input file. This would happen when the Output task obtains a partially updated value from shared_variable, a value that is a mixture of an old value and a new one. One way to avoid this interference is to arrange for Input and Output to have mutually exclusive access to an intermediate buffer.

Now let's consider the issue of synchronization. The probability of Input and Output running at exactly the same speed is very low. If Output runs faster than Input, then it may print out the same string several times before Input updates the shared variable. On the other hand, if Output runs slower than Input, then it may miss printing some values of the shared variable altogether, printing only every second or third string.

One way to avoid the problems of interference and lack of synchronization is to use the Ada rendezvous and avoid the shared buffer altogether. This is the approach taken in the following program. This program also supplies the code for terminating the tasks.

```
with Text_IO; use Text_IO;
procedure copy_program is
  subtype String_80 is String(1..80);

  task Input;

  task Output is
    entry print(s : String_80);
  end Output;

  task body Input is
    local_buffer : String_80;
  begin
    while not end_of_file loop
      get(local_buffer);                    -- Get the next string.
      skip_line;
      Output.print(local_buffer);           -- Send string to Output.
    end loop;
    local_buffer(1) := ASCII.eot;           -- Form a stop message.
    Output.print(local_buffer);             -- Send stop message to Output
  end Input;

  task Output;
  task body Output is
    local_buffer : String_80;
  begin
    loop
      accept print(s : String_80) do
        local_buffer := s;                  -- Receive string from Input.
      end;
      exit when local_buffer(1) = ASCII.eot; -- Exit when stop message.
      put(local_buffer);                    -- Print the string.
      new_line;
    end loop;
  end Output;
begin
  -- Both tasks are activated here.
  null;
  -- Wait here for both tasks to terminate.
end copy_program;
```

We will describe the operation of this program by frequent reference to the timing diagram in Figure 3.2. This is one of many possible patterns: it assumes that the put operation takes about fifty percent longer than the get operation. It also assumes that the rendezvous takes about one-quarter of the time a put operation takes. This is unrealistically pessimistic; but even so, the program copies a file considerably faster than a purely sequential program.

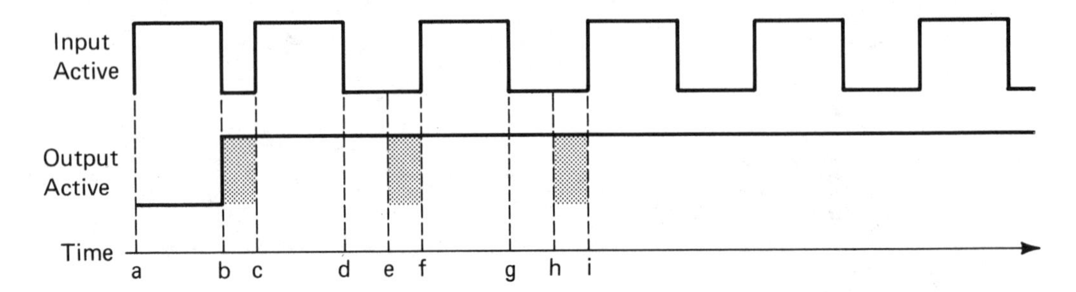

Figure 3.2. Possible timing diagram for tasks in copy_program

Input issues print entry calls to Output at times b, d, g, and so on. Output accepts Input's entry calls at times b, e, h, and so on. Output completes rendezvous with Input at times c, f, i, and so on. Therefore, Input and Output are synchronized in rendezvous during time intervals b-c, e-f, and h-i, and so on. The crosshatched regions represent the periods of rendezvous. Input is inactive from the time it issues an entry call until Output has completed execution of its accept statement for that call.

The entry declaration (its identifier is print) in the specification of Output allows Input to pass a string to Output by means of a rendezvous.

Both tasks start their execution (time a) at the first statement in their loops. (Of course, Input tests end_of_file before each execution of its while loop.) Input starts its input activity by calling a get procedure in Text_IO. Output tries to execute its accept statement but is blocked and immediately suspended because Input hasn't issued a print entry call. As soon as Input completes the execution of the procedure skip_line (time b), it issues an entry call to Output, associating the call's actual parameter, local_buffer, with Output's formal parameter, s. Output has, of course, been waiting for this call; Output immediately executes its accept statement, assigning the value in s to its own local buffer. Input is suspended from the time it issues the entry call to Output until Output completes the execution of its accept statement.

We can now understand how the rendezvous mechanism prevents interference of Input's updating of its local_buffer with Output's reading of this variable. Input updates local_buffer by executing the get procedure. It later issues a print entry call and thereby associates the value in local_buffer with prints's formal parameter. Input is suspended from the time it issues the entry call (time b) until the time that Output completes the rendezvous (time c). Note that Input updates local_buffer during the intervals a-b, c-d, and f-g; Output reads this variable during the intervals b-c, e-f, and h-i. These intervals do not overlap. Output can't possibly read the value in local_buffer while Input is updating it; Input can't possibly update the value in local_buffer while Output is reading it. The rendezvous mechanism guarantees mutually exclusive access by Input and Output to Input.local_buffer.

Now that we have seen how the rendezvous mechanism prevents interference of Input with Output, let's see how this mechanism provides synchronization of Input and Output. Input is capable of running faster than Output. If allowed to do this, the Output task could miss strings. But, of course, Input cannot run faster than Output because it is held up by each and every print entry call until Output is ready to accept its datum. The rendezvous mechanism guarantees synchronization between Input and Output. Notice that synchronization is achieved by Output's blocking Input's "progress".

We have established that copy_program is free of the defects of interference and desynchronization. What about performance? Notice that Output, the slower task, is active continually from time b on and that its execution completely overlaps Input's execution. This is desirable because it keeps the slower device almost continually busy. In a sequential program the slower device would be idle while the faster device operated. This would reduce the system throughput. The more nearly equal the time required for an input operation and an output operation, the better the performance of copy_program relative to a sequential program. Compared to the concurrent program on page 43, our new program is probably more efficient because it substitutes one rendezvous per copy cycle for the two task activations required each cycle in the earlier program. However, an advantage of the earlier program is that it avoids copying string values from the Input task to the Output task; instead it uses buffer switching. The larger the elements of the file, the more important this advantage is. At any rate we can combine buffer switching with the rendezvous approach; we show how to do this in an exercise at the end of this chapter.

SINGLE-SLOT AND PIPELINE BUFFERS

In the copy program in the previous section the Input task produced strings and the Output task consumed the strings (by printing them). The producer/consumer problem is a common one in computing.

Often the producer and consumer run at fluctuating speeds. For example, the input task may slow down because it reaches the end of a disk page, or the output task may slow down because it has to execute a form feed. The way we interfaced Input to Output in the previous section synchronized them very tightly. It was impossible for Input to produce extra strings and stockpile them. Input had to wait for Output to consume each string before it could produce another string. In most real-time systems devices run at fluctuating speeds. Therefore, it's realistic to allow for fluctuations in the times required by devices and processes.

Our previous copy program made no assumption about the timing of processes; and therefore it works for any timing pattern; but if the get and put operations fluctuate greatly, that program's performance will not be as good as it could be.

We will now illustrate how to decouple Input and Output slightly, at least to the extent that Input can "get ahead" of Output by one string. Then, if Input has to slow down for a moment, at least one string has been stockpiled for use by Output. Of course, our decoupling mechanism must also provide mutual exclusion and synchronization between Input and Output.

Our solution is the task type below, SynchronizingBuffer. A task of this type can serve as a synchronizing buffer between two other tasks, a producing task and a consuming task. The producing task can call the synchronizing buffer's put entry; the consuming task can call the synchronizing buffer's get entry. Since the synchronizing buffer has only a single slot, it must alternately accept a put call and a get call. The synchronizing buffer task blocks the producer task when the single slot is full; it blocks the consumer task when the single slot is empty. This task can provide a safe intermediate buffer between Input and Output, in contrast to the unsafe buffer on page 93 in the section entitled "The Hazards of Shared Variables." Notice that the only access to the "shared" buffer (slot in the task body) is via the entries put and get.

```
task type SynchronizingBuffer is
  entry put(line : in  String_80);
  entry get(line : out String_80);
end;
```

```
task body SynchronizingBuffer is
  slot : String_80;
begin
  loop
    accept put(line : in  String_80) do    -- accept another line
      slot := line;                         -- update slot
    end;
    accept get(line : out String_80) do    -- dispense the line
      line := slot;                         -- read slot
    end;
  end loop;
end SynchronizingBuffer;
```

The text of this task body makes remarkably clear that the updating of slot by the producer and the reading of slot by the consumer are executed in mutual exclusion: These operations are in different accept statements; these accept statements are executed one after another. It is impossible for the two operations to interfere with each other.

The text also makes remarkably clear that the producer and consumer are correctly synchronized. First, the task accepts a put entry call, filling the buffer; and then it accepts a get entry call, emptying the buffer; and then it accepts a put entry call, filling the buffer again; and so on. The producer cannot race too far ahead of the consumer because it will be held up on the put entry while the Buffer task is waiting for a get entry call from the consumer.

Here is our copy program, rewritten with SynchronizingBuffer.

```
procedure copy_text_concurrently is
  subtype String_80 is String(1..80);

  task Input;

  task type SynchronizingBuffer is
    entry put(line : in  String_80);
    entry get(line : out String_80);
  end;

  task Output;

  Buffer : SynchronizingBuffer;

  task body Input is separate;
  task body SynchronizingBuffer is separate;
  task body Output is separate;
begin
  null;
end copy_text_concurrently;
```

```
with Text_IO;
separate (copy_text_concurrently)
task body Input is
  line : String_80;
begin
  while not Text_IO.end_of_file loop
    Text_IO.get(line);
    Text_IO.skip_line;
    Buffer.put(line);
  end loop;
  line(1) := ASCII.eot;
  Buffer.put(line);
end Input;

separate (copy_text_concurrently)
task body SynchronizingBuffer is
  slot : String_80;
begin
  loop
    accept put(line : in  String_80) do
      slot := line;
    end;
    accept get(line : out String_80) do
      line := slot;
    end;
    exit when slot(1) = ASCII.eot;
  end loop;
end SynchronizingBuffer;

with Text_IO;
separate (copy_text_concurrently)
task body Output is
  line : String_80;
begin
  loop
    Buffer.get(line);
    exit when line(1) = ASCII.eot;
    Text_IO.put(line);
    Text_IO.new_line;
  end loop;
end Output;
```

Figure 3.3 is a Petri net of this program. The graph depicts the state of the program where Input is just beginning a new Text_IO.get operation; Output is just beginning a new Text_IO. put operation; and Buffer, which stores a line in slot, is waiting for Output to get this line. You can show this state is reachable by marking the net for its start state and then firing the appropriate sequence of enabled transitions.

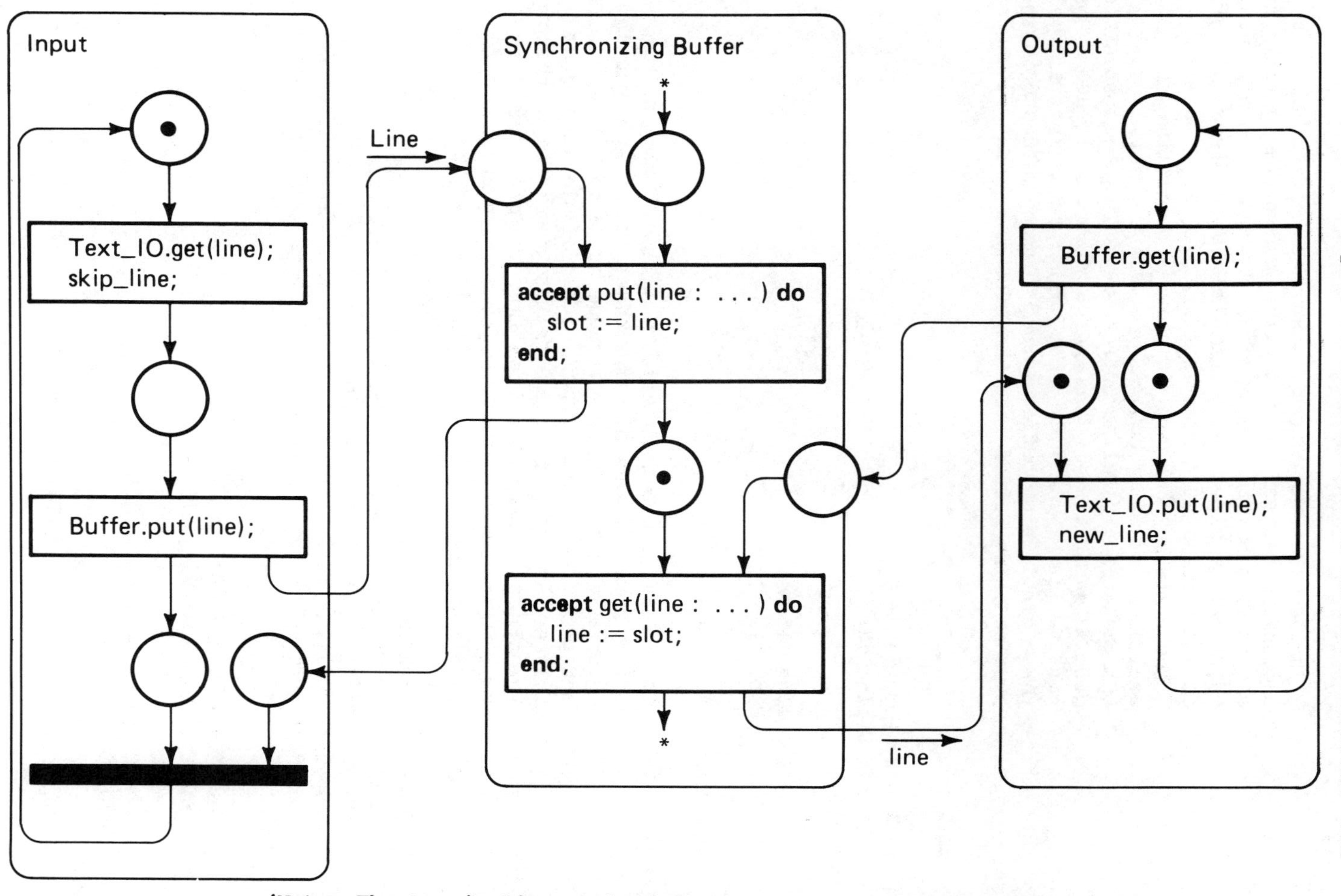

(Note: The termination mechanisms have not been illustrated.)

Figure 3.3. Petri net of copy_text_concurrently (see pages 99-100)

Suppose that we want to program a buffer that permits more decoupling between the producing and consuming tasks than our single-slot buffer does. One way to make such a program is to construct a pipeline of single-slot buffers. The pipeline constitutes a multi-slot buffer.

There are several ways to program a pipeline buffer. (In the exercises we show how to program a generic package which encapsulates a pipeline buffer whose length is specified by a generic parameter.) Our approach here is to use a "pumping" task to link two single-slot buffer tasks into a pipeline of three single-slot buffers. Pump "pumps" values from the first synchronizing buffer into the second.

```
task Pump;

task body Pump is
  line : String_80;
begin
  loop
    Buffer_1.get(line);
    Buffer_2.put(line);
  end loop;
end Pump;
```

To present a clean interface to the clients of the pipeline buffer, we encapsulate the three tasks in a package. (This interface is interesting because it permits simultaneous puts and gets under certain conditions: if the pipeline is neither full nor empty (either one or two items are in the pipeline), the producer can put a item into the pipeline at exactly the same time that the consumer is getting another item from the pipeline.)

```
package PipelineBuffer is
  -- This is a three-slot blocking buffer.
  subtype String_80 is String(1..80);
  procedure put(line :  in String_80); -- blocks caller if buffer full
  procedure get(line : out String_80); -- blocks caller if buffer empty
end;

package body PipelineBuffer is
  task type SynchronizingBuffer is
    entry put(line :  in String_80);
    entry get(line : out String_80);
  end;

  Buffer_1, Buffer_2 : SynchronizingBuffer;
```

```
  task body SynchronizingBuffer is
    slot : String_80;
  begin
    accept put(line :  in String_80) do
      slot := line;
    end;
    accept get(line : out String_80) do
      line := slot;
    end;
  end SynchronizingBuffer;

  task Pump;

  task body Pump is
    -- this task "pumps" objects from Buffer_1 to Buffer_2
    line : String_80;
  begin
    loop
      Buffer_1.get(line);
      Buffer_2.put(line);
    end loop;
  end Pump;

  procedure put(line :  in String_80) is
  begin
    Buffer_1.put(line);
  end;

  procedure get(line : out String_80) is
  begin
    Buffer_2.get(line);
  end;
end PipelineBuffer;
```

Figure 3.4 is the Petri net for the pipeline buffer. It illustrates the state of the buffer when there have been six consecutive put operations without a single get operation. The buffer is completely full (one item in each element of the pipeline) and there are three entry calls pending on the put entry (three tokens in the put entry place). Of course, this state assumes at least three different producing tasks are calling the put procedure. Why? Because as soon as a program unit issues an entry call, it is suspended; it cannot continue its execution until the requested rendezvous has been completed. Therefore, a program unit can appear on an entry queue only once (and it can appear on only one entry queue).

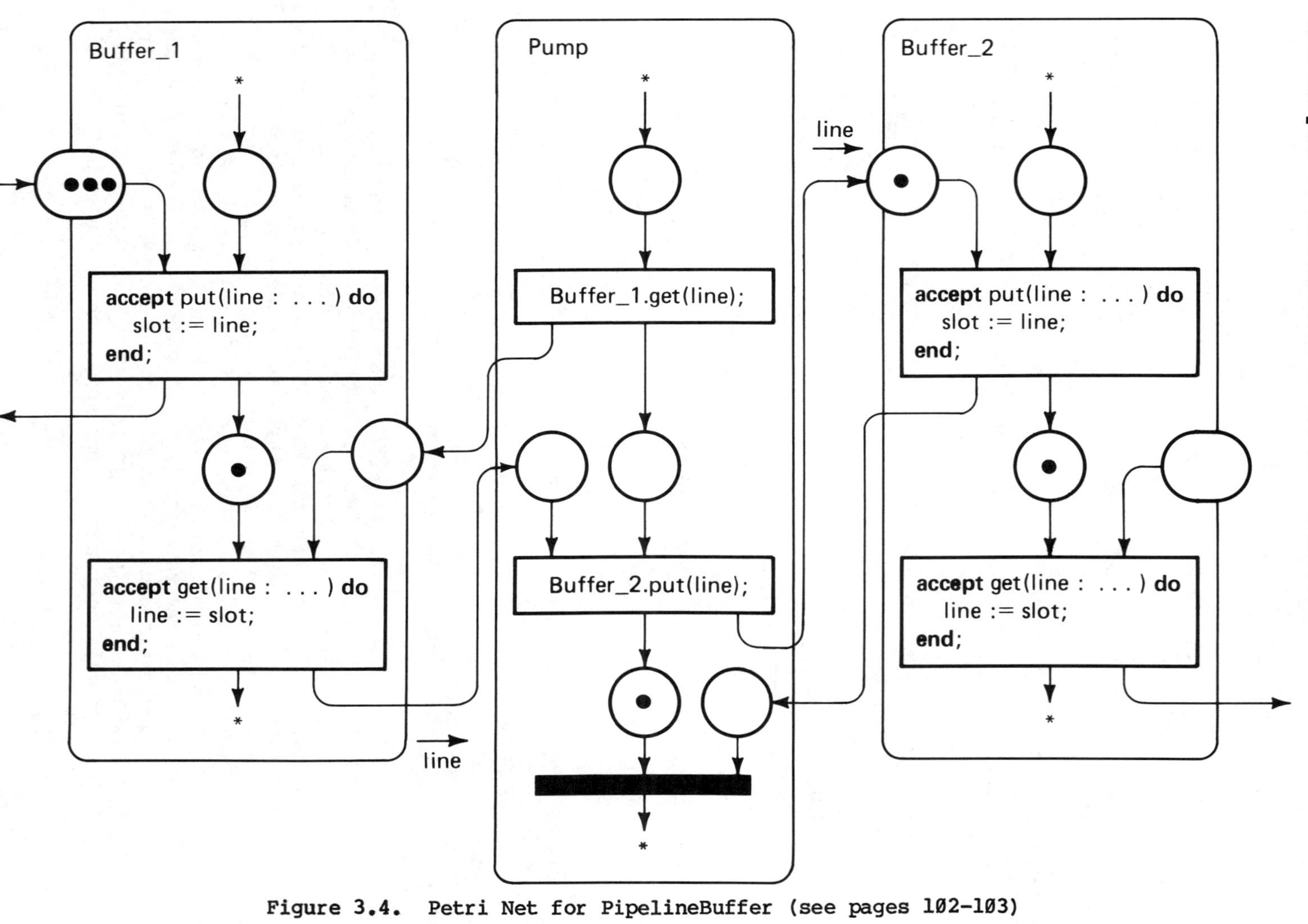

Figure 3.4. Petri Net for PipelineBuffer (see pages 102–103)

To illustrate using PipelineBuffer, we program our old friend, the copy program, in still another way.

```
with Text_IO, PipelineBuffer;
procedure copy_text_concurrently is
  package Buffer renames PipelineBuffer;

  task Input;

  task Output;

  task body Input is
    line : Buffer.String_80;
  begin
    while not Text_IO.end_of_file loop
      Text_IO.get(line);
      Text_IO.skip_line;
      Buffer.put(line);
    end loop;
    line(1) := ASCII.eot;
    Buffer.put(line);
  end Input;

  task body Output is
    line : Buffer.String_80;
  begin
    loop
      Buffer.get(line);
      exit when line(1) = ASCII.eot;
      Text_IO.put(line);
      Text_IO.new_line;
    end loop;
  end Output;
begin
  -- The Input and Output tasks are activated here.
  null;
  -- Wait here for Input and Output to terminate.
end copy_text_concurrently;
```

This is the first program we've encountered that depends on a library unit (PipelineBuffer) containing tasks. Note that these tasks have no mechanism for termination.

The library unit PipelineBuffer raises several questions. What program unit is the master of the three tasks? When are these tasks activated? Does the copy program have to wait for the tasks in the library unit to terminate before it can complete its execution? If so, the copy program is in trouble!

The master of the three tasks in the library unit Pipeline-Buffer is the library package itself. It would be unreasonable to require a program unit that depends on library packages to be the master of tasks declared in these library packages. If a program unit could be the master of such tasks it could be indefinitely held up by tasks it couldn't control and didn't even know existed. (Incidentally, a library package can be the master of tasks, but a package declared within another program unit cannot be a master. This means that if we had declared the PipelineBuffer package within the copy program, the copy program would have been the master of the three tasks inside the package. In this configuration, the copy program could never complete its execution because three of its dependent tasks would never terminate. Of course, if we wanted to declare the PipelineBuffer package inside the copy program we would code its tasks so that they terminated properly. It is very difficult to program library packages so that their encapsulated tasks terminate when their clients no longer want them. To do so would require the library unit to know a great deal about its clients or the clients to have detailed control over the mechanisms of its library resource, or both. Such knowledge and control would not be in the spirit of library resources.)

The three tasks in PipelineBuffer are activated before the execution of the main program. This follows from the rule that the library units needed by a main program are elaborated before the execution of the main program and the rule that the task objects occurring in the declarative part of the library package are activated after the elaboration of the package.

The termination of a main program (the copy program in our example) does <u>not</u> have to wait for the termination of tasks that depend on its library packages. This follows, of course, from the fact that a main program is not a master (direct or indirect) for tasks in library packages.

Finally, what can we say about the performance of a pipeline buffer? On a multi-microprocessor architecture where there is one processor per process, the pipeline buffer could be quite efficient. For example, the pipeline buffer permits simultaneous puts and gets when the buffer is neither full nor empty. On the other hand, it takes time to fill the buffer or pump an item from the first (input) to the last (output) process. If the buffer is lightly loaded, the pumping serves little purpose and takes time. It would not be advisable to run a pipeline buffer on a uniprocessor.

The concept of a pipeline of tasks is useful. We will apply this concept again in a later section in this chapter. (The second application will be to sorting a sequence of scalar values.)

THE SELECTIVE WAIT STATEMENT

In this section we introduce Ada's selective wait statement, which allows a task to wait for and select any one of a number of entry calls. To motivate the introduction, we first program a package that implements a ring buffer. We analyze the problems of using this package in a parallel program (such as our copy program). Then, we introduce the selective wait statement, and use it to develop a task that solves the problems we found in the ring buffer package. This task is a blocking ring buffer which provides the mutual exclusion and synchronization required by parallel programs. This task can be used as a multislot buffer coupling a producer and consumer.

Here is the package specification and body for a ring buffer (queue). Its capacity is eight items.

```
package RingBuffer is                -- This buffer's capacity is 8 items.
  procedure put(x : in  Item);       -- can raise buffer_full
  procedure get(x : out Item);       -- can raise buffer_empty
  buffer_full, buffer_empty : exception;
end;

package body RingBuffer is                               -- a queue
  slot     : array(0..7) of Item;                        -- it has 8 slots
  count    : Integer range 0..slot'length := 0;          -- number of occupied slots
  next_in  : Integer range slot'range     := 0;          -- next empty slot
  next_out : Integer range slot'range     := 0;          -- next item out

  procedure put(x : in Item) is
  begin
    if count = slot'length then
      raise buffer_full;
    end if;
    slot(next_in) := x;
    count := count + 1;
    next_in := (next_in + 1) mod slot'length;
  end put;

  procedure get(x : out Item) is
  begin
    if count = 0 then
      raise buffer_empty;
    end if;
    x := slot(next_out);
    count := count - 1;
    next_out := (next_out + 1) mod slot'length;
  end put;
end RingBuffer;
```

The ring buffer is implemented as an array of slots that wrap around so that slot'first directly follows slot'last. The index next_out points at the item in the front of the buffer (if count > 0). The index next_in points at the next available empty slot (if count < slot'length). The indexes next_in, next_out move clockwise as items are inserted (put operations) and removed (get operations) from the array. Figure 3.5 depicts the ring buffer for the values

```
next_in  = 2;
count    = 6;
next_out = 4.
```

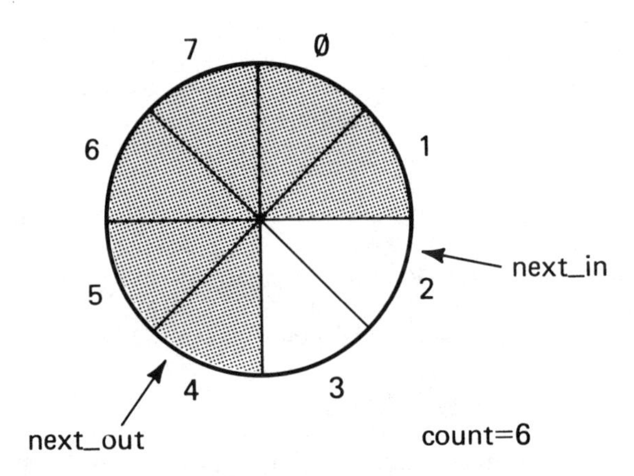

Figure 3.5. A ring buffer (queue) with a capacity of eight items

The shaded portion depicts the occupied portion of the slot array. The indexes next_in, next_out must be updated with modulo arithmetic (the modulus is slot'length) so that the slots wrap around.

This package is satisfactory--even elegant--for service in a *sequential* program. An attempt to use it in a *parallel* program could be disastrous. The package does encapsulate and protect from direct outside influence its buffering mechanism (e.g., slot, count, next_in, and next_out). But consider what would happen if we tried to use the package to couple concurrent producers and consumers. Since the procedures put and get are reentrant, many tasks can invoke get and put operations concurrently. These operations can interfere disastrously with one another. For example, suppose a producer invokes put at the same time that a consumer invokes get; the concurrent interfering updates of count can leave a meaningless value in that variable. Or, suppose two consumers invoke get simultaneously when count = 1; both invocations slip past the statement that would raise the buffer_empty exception and attempt to get a value from slot (but there is only one value in slot); and then the two invocations proceed to update count and next_out simultaneously, with possibly bizarre results.

We need an implementation that permits only one of the package's procedures to be executed at a time. (This kind of implementation is often called a monitor.)

But we need more than mutual exclusion on the executions of get and put operations. We also need some synchronism between these operations. For example, when the buffer is empty, we shouldn't accept a get call (nor should we raise a exception in any consumer who calls get at this time); instead, we should block consumers who call get until a producer puts an item into the empty buffer.

On the other hand, when our eight-slot buffer is neither empty nor full, we should be willing to accept either a put operation or a get operation. Let us sum up the requirements for a buffer for concurrent producers and consumers:

1. when the buffer is not full, accept a put operation;

2. when the buffer is not empty, accept a get operation;

3. when the buffer is neither empty nor full
   accept either a put operation or a get operation

4. execute all get and put operations in strict
   mutual exclusion with respect to each other

The selective wait statement satisfies all our requirements.

```
select
  when count < slot'length =>
  accept put(x : in Item) do                    -- \
    slot(next_in) := x;                         --  \  accept alternative
  end put;                                      --   > for put operation
  count := count + 1;                           --  /
  next_in := (next_in + 1) mod slot'length;     -- /
or
  when count > 0 =>
  accept get(x : out Item) do                   -- \
    x := slot(next_out);                        --  \  accept alternative
  end get;                                      --   > for get operation
  count := count - 1;                           --  /
  next_out := (next_out + 1) mod slot'length;   -- /
end select;
```

We particularly require the selective wait statement to satisfy the third requirement. This requirement implies _nondeterministic_ waiting (at least sometimes) for entry calls. The selective wait statement introduces the required nondeterminism: that is, the programmer does not have to determine--when both guarding conditions are true--whether the selective wait statement should select a put or get rendezvous next.

Note that the accept alternatives are both preceded by

when condition =>

Some writers call this clause a "guard". The => is the arrow delimiter. (Do not confuse it with less than or equal to, <=.)

Execution of the selective wait statement proceeds as follows.

First, the execution evaluates the conditions following each **when** to determine which accept alternatives are _open_ and which are _closed_. If a given condition is true, its accept alternative is open; otherwise, its accept alternative is closed.

Second, the execution selects and executes one of the open accept alternatives, according to the following rules.

If an entry call has been issued for an entry corresponding to one of the open accept alternatives, the execution immediately selects that alternative, holds a rendezvous with the caller by executing the alternative's accept statement, and then executes the statements which follow the accept statement in the accept alternative, thereby completing execution of the selective wait statement.

If several accept alternatives are selectable (i.e., entry calls have been issued for several open accept alternatives) then the execution _arbitrarily_ selects one of them for rendezvous, and executes it as described in the previous paragraph.

If no open accept alternative can be selected because no entry call has been issued for an open alternative, the task owning the selective wait statement can be suspended. When a process finally issues an entry call for one of this task's open accept alternatives, the waiting task can execute the corresponding accept alternative and complete its execution of the selective wait statement.

It is important to note that each execution of a selective wait statement evaluates only once the conditions following the whens. If all these conditions were false at the time of evaluation (and the selective wait statement has no else part) then the task owning the selective wait statement would be permanently blocked. This could deadlock an entire system since all tasks issuing an entry call to the blocked task could also be permanently blocked. Therefore, this situation raises a program_error exception.

Armed with the selective wait statement, we will program a ring buffer suitable for connecting parallel producers and consumers. This buffer must be implemented as a task because only a task can contain a selective wait statement.

The specification of the task looks very similar to the specification of the ring buffer package. There aren't any buffer_full or buffer_empty exceptions: the task's correct response to a request it presently can't fulfill is to block the requestor until other operations it carries out make possible the request's fulfillment. Because of the task's ability to block and queue the calls it can't immediately service, we name it BlockingRingBuffer.

```
task BlockingRingBuffer is
  entry put(x : in  Item);
  entry get(x : out Item);
end;

task body BlockingRingBuffer is
  slot      : array(0..7) of Item;                  -- it has 8 slots
  count     : Integer range 0..slot'length := 0; -- number of occupied slots
  next_in   : Integer range slot'range     := 0; -- next empty slot
  next_out  : Integer range slot'range     := 0; -- next item out
begin
  loop
    select
      when count < slot'length =>
      accept put(x : in Item) do                    -- \
        slot(next_in) := x;                         --  \  accept alternative
      end put;                                      --   > for put operation
      count := count + 1;                           --  /
      next_in := (next_in + 1) mod slot'length;     -- /
    or
      when count > 0 =>
      accept get(x : out Item) do                   -- \
        x := slot(next_out);                        --  \  accept alternative
      end get;                                      --   > for get operation
      count := count - 1;                           --  /
      next_out := (next_out + 1) mod slot'length;   -- /
    end select;
  end loop;
end BlockingRingBuffer;
```

The task body makes remarkably clear that the task satisfies both the mutual exclusion requirement and the synchronization requirement.

Since the task can execute only one accept alternative at a time, the task ensures mutually exclusive access to the buffer, its counter, and its indexes.

The task body makes equally clear that the task satisfies the synchronization requirements. The explicit synchronization conditions that follow each **when** and precede each accept alternative is one of Ada's most elegant features. The guarding conditions are particularly clear and require no further explanation. Figure 3.6 is a Petri net of the task.

Note that each accept alternative in the task's selective wait statement has two parts: (1) an accept statement and (2) an (optional) sequence of statements. This syntax allows us to burden the rendezvous with only those actions that must be effected (e.g., communication) while the calling and called tasks are locked in synchronism. The called task should relegate to the (optional) sequence of statements actions (if any) that do not require synchronism with the caller but do require completion before the next execution of the selective wait statement. This policy minimizes the calling task's suspension.

A COMPARISON OF PACKAGES AND SERVER TASKS

In chapter two we compared tasks without entries to concurrent parameterless procedures. In this section we compare packages and server tasks (e.g., RingBuffer and BlockingRingBuffer) and point out their similarities and differences.

The package RingBuffer and the task BlockingRingBuffer both offer a service to their clients. The clients' interfaces to these program units are specified in the package and task declarations, which are remarkably similar. The formal parts of the procedure and entry declarations are identical, the semantics of the formal parameter modes and the semantics of associating actual and formal parameters are identical, and the syntax for invoking the get and put operations are also identical with the exception that a use clause can be used to simplify the naming of the package's procedure calls but not the naming of the task's entry calls.

The data structures encapsulated in the two program bodies are identical.

The procedure bodies in the package body are analogous to the accept statements in the task body. A procedure body (accept statement) describes the actions that take place as the result of a procedure call (entry call). (An accept statement is like an "entry body".)

But there are the following profound differences.

The caller of a procedure can immediately execute the procedure body; but the caller of an entry must wait for the called task to execute a corresponding accept statement. (Each entry has a queue where its blocked callers wait.)

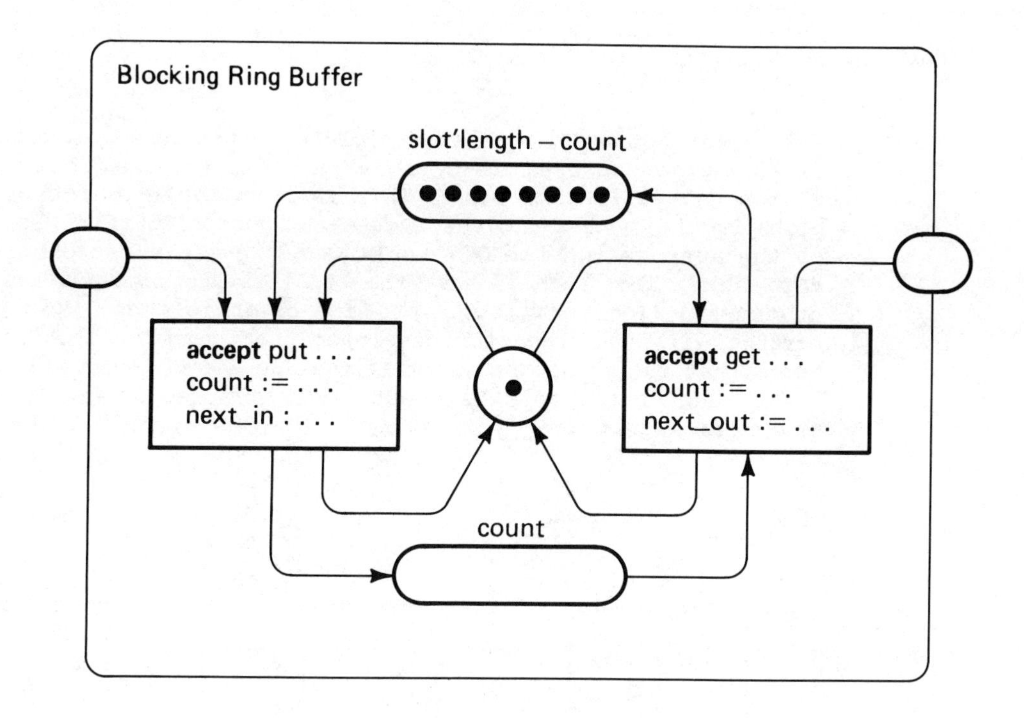

Figure 3.6. Petri net of BlockingRingBuffer (marked for initial state)

A procedure has a single body; but an entry may have several "bodies" (i.e., correponding accept statements). We haven't illustrated this possibility yet.

Procedures can be executed concurrently (no mutual exclusion); accept statements are executed in mutual exclusion.

There is no execution synchronism between the package's put and get operations. (However, there is synchronism via the state variable count: for example, if clients tried to invoke more get operations than put operations, the get procedure would raise the buffer_empty exception). Accept statements occur in the task body's sequence of statements; their execution is synchronized with each other and with other statements in the task. Conditions in select alternatives also synchronize the acceptance of entry calls.

The package containing the procedures is not a separate thread of control; the task is a separate thread of control.

PIPELINE SORT

Per Brinch Hansen, in his article on distributed processes (1978), gives an example of an array of processes that can sort n values in time O(n). This is remarkable: Quicksort, probably the most efficient sequential sort algorithm, sorts on the average in time O(n*log(n)) and in the worst case in time $O(n^2)$. The catch is that the parallel program requires n processes! (I hope that the promise of efficiency like O(n) sorting will encourage the development of computer architectures that fully support our multitasking Ada programs.)

The idea of the sort is beautifully simple. It is illustrated in Figure 3.7.

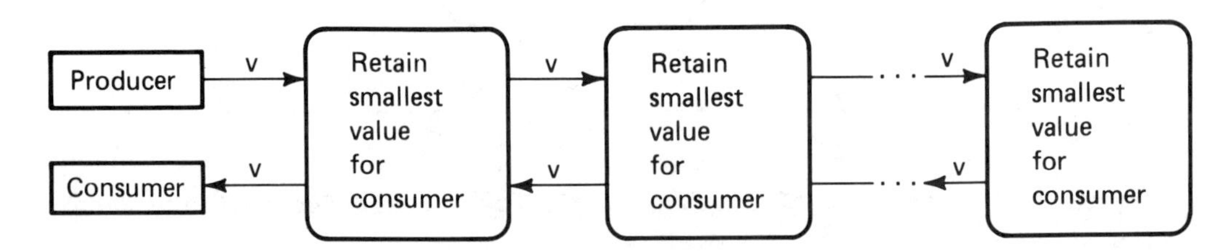

Figure 3.7. Object flow diagram for pipeline sort

Producer inputs values to the first process which retains the smallest value input so far, passing the rest of the values to its successor. The second process retains the second smallest value input so far, passing the rest of the values to its successor. When Producer has input all n values the processes 1, 2, ..., n will contain the n values stored in ascending order. Now Consumer can output the sorted values in ascending order through process 1. Of course, the internal logic of the processes must support the flow of values into the pipeline and then back out.

We assume the pipeline sort is encapsulated in a package with the following specification. (A more useful packaging would be a generic. This we do in the exercises.)

```
package PipelineSort is
  capacity : constant Positive := any_constant; -- maximum number of values
  procedure sort_this_value(value : Integer);
    -- blocks the caller if the pipeline is full.
  procedure give_me_your_smallest_value(value : out Integer);
    -- blocks the caller if the pipeline is empty
end;
```

Care must taken by the user of the package not to exceed its capacity. The procedure sort_this_value blocks its caller when the pipeline is already full. (give_me_your_smallest_value blocks its caller when the pipeline is already empty.) For many applications, a more appropriate interface would raise exceptions (buffer_full, buffer_empty) in the erring clients. We address this issue in the next chapter.

Here is a program which uses this package to sort an array.

```
with PipelineSort;
procedure sort_array is
  n : constant :=   ;                       -- n <= PipelineSort.capacity
  a : array(1..n) of Integer;
  . . .
begin
  -- fill the array

  for j in a'range loop                     -- Producer
    PipelineSort.sort_this_value(a(j));
  end loop;

  for j in a'range loop                     -- Consumer
    PipelineSort.give_me_your_smallest_value(a(j));
  end loop;

  -- use the sorted array
end sort_array;
```

The package body is relatively straightforward. We program the pipeline as an array of identical tasks. The package's initializing sequence of statements issues an entry call to every task in order to pass each one its process number. Sort_this_value and give_me_your_smallest_value call the first process in the pipeline, Process(1).

```
package body PipelineSort is
  subtype ProcessNumber is Integer range 1..capacity;

  task type Retain_smallest_value_for_consumer is
    entry here_is_your_process_number(process_number : ProcessNumber);
    entry sort_this_value(value : Integer);
    entry give_me_your_value(value : out Integer);
  end;

  Process : array(ProcessNumber) of Retain_smallest_value_for_consumer;

  task body Retain_smallest_value_for_consumer is separate;

  procedure sort_this_value(value : Integer) is
  begin
    Process(1).sort_this_value(value);
  end;

  procedure give_me_your_smallest_value(value : out Integer) is
  begin
    Process(1).give_me_your_value(value);
  end;
begin  -- All tasks are activated here.
  for j in ProcessNumber loop
    Process(j).here_is_your_process_number(process_number => j);
  end loop;
end PipelineSort;
```

Each task strives to maintain exactly one value in its local storage. A task has storage (the slot array) for two values; but a task will contain two values only temporarily--it will pass on the larger. A task can be disturbed from its equilibrium only by its predecessor--except for Process(1) which is disturbed by the two procedures. When its predecessor disturbs a task, it takes an action to restore its equilibrium:

(1) if the predecessor gives it a value with the result that it now contains two values, it keeps the smaller one and passes the other one to its successor;

(2) if the predecessor takes a value from it with the result that it now contains no value and its successor has a value, it gets a value from its successor.

Each task requires two state variables:

(1) my_count: the number of values contained in the task;

(2) our_count: the number of values contained in the task and all of its successors.

Here is the task body for Retain_smallest_value_for_consumer.

```
with increment, decrement;  -- library procedures for integers
separate (PipelineSort)
task body Retain_smallest_value_for_consumer is
  slot         : array(0..1) of Integer;          -- task's storage for values
  my_count     : Integer range 0..2 := 0;          -- number of values in slot
  my_number    : ProcessNumber;                    -- assigned by master
  our_count    : Integer range 0..capacity := 0;-- number of values in this
                                                   --  task and its successors
  my_successor : Integer range 2..capacity + 1; -- this task's successor
  our_capacity : Integer range 1..capacity;      -- capacity - my_number + 1;
begin
  accept here_is_your_process_number(process_number : ProcessNumber) do
    my_number := process_number;
  end here_is_your_process_number;
  my_successor := ProcessNumber'succ(my_number);
  our_capacity := capacity - my_number + 1;

  loop
    select
      when our_count < our_capacity => -- not needed for Process(j), j > 1
      accept sort_this_value(value : Integer) do
        slot(my_count) := value;         -- my_count = 0 or my_count = 1
      end;
      increment(my_count);
      increment(our_count);
      if my_count = 2 then               -- pass on the larger value
        if slot(0) <= slot(1) then
          Process(my_successor).sort_this_value(slot(1));
        else
          Process(my_successor).sort_this_value(slot(0));
          slot(0) := slot(1);
        end if;
        my_count := 1;
      end if;
    or
      when our_count > 0 =>              -- not needed for Process(j), j > 1
      accept give_me_your_value(value : out Integer) do
        value := slot(0);
      end;
      decrement(our_count);
      my_count := 0;
      if our_count > 0 then              -- get a value from successor
        Process(my_successor).give_me_your_value(slot(0));
        my_count := 1;
      end if;
    end select;
  end loop;
end Retain_smallest_value_for_consumer;
```

REFERENCES

Brinch Hansen, P. Distributed processes: a concurrent programming concept. Communications of the ACM, 1978, 934-941.

Yemini, S. On the suitability of Ada Multitasking for expressing parallel algorithms. Proceedings of the AdaTEC Conference on Ada, 1982, 91-97.

EXERCISES

3.1. Draw a Petri net graph for the following program. Do not show uninteresting syntactic details like "sequential" **begins** and **ends**. By "sequential" I mean a **begin** that does not radiate multiple threads of control or an **end** that does not collect terminating multiple threads of control.

```
procedure execute_project is
  task For_s2_s4 is
    entry start_s4;
  end;

  task body For_s2_s4 is
  begin
    s2;
    accept  start_s4 do
      s4;
    end;
  end;
begin
  s1;
  block:
  declare
    task For_s3;
    task body For_s3 is
    begin
      s3;
    end For_s3;
  begin
    For_s2_s4.start_s4;
  end block;
end execute_project;
```

(Here are a few words in explanation of execute_project. Note that the master holds a rendezvous with one of its dependent tasks; but the master doesn't pass any data to this task. (An entry can be parameterless.) So why does the master bother to issue an entry call to this task and then wait for a rendezvous with it? The master does this in order to synchronize with For_s2_s4. The master starts s1 and s2 in parallel; starts s3 as soon as s1 is completed; and starts s4 when s1 <u>and</u> s2 are completed. Note that this program is more complex than the one in exercise 2.2--because execution of the action s4 depends on two separate threads of control, requiring one thread to synchronize with the other. The rendezvous carries out this synchronization. The graphical Petri net makes much clearer than the linear Ada text the concurrent execution of s1 and s2, the concurrent execution of s3 and the master's request (For_s2_s4.start_s4) for a synchronizing rendezvous, and the preconditions for the execution of s4.)

3.2. Consider the following program.

```
with Text_IO;
procedure test_the_selective_wait_statement is
  task Arbitrary is
    entry give_me_a_number(number : out Integer);
  end;

  task body Arbitrary is separate;
begin
  declare
    number : Integer;
  begin
    for j in 1..30 loop
      Arbitrary.give_me_a_number(number);
      Text_IO.put(Integer'image(number));
    end loop;
  end;
end test_the_selective_wait_statement;
```

Study the task body of Arbitrary (on next page) and try to predict the output produced by this program. The selective wait statement in this task has six unguarded accept statements corresponding to the entry give_me_an_number. Remember that, in the words of the Language Reference Manual (page 9-13), "If several [accept] alternatives can ... be selected, one of them is selected arbitrarily (that is, the language does not define which one)".

If you have an Ada compiler, compile and run this program to determine what output it produces.

```
separate (test_the_selective_wait_statement)
task body Arbitrary is
begin
  loop
    select
      accept give_me_a_number(number : out Integer) do
        number := 1;
      end;
    or
      accept give_me_a_number(number : out Integer) do
        number := 2;
      end;
    or
      accept give_me_a_number(number : out Integer) do
        number := 3;
      end;
    or
      accept give_me_a_number(number : out Integer) do
        number := 4;
      end;
    or
      accept give_me_a_number(number : out Integer) do
        number := 5;
      end;
    or
      accept give_me_a_number(number : out Integer) do
        number := 6;
      end;
    end select
  end loop;
end Arbitrary;
```

3.3. Draw a Petri net graph to show the state of a task that has called its own entry e in an attempt to rendezvous with itself.

3.4. Write a package for safely reading and updating a shared variable. Meet the following specifications in your package:

(1) do not accept a read operation until after the first update operation;

(2) allow simultaneous read operations on the variable;

(3) conduct every update operation in mutual exclusion with respect to every other operation;

(4) do not permit new read operations to start when an update operation is waiting to start.

The 1st requirement prevents read operations on an uninitialized variable. The 2nd requirement increases concurrency. The 3rd requirement is necessary to prevent interference. The 4th requirement prevents read operations on outdated values.

(This classic problem is usually called the readers-writers problem. Some authors add a 5th requirement: after an update operation, do not accept another update until all the readers who were waiting during that update operation have been given a chance to conduct a read operation. If a system is not grossly overloaded with too many readers and especially too many writers, the 5th requirement may be dismissed.)

The Ada package specification is simple.

```
package SharedVariable is
  procedure read(variable : out Item);
  procedure update(value  : in  Item);
end;
```

Use the following task in your package body.

```
task Controller is
  entry start_update;
  entry end_update;
  entry start_read;
  entry end_read;
end

task body Controller is
  s : Integer := 0;        -- Controller's state variable
begin
  accept start_update;     -- \  1st requirement
  accept end_update;       -- /
  loop
    select
      when s > -1 and start_update'count = 0 =>
      accept start_read;
      s := s + 1;
    or
      accept end_read;
      s := s - 1;
    or
      when s = 0 =>
      accept start_update;
      s := -1;
    or
      accept end_update;
      s := 0;
    end select
  end loop;
end Controller;
```

3.4. (continued) The values of the state variable s have these meanings:

s = -1	A writer is performing an update operation.
s = Ø	There are no operations currently underway.
s = 1	One reader is performing a read operation.
s = 2	Two readers are performing read operations.
. . .	
s = J	J readers are performing read operations.

What is the meaning of the condition start_update'count = Ø? Start_update'count names an attribute of Controller's entry start_update. It yields the number of entry calls presently queued on the entry start_update. Thus, the condition

s > -1 **and** start_update'count = Ø

means "no writer is conducting an update and no writer is waiting to start an update." This is precisely the condition for a reader starting a read operation.

3.5. On page 95 we developed a copy program which improved on the program on page 43 by substituting one rendezvous each copy cycle for two task activations. The eariler program did have one advantage: it avoided copying values from the input task to the output task by using switched buffers. Incorporate switched buffers in the program on page 95. Use a rendezvous to synchronize the buffer switch.

3.6. Write the package body corresponding to the following generic specification. Implement the body so that all the pipeline elements (processes) are identical

```
generic
  n : in Postive;      -- number of storage elements in pipeline
  type T is private; -- the type of object stored in buffer
package PipelineBuffer is
  procedure put(x : in  T); -- blocks caller if buffer full
  procedure get(x : out T); -- blocks caller if buffer empty
end;
```

3.7. Write the package body corresponding to the following generic specification.

```
generic
  capacity : in Positive;
  type ItemType is private;
  with function "<"(x, y : ItemType) return Boolean;
package
PipelineSort is
  procedure insert_this_item(item : ItemType);
  procedure give_me_the_item_with_smallest_key(item : out ItemType);
end;
```

3.8. Draw a Petri net for the following task.

```
task T is
  entry e;
end;

task body T is
begin
  s1;
  accept e;
  s2;
  accept e;
  s3;
end T;
```

Note that there are two accept statements for the same entry. Be sure to draw only one place (i.e., entry queue) for this entry.

ANSWERS TO EXERCISES

3.1.

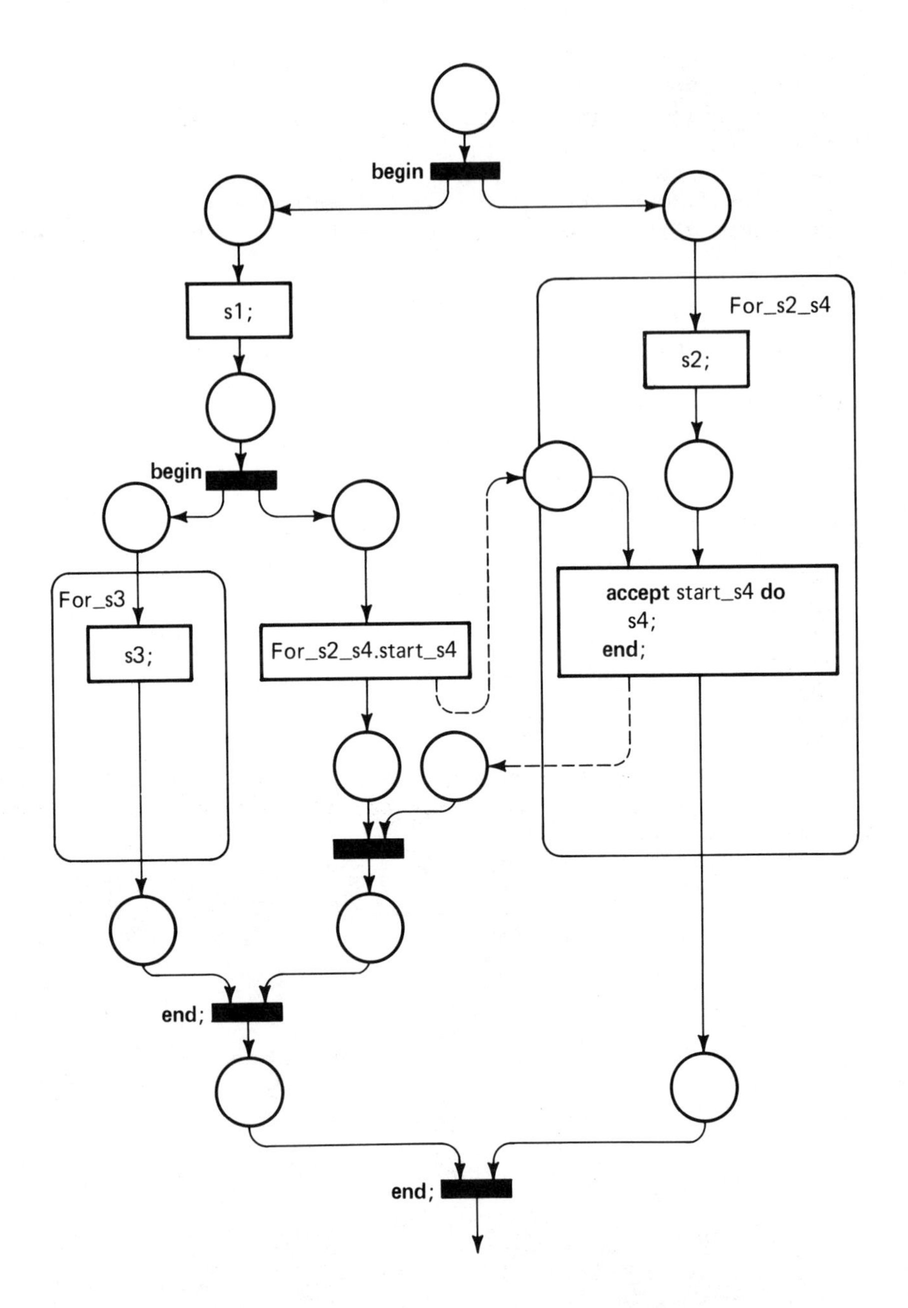

Figure 3.8. Petri net for the execute_project procedure on page 118

3.2 The language reference manual states that one of the selectable accept alternatives "is selected arbitrarily." This gives the implementor freedom to choose an efficient mechanism.
I know of at least one implementation that prints

1 1 1 1 1 1 1 1 1 1 1 1 1 1 1 1 1 1 1 1 1 1 1 1 1 1 1 1 1 1

Now I ask you, is that _fair_? (Of course, the language reference manual, says "arbitrarily", not _fairly_; and, certainly, this implementation is choosing arbitrarily!) One problem with this mechanism of selection is that the programmer may find out about it and begin to write code whose desired effect depends on the implementation's always choosing the first selectable accept alternative.
Perhaps not much harder to implement would be round-robin which has the advantage of being fair:

1 2 3 4 5 6 1 2 3 4 5 6 1 2 3 4 5 6 1 2 3 4 5 6 1 2 3 4 5 6

But I don't know of any implementor using round-robin.
The Preliminary Language Reference Manual (June 1979) used "at random" rather than "arbitrarily": "In such cases [where more than one accept alternative is selectable] one of these alternatives is selected at random." This rule would be fair and would prevent the programmer from writing implementation dependent code. It would also be harder to implement; that is no doubt why "at random" was later changed to "arbitrarily".

3.3. A Petri net graph of a task that has called one of its own entries is shown below. The task is deadlocked: it can't fire t2 until it receives a token from the firing of **accept** e and it can't fire **accept** e until it fires t2. A task that issues an entry call to one of its own entries will always deadlock (unless the entry call is conditional or timed (see sections 9.7.2 and 9.7.3 of the Language Reference Manual). Nevertheless, the Language Reference Manual does not forbid a task from calling one of its own entries.

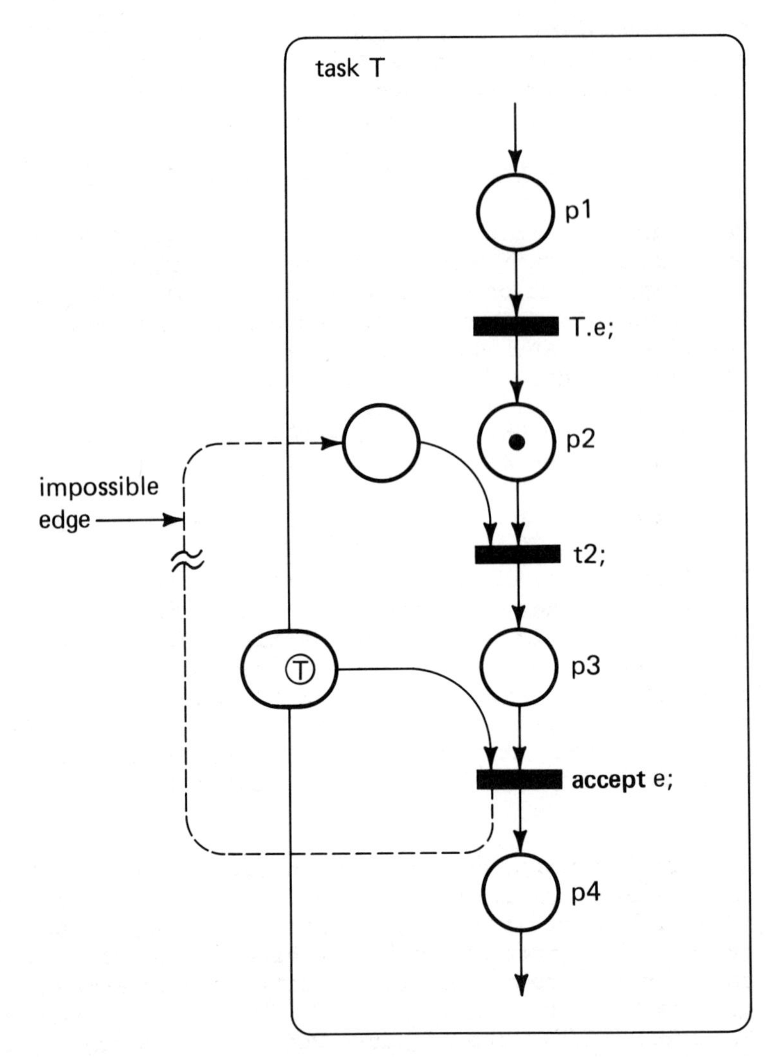

Figure 3.9. Petri net graph of a task T that has called its own entry e

3.4.

```
package SharedVariable is
  procedure read(variable : out Item);
  procedure update(value  : in  Item);
end;
```

```
package body SharedVariable is
  shared_variable : Item;

  task Controller is
    entry start_update;
    entry end_update;
    entry start_read;
    entry end_read;
  end;

  task body Controller is
    s : Integer := 0;       -- Controller's state variable
  begin
    accept start_update;  -- \  1st requirement
    accept end_update;    -- /
    loop
      select
        when s > -1 and start_update'count = 0 =>
        accept start_read;
        s := s + 1;
      or
        accept end_read;
        s := s - 1;
     or
        when s = 0 =>
        accept start_update;
        s := -1;
      or
        accept end_update;
        s := 0;
      end select
    end loop;
  end Controller;

  procedure read(variable : out Item) is
  begin
    Controller.start_read;
    variable := shared_variable;
    Controller.end_read;
  end read;

  procedure update(value   : in Item) is
  begin
    Controller.start_update;
    shared_variable := value;
    Controller.end_update;
  end update;
end SharedVariable;
```

3.5. There are two approaches we can take: (1) let Input issue an entry call to Output and let Output switch the buffers during its rendezvous with Input; (2) let Input and Output issue entry calls to a third task, SwitchBuffers, that switches the buffers during its "rendezvous à trois" with Input and Output. Whichever approach we take, we must ensure that neither Input nor Output starts using its buffer until the switching has been completed.

Here's the first approach. (The second approach, shown later, uses a selective wait statement with a terminate alternative to terminate the buffer-switching task.)

```
with Text_IO; use Text_IO;
procedure copy_program is
  buffer      : array(1..2) of String(1..80);  -- 2 buffers indexed
  for_reading : Integer range 1..2 := 1;       -- by for_reading
  for_writing : Integer range 1..2 := 2;       -- and for_writing

  procedure switch_buffers is                  -- which are switched
    tmp_reading : Integer range 1..2;          -- between Input and
  begin                                        -- and Output by this
    tmp_reading := for_reading;                -- procedure
    for_reading := for_writing;
    for_writing := tmp_reading;
  end switch_buffers;
  pragma inline(switch_buffers);

  task Input is
    -- calls Output.Input_is_ready_to_switch (when it is ready to switch)
  end;

  task Output is
    entry Input_is_ready_to_switch;
  end;

  task body Input is
  begin
    while not end_of_file loop
      get(buffer(for_reading));
      skip_line;
      Output.Input_is_ready_to_switch;
    end loop;
    buffer(for_reading)(1) := ASCII.eot;
    Output.Input_is_ready_to_switch;
  end Input;
```

```
  task body Output is
  begin
    loop;
      -- Output is ready to switch.
      accept Input_is_ready_to_switch do   -- Hold Input in the
        switch_buffers;                      -- rendezvous until the
      end;                                   -- switching is complete.
      exit when buffer(for_writing)(1) = ASCII.eot;
      put(buffer(for_writing));
      new_line;
    end loop;
  end Output;
begin
  null;
end copy_program;
```

3.5. (continued) Here is the second approach. Note the nested accept statement in the task that switches the buffers. The switching task, SwitchBuffers, waits for both Input and Output to issue entry calls to it and then holds both these tasks in a rendezvous until the switching has been completed. This program is more symmetric than the first one; but it requires an additional rendezvous each copy cycle.

```
with Text_IO; use Text_IO;
procedure copy_program is
  buffer      : array(1..2) of String(1..80); -- 2 buffers indexed
  for_reading : Integer range 1..2 := 1;      -- by for_reading
  for_writing : Integer range 1..2 := 2;      -- and for_writing

  task SwitchBuffers is
    entry Input_is_ready_to_switch;
    entry Output_is_ready_to_switch;
  end SwitchBuffers;

  task Input is
    -- calls SwitchBuffers.Input_is_ready_to_switch;
  end Input;

  task Output is
    -- calls SwitchBuffers.Output_is_ready_to_switch;
  end Output;

  task SwitchBuffers is separate;
  task Input         is separate;
  task Output        is separate;
begin
  null;
end copy_program;
```

3.5. (continued) We have programmed SwitchBuffers to terminate by the mechanism of a selective wait statement with a terminate alternative. See the Language Reference Manual (sections 9.7.1 and 9.4) for a description of the semantics of the terminate alternative. SwitchBuffers will terminate on the selective wait statement when the master completes the execution of the null statement and the other two tasks have terminated.

```
separate (copy_program)
task body SwitchBuffers is
  tmp_reading : Integer range 1..2;
begin
  loop
    select
      accept Input_is_ready_to_switch do
        accept Output_is_ready_to_switch do
          tmp_reading := for_reading;       -- \  Switch buffers
          for_reading := for_writing;       --  > during this
          for_writing := tmp_reading;       -- /  "rendezvous à trois"
        end;
      end;
    or
      terminate;
    end select;
  end loop;
end SwitchBuffers;

separate (copy_program)
task body Input is
begin
  while not end_of_file loop
    get(buffer(for_reading));
    skip_line;
    SwitchBuffers.Input_is_ready_to_switch;
  end loop;
  buffer(for_reading)(1) := ASCII.eot;
  SwitchBuffers.Input_is_ready_to_switch;
end Input;

separate (copy_program)
task body Output is
begin
  loop
    SwitchBuffers.Output_is_ready_to_switch;
    exit when buffer(for_writing)(1) = ASCII.eot;
    put(buffer(for_writing));
    new_line;
  end loop;
end Output;
```

3.6.

```
package body PipelineBuffer is
  subtype IndexType is Integer range 1..n;

  task type Element is
    entry here_is_your_index(index : IndexType);
    entry here_is_an_x(x : in  T);
    entry give_me_an_x(x : out T);
  end;

  Buffer : array(IndexType) of Element;

  task body Element is
    my_index : IndexType;
    my_slot  : T;
  begin
    accept here_is_your_index(index : IndexType) do
      my_index := index;
    end;
    loop
      accept here_is_an_x(x : in  T) do
        my_slot := x;
      end;
      if my_index < n then
        Buffer(my_index + 1).here_is_an_x(my_slot);
      else
        accept give_me_an_x(x : out T) do
          x := my_slot;
        end;
      end if;
  end Element;

  procedure put(x : in  T) is
  begin
    Buffer(1).here_is_an_x(x);
  end put;

  procedure get(x : out T) is
  begin
    Buffer(n).give_me_an_x(x);
  end get;
begin
  for j in IndexType loop
    Buffer(j).here_is_your_index(index => j);
  end loop;
end PipelineBuffer;
```

3.7. We have programmed Process_1 differently from all the other processes since only the first process need guard against the caller overfilling or underfilling the pipeline. Once again, I mention that for some applications it might be more appropriate to raise an exception in a caller who tries to overfill the pipeline rather than block this caller. Indeed, blocking the caller may deadlock the system.

```
package body PipelineSort is
  subtype ProcessNumber is Integer range 2..capacity;

  task Process_1 is
    entry here_is_an_item(item : ItemType);
    entry give_me_your_item(item : out ItemType;
  end;

  task type ProcessType is
    entry here_is_your_process_number(process_number : ProcessNumber);
    entry here_is_an_item(item : ItemType);
    entry give_me_your_item(item : out ItemType);
  end;

  Process : array(ProcessNumber) of ProcessType;

  task body Process_1   is separate;
  task body ProcessType is separate;

  procedure insert_this_item(item : ItemType) is
  begin
    Process_1.here_is_an_item(item);
  end;

  procedure give_me_the_item_with_smallest_key(item : out ItemType) is
  begin
    Process_1.give_me_your_item(item);
  end;
begin  -- All tasks are activated here.
  for j in ProcessNumber loop
    Process(j).here_is_your_process_number(process_number => j);
  end loop;
end PipelineSort;
```

3.7. (continued)

```
with increment, decrement;  -- library procedures for integers
separate (PipelineSort)
task body Process_1 is
  slot     : array(0..1) of ItemType;          -- task's storage for items
  my_count : Integer range 0..2 := 0;          -- number of items in slot
  count    : Integer range 0..capacity := 0;   -- total count for pipeline
begin
  loop
    select
      when count < capacity =>
      accept here_is_an_item(item : ItemType) do
        slot(my_count) := item;                -- my_count contains 0 or 1
      end;
      increment(my_count);
      increment(count);
      if my_count = 2 then                     -- pass on the larger item
        if slot(0) <= slot(1) then
          Process(2).here_is_an_item(slot(1));
        else                                   -- slot(0) holds larger item
          Process(2).here_is_an_item(slot(0));
          slot(0) := slot(1);
        end if;
        my_count := 1;
      end if;
    or
      when count > 0 =>
      accept give_me_your_item(item : out ItemType) do
        item := slot(0);
      end;
      decrement(count);
      my_count := 0;
      if count > 0 then              -- get a item from successor
        Process(2).give_me_your_item(slot(0));
        my_count := 1;
      end if;
    end select;
  end loop;
end Process_1;
```

3.7. (continued)

```
with increment, decrement;  -- library procedures for integers
separate (PipelineSort)
task body ProcessType is
  slot         : array(0..1) of ItemType;
  my_count     : Integer range 0..2 := 0;
  my_number    : ProcessNumber;
  our_count    : Integer range 0..capacity - 1 := 0;
  my_successor : Integer range 3..capacity + 1;
  our_capacity : Integer range 1..capacity - 1;
begin
  accept here_is_your_process_number(process_number : ProcessNumber) do
    my_number := process_number;
  end here_is_your_process_number;
  my_successor := ProcessNumber'succ(my_number);
  our_capacity := capacity - my_number + 1;

  loop
    select
      accept here_is_an_item(item : ItemType) do
        slot(my_count) := item;         -- my_count = 0 or my_count = 1
      end;
      increment(my_count);
      increment(our_count);
      if my_count = 2 then              -- pass on the larger item
        if slot(0) <= slot(1) then
          Process(my_successor).here_is_an_item(slot(1));
        else
          Process(my_successor).here_is_an_item(slot(0));
          slot(0) := slot(1);
        end if;
        my_count := 1;
      end if;
    or
      accept give_me_your_item(item : out ItemType) do
        item := slot(0);
      end;
      decrement(our_count);
      my_count := 0;
      if our_count > 0 then             -- get a item from successor
        Process(my_successor).give_me_your_item(slot(0));
        my_count := 1;
      end if;
    end select;
  end loop;
end ProcessType;
```

3.8.

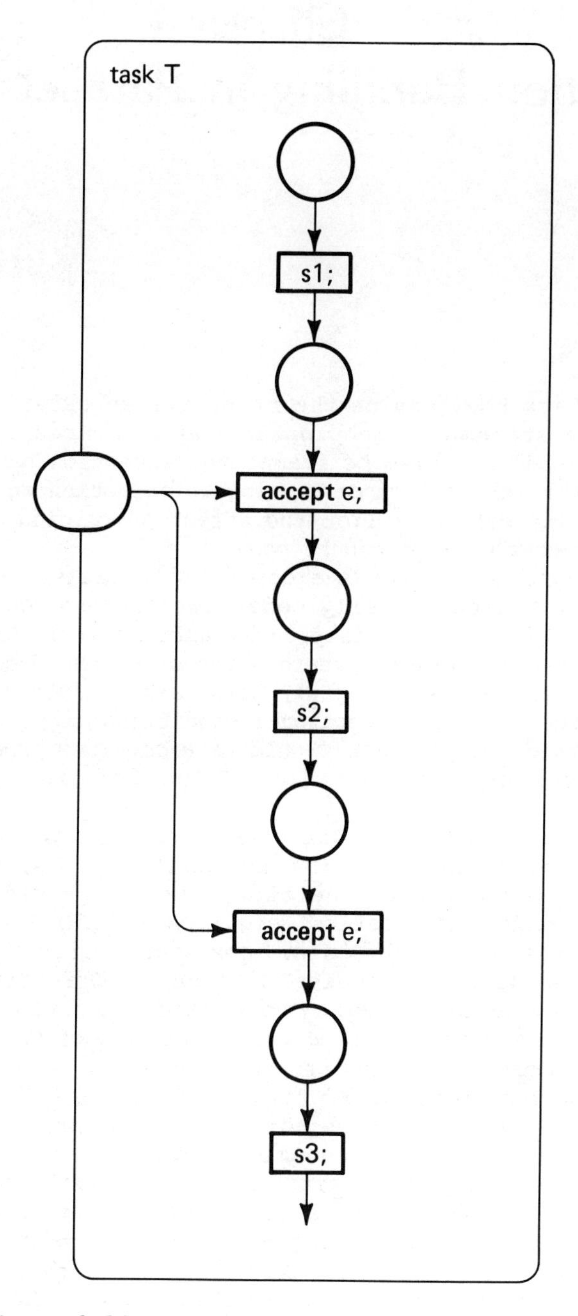

Figure 3.10. Petri net for task T on page 123

Chapter 4
Exception Handling in Parallel Programs

A task body can be the frame for an exception handler. (A block statement, subprogram body, package body, or generic unit body can also be frames for exception handlers.) We will see that the effect of raising an exception in a task body can be quite different from the effect of raising an exception in, for example, a procedure body.

In order to discuss exceptions in tasks, we will look at a somewhat artificially coded two-process root-searching program. What makes this program artificial is that one task has an exception handler whereas the other one does not. If exception handlers are helpful, both tasks should have them.

Evidently, the exceptional conditions likely to arise in the execution of the tasks would be exceptions propagated to these tasks from the execution of the function calls f(x1) and f(x2).

Let us first consider task Compute_fx1. The coder of this task has assumed that the computation of f(x) is very accurate but failure-prone; therefore, he has provided a cruder but more robust alternative: sign_f(x). If f(x1) fails and raises an exception in the task, then control is transferred to the task's exception handler. If sign_f(x1) returns normally the task terminates, having performed, we suppose, a reasonable job. At any rate, the master is unaware of Compute_fx1's extra effort and everything proceeds normally.

But what happens if f(x2) in Compute_fx2 fails? The task body of this task does not have an exception handler. Consequently, this task becomes completed (and since it has no dependent tasks it terminates). No value of fx2 has been computed; and so the value is the old one, the one remaining from the last cycle through the loop. The important point to note is that Compute_fx2 terminates without propagating the exception to its master. In this respect the behavior of the task is very different from the behavior of a procedure that

```
function root_of_f(a, b : Float) return Float is
  x0, x1, x2, x3, fx0, fx1, fx2, fx3, : Float;
begin
  x0 := a; fx0 := f(x0);
  x3 := b; fx3 := f(x3);

  if x3 - x0 <= epsilon and fx0*fx3 > 0.0 then
    raise no_root;
  end if;

  while x3 - x0 > epsilon loop
    declare                          -- Elaborate a block (task master) to
      task Compute_fx1;              -- concurrently compute x1, x2, f(x1),
      task Compute_fx2;              -- and f(x2).

      task body Compute_fx1 is
      begin
        x1  := x0 + (1.0/3.0)*(x3 - x0);
        fx1 := f(x1);
      exception
        when others => fx1 := sign_f(x1);
      end;

      task body Compute_fx2 is
      begin
        x2  := x0 + (2.0/3.0)*(x3 - x0);
        fx2 := f(x2);
      end;
    begin
      null;
    end;

    if fx0*fx1 <= 0.0 then         -- Shrink search interval to x0..x1.
      x3  := x1;
      fx3 := fx1;
    elsif fx1*fx2 <= 0.0 then      -- Shrink search interval to x1..x2.
      x0  := x1;
      x3  := x2;
      fx0 := fx1;
      fx3 := fx2;
    elsif fx2*fx3 <= 0.0 then      -- Shrink search interval to x2..x3.
      x0  := x2;
      fx0 := fx2;
    else
      raise no_root;
    end if;
  end loop;
  return (x0 + x3)/2.0;
end root_of_f;
```

the master might call. If a program unit calls a procedure and the procedure fails (has an unhandled exception), the caller very well knows about it because the unhandled exception is raised again at the point of call. But if a master activates a task and the task subsequently terminates abnormally because of an unhandled exception, the master is not informed by the exception mechanism.

If this seems surprising to you, consider the alternative. The alternative is the propagation of every dependent task's unhandled exceptions back to the master. This means that every dependent task could interfere asynchronously with its master. This kind of interference could result in utter chaos. To avoid this potential chaos, if an exception is not handled within a task, the exception is not propagated further; and the task's execution is "quietly" completed.

(On the other hand, If an unhandled exception occurs during a program unit's attempt to communicate with a task, then the propagation of the exception to the caller does not constitute asynchronous interference. Therefore, when an exception is raised within an accept statement and the exception is not handled within an inner frame of the accept statement, the exception is synchronously propagated to the calling task, at the point of the entry call. We discuss the effects of exceptions raised during task communication in the next section.)

EXCEPTIONS RAISED DURING TASK COMMUNICATION

Given that the failure of Compute_fx1 or Compute_fx2 will not be automatically communicated to the master, we may want to provide a means for each task to communicate success or failure--synchronously--to the master. The following version of root_of_f does this. In this program each task first tries to compute f(x); if f(x) fails, the task next tries to compute sign_f(x); if sign_f(x) also fails, the task gives up and subsequently raises an exception in the master when it responds to the master's request for f(x).

This program represents several improvements and innovations over the program in the previous section: it eliminates global variables; it computes f(a) and f(b) in parallel; it substitutes task rendezvous for task activations; and it uses the terminate option in a selective wait statement to effect an orderly termination of the two dependent tasks.

Note that ProcessType has two entries. Of course, we could have used a single entry to pass in x and then pass out f(x).

```
entry compute_fx(x : in Float; fx : out Float);
```

But this would have defeated the quest for parallelism because the master would have to wait while the called task computes f(x). We have written the tasks so that the master can call them in quick succession to pass in their respective x values; then the master calls their other entries and waits for them to pass out their results.

After each task obtains its x value, it attempts to compute the corresponding f(x); if this computation fails for any reason the local exception handler attempts sign_f(x); if this fails, control is transferred to to the exception handler at the end of the task body. The same kinds of statements are allowed in an exception handler's sequence of statements as

```
function root_of_f(a, b : Float) return Float is
  task type ProcessType is
    entry here_is_an_x(x : Float);
    entry give_me_the_fx(fx : out Float);
  end;

  Process : array(1..2) of ProcessType;

  task body ProcessType is
    my_x, my_fx : Float;
  begin
    loop
      select
        accept here_is_an_x(x : Float) is
          my_x := x;
        end;
      or
        terminate;
      end select;

      begin
        my_fx := f(my_x);                     -- f may raise an exception
      exception
        when others => my_fx := sign_f(my_x); -- sign_f may raise an exception
      end;

      accept give_me_the_fx(fx : out Float) do
        fx := my_fx;
      end;
    end loop;
  exception
    when others =>
    accept give_me_the_fx(fx : out Float) do
      raise; -- This statement propagates the exception to the caller.
    end;
  end ProcessType;
```

```
begin
  declare
    xØ, x1, x2, x3, fxØ, fx1, fx2, fx3 : Float; -- master's local variables
  begin
    xØ := a;
    x3 := b;

    Process(1).here_is_an_x(xØ);        -- \  Set the processes to work
    Process(2).here_is_an_x(x3);        -- /  computing f(a) and f(b).

    Process(1).give_me_the_fx(fxØ);     -- \  Collect f(xØ) = f(a)
    Process(2).give_me_the_fx(fx3);     -- /      and f(x3) = f(b)

    if x3 - xØ <= epsilon and fxØ*fx3 > Ø.Ø then
      raise no_root;
    end if;

    while x3 - xØ > epsilon loop
      x1 := xØ + (1.Ø/3.Ø)*(x3 - xØ); -- \  Divide the search
      x2 := xØ + (2.Ø/3.Ø)*(x3 - xØ); -- /  interval into thirds.

      Process(1).here_is_an_x(x1);      -- \  Set the processes to work
      Process(2).here_is_an_x(x2);      -- /  computing f(x1) and f(x2).


      Process(1).give_me_the_fx(fx1); -- \  Collect f(x1)
      Process(2).give_me_the_fx(fx2); -- /      and f(x2)

      if fxØ*fx1 <= Ø.Ø then            -- Shrink search interval to xØ..x1.
        x3  := x1;
        fx3 := fx1;
      elsif fx1*fx2 <= Ø.Ø then         -- Shrink search interval to x1..x2.
        xØ  := x1;
        x3  := x2;
        fxØ := fx1;
        fx3 := fx2;
      elsif fx2*fx3 <= Ø.Ø then         -- Shrink search interval to x2..x3.
        xØ  := x2;
        fxØ := fx2;
      else
        raise no_root;
      end if;
    end loop;

    return (xØ + x3)/2.Ø;
  end;
exception
  when others => raise no_root;
end root_of_f;
```

are allowed in the task body's normal sequence of statements. Therefore, an accept statement is allowed in a task's exception handler. In our program, the exception handler's accept statement is substituted for the normal one. The normal accept statement returns the computed value (either f(x) or sign_f(x)). The exception handler's accept statement raises again the exception (originally raised by sign_f) which caused transfer to the handler. Because the handler raises the original exception again, the task terminates abnormally. But this is not enough to propagate the exception to the master. Because the master is in a rendezvous with the task when the exception is raised (and not handled), the exception is propagated to the calling task (the master) at the point of the entry call.

Thus any one of give_me_the_fx entry calls could result in an exception (originally raised by sign_f) propagating to the master. The master's response in these cases is to terminate abnormally by raising the no_root exception.

There is another way an exception can be propagated to a program unit attempting to communicate with a task. If a task has already completed its execution at the time of an entry call to it or if it completes its execution before it accepts an entry call to it, then the exception tasking_error is raised in the caller at the place of the entry call. As an example, consider the body of ProcessType rewritten this way

```
task body ProcessType is
  my_x, my_fx : Float;
begin
  loop
    select
      accept here_is_an_x(x : Float) is
        my_x := x;
      end;
    or
      terminate;
    end select;

    begin
      my_fx := f(my_x);                        -- f may raise an exception
    exception
      when others => my_fx := sign_f(my_x); -- sign_f may raise an exception
    end;

    accept give_me_the_fx(fx : out Float) do
      fx := my_fx;
    end;
  end loop;
end ProcessType;
```

This version of ProcessType has no exception handler for exceptions that might be raised by sign_f. Therefore, if such an exception arises in an object of type ProcessType, this task will abnormally terminate without any immediate notification to the master. However, when the master next tries to communicate with it (by calling its entry give_me_the_fx), the exception tasking_error will be raised in the master. The program as previously written will still work with this version of ProcessType because the exception handler in the master,

```
when others => raise no_root;
```

handles all exceptions raised as a result of entry calls to tasks, including, of course, tasking_error exceptions.

Finally, we offer a few words in explanation of the terminate alternative in the selective wait statement. This selective wait alternative is a neat way Ada provides for terminating tasks--particularly server tasks--that are no longer needed. The terminate alternative in a selective wait statement is taken, that is the task owning the statement is terminated, if the following conditions hold:

The task in question is waiting to execute a selective wait statement that contains an open terminate alternative.

Every other task that depends on this master is either terminated or is also waiting to execute a selective wait statement with an open terminate alternative.

This task depends on a master whose execution is completed.

When all three conditions hold, the task in question--along with all the other tasks that depend on the master--are terminated. Notice that both tasks, Process(1) and Process(2), wait to execute a selective wait statement at the top of their respective loops. Consequently, the first two conditions hold after each execution of the loop's sequence of statements. The third condition holds when the master completes its execution, which can happen two ways: the master can evaluate the expression in a return statement or the master can raise an exception (**raise** no_root) for which there is no handler. (If the master raises an exception for which it does have a handler, it completes its execution after it finishes executing the corresponding handler.)

The effect of the above semantics is that when the master no longer requires its dependent tasks, they obligingly terminate.

EXCEPTION HANDLING AND TERMINATION IN A PIPELINE OF TASKS

To illustrate exception handling and termination in a task pipeline, we will solve the "telegram analysis" problem, first posed by Henderson and Snowdon (1972) and further treated by (among others) Michael Jackson (1980). (This problem is an example of what Jackson (1980) calls a "structure clash." Ada tasks are exquisitely effective at decomposing and resolving "structure clash" problems.)

The Telegram Analysis Problem

An input file contains the text of a number of telegrams. Each telegram consists of a number of words followed by the word "ZZZZ".

The input file is composed of a sequence of lines. The lines can vary in length; but the length of a line cannot exceed 40 characters. Each line contains a number of words, separated by blanks (space characters).

The length of a word cannot exceed 26 characters. There may be one or more blanks between adjacent words; and there may (but need not) be one or more additional blanks at the beginning and end of a line .

There is no particular relationship between telegrams and lines: a telegram may begin and end anywhere in a line and may span several lines. Furthermore, several telegrams may share a line.

The problem is to analyze the set of telegrams and print a report, showing for each telegram its ordinal number and the number of words it contains. Of course, the special "word" "ZZZZ" should not be counted as a word in the statistics.

It may be helpful to the reader to see a short example of a set of telegrams:

```
Dear Mom: Happy Birthday! Love, Tim ZZZZ
Dad: Send money. Joe ZZZZ Mr. President:
 Please restore the budget for STARS.
Vance Druffel ZZZZ Dear Elizabeth: Best
wishes on your latest matrimonial try.
J. Warner ZZZZ Dear J. Go to h---! E. T.
ZZZZ Dear George: Go for it! J. I. ZZZZ
Dear Jean: Roses are read; violets are
blue; Ada is green. D. F. ZZZZ Dear 007:
009 has been assassinated; your new
contact is 008. Control ZZZZ
```

Here is the report for this set of telegrams.

```
            TELEGRAMS REPORT
Telegram number 1 contains 6 words.
Telegram number 2 contains 4 words.
Telegram number 3 contains 10 words.
Telegram number 4 contains 11 words.
Telegram number 5 contains 7 words.
Telegram number 6 contains 7 words.
Telegram number 7 contains 13 words.
Telegram number 8 contains 12 words.
             END OF REPORT
```

An effective approach to this problem is to transform the requirements into a pipeline of processes. The first process should break the lines into words, the second process (not strictly necessary) should buffer a word, and the third and final process should transform its input stream of words into the required report. Here is the object flow diagram for this approach.

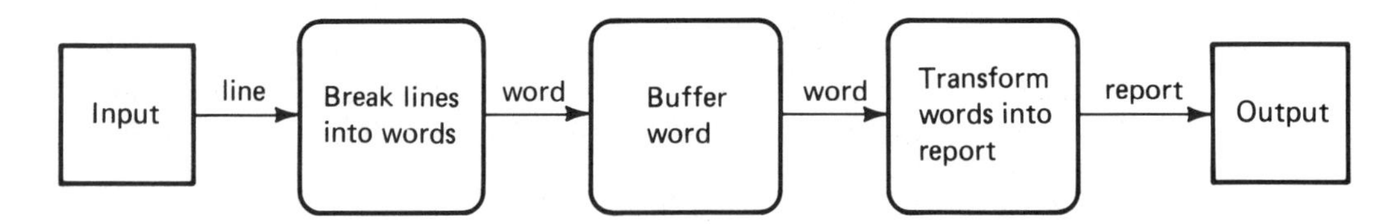

Figure 4.1. Object flow diagram for telegrams analysis problem

The first step we take in implementing this object flow diagram is to write a master procedure which defines the tasks that will realize the process abstractions. We make an important design decision at this stage of development: how should the objects flow from one process to the next? This is the crucial interface decision: how should one task communicate with another? The designer must decide which task owns the entry which the other task calls. In this design, for example, we have decided that the second task, Buffer_word, should be passive and own two entries which the first and third tasks call. Please note that we can decide which task owns an entry quite independently of the direction of object flow, since an entry can have **in**, **out**, or even **in out** parameters.

Note the use of the discriminated record to define the type of a word object. We are concerned in the object flow method of design about the width of the objects which flow between tasks. If the objects are unnecessarily wide, the burden of rendezvous and object flow is unnecessarily high. WordType, a discriminated record type, permits the passed string object to be the optimum length.

Note the top-down nature of our development. First we transformed the requirements into an object flow diagram, then we transformed the object flow diagram into an Ada master procedure which defines the objects and the task interfaces, and finally we will define the internal logic of the primitive processes (the three tasks).

```
procedure analyze_telegrams_file is
  max_length : constant := 26; -- the maximum length of a word
  subtype WordLength is Integer range 1..max_length;

  type WordType(length : WordLength := max_length) is  -- for word objects
    record
      letter : String(1..length);
    end record;

  ZZZZ : constant WordType(4) := (4, "ZZZZ");
  eof  : constant WordType(1) := (1, (1 => ASCII.eot));

  task Break_lines_into_words is
    -- calls Text_IO.open, Text_IO.get_line, and Text_IO.close
    -- calls Buffer_word.here_is_a_word
  end Break_lines_into_words;

  task Buffer_word is
    entry here_is_a_word(word : in  WordType);
    entry give_me_a_word(word : out WordType);
    entry halt;
  end Buffer_word;

  task Tranform_words_into_report is
    -- calls Buffer_word.give_me_a_word
    -- calls Text_IO.create, Text_IO.put_line, and Text_IO.close
    -- calls Buffer_word.halt (when it encounters a fatal error)
  end Tranform_words_into_report;

  task body Break_lines_into_words     is separate;
  task body Buffer_word                is separate;
  task body Tranform_words_into_report is separate;
begin
  null; -- There is nothing for master to do except create its subordinates.
end analyze_telegrams_file;
```

Ada does not require us to document in the "interface" specification of a task the other processes which the task calls. If we are documenting a library unit, this makes eminent sense: we don't need to know how the library unit implements its services. Indeed, the principle of information hiding requires that such information be deliberatedly withheld from us. But when we are documenting a program design, we are vitally interested in documenting the other processes which a task calls. This information is just as important to our understanding of the task's interface as the task's entries. We document the outgoing calls from a task as comments in its specification. (Unfortunately, the compiler will not check these informal interface specifications for us.) Two of the three tasks in our current program have examples of such informal (commentary) interface specifications.

Here are the internal entities and internal logic of the first task, Break lines into words.

```
with Text_IO; use Text_IO;
separate (analyze_telegrams_file)
task body Break_lines_into_words is
  type StateType is (not_in_word, in_word); -- for finite state machine
  state      : StateType := not_in_word;
  telegrams  : File_Type;              -- internal name of "Telegrams" file
  last       : Integer range 0..40;   -- index of last character from get_line
  line       : String(1..41);          -- buffer for letters of line, plus ' '
  i          : Integer range 1..40;   -- index of first character in a new word
begin
  open(telegrams, mode => in_file, name => "Telegrams");

  while not end_of_file(telegrams) loop
    get_line(telegrams, line, last);
    line(last + 1) := ' ';     -- The line end is represented by a blank.
    for j in 1..last + 1 loop
      case state is            -- This is a finite state machine to find words.
        when not_in_word =>
        if line(j) /= ' ' then
          state := in_word;
          i := j;              -- i saves the index of beginning of new word.
        end if;

        when in_word =>
        if line(j) = ' ' then
          Buffer_word.here_is_a_word((j - i,  line(i..j - 1)));
          state := not_in_word;
        end if;
      end case;
    end loop;
  end loop;
```

```
  Buffer_word.here_is_a_word(eof);
  close(telegrams);
exception
  when status_error | name_error | use_error | device_error =>
  put_line("Break lines into words terminated due to an input error.");
  Buffer_word.here_is_a_word(eof);

  when tasking_error =>
  put_line("Break lines into words terminated due to tasking_error.");
  close(telegrams);

  when others =>
  put_line("Break lines into words terminated due to an unknown exception.");
  Buffer_word.here_is_a_word(eof);
  close(telegrams);
end Break_lines_into_words;
```

During normal processing, Break_lines_into_words gets a line, finds the words on the line, and sends each word (along with its length) to its successor task, Buffer_word.

Break_lines_into_words is specialized to perform a transformation upon the input lines; it doesn't test the words it finds: it merely passes them down the pipeline. When it detects end_of_file, it doesn't know whether it's a normal or premature end of file; so it sends an eof message down the pipeline for successor tasks to use as they see fit.

Break_lines_into_words may encounter a fatal condition. Especially likely are input exceptions like status_error and name_error. (The procedure call statement open(...) will raise a name_error exception if there is no external file with the name "Telegrams".) If Break_lines_into_words merely terminated when it encountered one of these exceptions, it would leave its successor tasks stranded. Therefore, when it encounters an input exception, it sends an eof message down the pipeline.

Break_lines_into_words' successor, Buffer_word, may also encounter a fatal condition. How can Buffer_word communicate a fatal condition to Break_lines_into_words? If Buffer_word encounters a fatal condition and consequently terminates, then Break_lines_into_words will encounter a tasking_error exception when it issues an entry call to Buffer_word.

The internal logic of Buffer_word (on the next page) is fairly straightforward. Its selective wait statement has a guarded (**when not** filled) accept statement for here_is_a_word and another guarded (**when** filled) accept statement for give_me_a_word. The normal way for Buffer_word to terminate is for it to take the terminate alternative in its selective wait statement after both its predecessor and successor have terminated. (The terminate alternative also covers the abnormal case when the eof message denotes a premature end_of_file.)

```
with Text_IO; use Text_IO;
separate (analyze_telegrams_file)
task body Buffer_word is
  buffer : WordType;  -- unconstrained
  filled : Boolean := false;
begin
  loop
    select
      when not filled =>
      accept here_is_a_word(word : in WordType) do
        buffer := word;
      end;
      filled := true;
    or
      when filled =>
      accept give_me_a_word(word : out WordType) do
        word := buffer;
      end;
      filled := false;
    or
      accept halt;
      put_line("Buffer_word halting due to halt entry call.");
      exit;
    or
      terminate;
    end select;
  end loop;
end Buffer_word;
```

What is the purpose of the third entry in Buffer_word? If Buffer_word's successor, Transform_words_into_report, encounters a fatal error (for example, while trying to create the report file), it must cause its predecessor tasks in the pipeline to terminate. Otherwise, it would leave these tasks stranded. Of course, Transform_words_into_report could simply abort Buffer_word. But we should usually take a firm stand against aborting a task, because aborting a task prevents its carrying out last wishes or clean-up operations by means of an exception handler:

```
when others => perform_last_wishes;
```

In the case of the buffer under consideration, it need perform no clean-up operation. Therefore, its successor could abort the buffer task in order to propagate a fatal exception toward the input end of the pipeline. However, this is not a general solution because very often a task does have to perform a clean-up operation. The halt entry in Buffer_word provides a better way for its successor to stop Buffer_word. We can place clean-up operations, if any are required, between the **accept** halt and **exit** statements.

We note in passing that the terminate alternative does not make provisions for any final (for example, clean-up) operations; this will sometimes limit its usefulness.

The internal logic of Transform_words_into_report follows. It's relatively simple because we don't have to worry about the mechanism for producing its incoming stream of words.

```
with increment;
with Text_IO; use Text_IO;
separate (analyze_telegrams_file)
task body Transform_words_into_report is
  report           : File_Type;
  word             : WordType; -- unconstrained
  telegram_number  : Natural := 0;
  word_count       : Positive;
  premature_eof    : exception;
begin
  create(report, mode => out_file, name => "TELEGRAMS_REPORT");

  put_line(report, "    TELEGRAMS REPORT    ");

  loop                                 -- This is the telegram analysis loop.
    Buffer_word.give_me_a_word(word);  -- Get the 1st word of next telegram.
    if word = eof then                 -- If end of file then
      exit;                            -- exit the analysis loop.
    elsif word = ZZZZ then             -- If it's a null telegram then
      null;                            -- ignore the telegram.
    else                               -- else, its another telegram.
      increment(telegram_number);      -- Compute its number, and note that
      word_count := 1;                 -- we've read one word in it already.

      loop                             -- Count any more words in it.
        Buffer_word.give_me_a_word(word);
        if word = eof then             -- eof should not occur here.
          raise premature_eof;
        end if;
        exit when word = ZZZZ;
        increment(word_count);
      end loop;
                                       -- When through counting words, report.
      put_line(report, "Telegram number" & Integer'image(telegram_number) &
                       " contains" & Integer'image(word_count) & " words.");
    end if;
  end loop;

  put_line(report, "      END OF REPORT      "); close(report);
```

```
exception
  when name_error | use_error | device_error =>
  Buffer_word.halt;  -- Halt this task's predecessor(s).
  put_line("Transform words into report terminated due to output error.");

  when premature_eof =>
  put_line("Transform words into report terminated due to premature eof.");
  put_line(report, "END OF REPORT DUE TO INPUT ERROR.");
  close(report);

  when others =>
  put_line("Transform words into report terminated due to unknown exception.");
  if Buffer_word'callable then -- Ensure that Buffer_word is still callable.
    Buffer_word.halt;
  end if;
  put_line(report, "END OF REPORT DUE TO UNKNOWN EXCEPTION");
  close(report);  -- Attempt to close report.
end Transform_words_into_report;
```

Some care must be taken in writing the exception handlers:

Consider the first handler. If this handler tried to write on the report file before it called Buffer_word.halt, the put_line procedure would almost surely raise another exception and thus prevent the execution of the entry call statement, Buffer_word.halt. (If an exception is raised in the sequence of statements of an exception handler, then the execution of this sequence of statements is abandoned.) This would leave the first two tasks stranded.

Consider the second handler. It has no need to halt this task's predecessor since the problem originated at the input end of the pipeline. (Buffer_word's terminate alternative will terminate Buffer_word after the other tasks in the pipeline have terminated.)

Finally, consider the **others** handler. We aren't sure where this exception originated. So, it may be important to call Buffer_word.halt; it may also be important to invoke close. If we invoke close first, and it raises an exception, then we wouldn't have the opportunity to call Buffer_word.halt. If we call Buffer_word.halt first, and it causes an exception, then we wouldn't have the opportunity to invoke close. The only way Buffer_word.halt can cause an exception is for Buffer_word to be completed, terminated, or abnormal. The solution is to call Buffer_word.halt first--but only if Buffer_word is in none of these states. The attribute T'callable (where T must be a task) yields true if the task T is in none of these states; it yields false if it's in any of these states.

REFERENCES

Henderson, P., & Snowdon, R. An experiment in structured programming. *Bit*, 1972, *12*, 38-53.

Jackson, M. A. The design and use of conventional programming languages. In H. T. Smith & T. R. G. Green (Eds.), *Human interaction with computers*. New York: Academic Press, 1980.

EXERCISES

4.1. Write a two-processor parallel function that returns the average of all the components of an object of type FloatArray.

```
type FloatArray is array(Integer range <>) of Float;
```

Provide your function with an exception handler that computes the average without accumulating large sums of floats.

4.2. Rewrite analyze_telegrams_file so that the first task analyzes lines into symbols of the following enumeration type

```
type SymbolType is (word, zzzz, eof);
```

where normal words are analyzed into word, "ZZZZ" is analyzed into zzzz, and end_of_file = true is analyzed into eof. This analysis at the front-end of the pipeline reduces the amount of data that has to be propagated through the pipeline and therefore increases the throughput of the program. (Are there any disadvantages of this approach?) For the symbol buffer use a multi-slot buffer like the one on page 52.

ANSWERS TO EXERCISES

4.1.

```
function average(a : FloatArray) return Float is
  task Sum_1st_half is
    entry give_me_your_sum(s : out Float);
  end;

  task Sum_2nd_half is
    entry give_me_your_sum(s : out Float);
  end;

  task body Sum_1st_half is
    sum : Float := 0.0;
  begin
    for j in a'first..(a'first + a'last)/2 loop
      sum := sum + a(j);
    end loop;
    accept give_me_your_sum(s : out Float) do
      s := sum;
    end;
  end Sum_1st_half;

  task body Sum_2nd_half is
    sum : Float := 0.0;
  begin
    for j in 1 + (a'first + a'last)/2..a'last loop
      sum := sum + a(j);
    end loop;
    accept give_me_your_sum(s : out Float) do
      s := sum;
    end;
  end Sum_2nd_half;
begin
  declare
    sum_1, sum_2 : Float;
  begin
    Sum_1st_half.give_me_your_sum(sum_1);    -- may raise tasking_error
    Sum_2nd_half.give_me_your_sum(sum_2);    -- may raise tasking_error
    return sum_1/a'length + sum_2/a'length; -- divide sums before adding
  end;
```

```
exception
  when tasking_error =>
  declare
    x : Float   := 0.0; -- for running average
    n : Integer := 0;   -- for running number of components
  begin
    for j in a'range loop
      n := n + 1;
      x := x + (a(j) - x)/float(n);
    end loop;
    return x;
  end;
end average;
```

Note: If either task encounters a numeric error (due to overflow of its summing operation), it will terminate abnormally since the tasks have no exception handlers. When the master issues an entry call to such a terminated task, the master (due to the tasking_error exception) will transfer control to its exception handler and execute the block statement which computes the average by the method of "running-averages". This method avoids large sums by repeated division.

4.2.

```
procedure analyze_telegrams_file_2 is
  type SymbolType is (word, zzzz, eof);

  task Analyze_lines_into_symbols is
    -- calls Text_IO.open, Text_IO.get_line, and Text_IO.close
    -- calls Buffer_symbol.here_is_a_symbol
  end Analyze_lines_into_symbols;

  task Buffer_symbol is
    entry here_is_a_symbol(symbol : in  SymbolType);
    entry give_me_a_symbol(symbol : out SymbolType);
    entry halt;
  end Buffer_symbol;

  task Tranform_symbols_into_report is
    -- calls Buffer_symbol.give_me_a_symbol
    -- calls Text_IO.create, Text_IO.put_line, and Text_IO.close
    -- calls Buffer.halt when it encounters a fatal error
  end Tranform_symbols_into_report;

  task body Analyze_lines_into_symbols   is separate;
  task body Buffer_symbol                is separate;
  task body Tranform_symbols_into_report is separate;
begin
  --        All three tasks are activated in parallel at this point.
  null; -- nothing for master to do except create its subordinates
  --        The procedure waits here for all three tasks to terminate.
end analyze_telegrams_file_2;
```

```
with Text_IO; use Text_IO;
separate (analyze_telegrams_file_2)
task body Break_lines_into_symbols is
  type StateType is (not_in_word, in_word); -- for finite state machine
  state      : StateType := not_in_word;
  telegrams  : File_Type;            -- internal name of "Telegrams" file
  last       : Integer range 0..40; -- index of last character from get_line
  line       :  String(1..41);       -- buffer for letters of line, plus ' '
  i          : Integer range 1..40; -- index of first character in a new word
```

```
begin
  open(telegrams, mode => in_file, name => "Telegrams");

  while not end_of_file(telegrams) loop
    get_line(telegrams, line, last);
    line(last + 1) := ' ';     -- The line end is represented by a blank.
    for j in 1..last + 1 loop
      case state is            -- This is a finite state machine to find words.
        when not_in_word =>
        if line(j) /= ' ' then
          state := in_word;
          i := j;              -- i saves the index of beginning of new word.
        end if;

        when in_word =>
        if line(j) = ' ' then
          if j - i = 4 and then line(i..j - 1)) = "ZZZZ" then
            Buffer_word.here_is_a_symbol(zzzz);
          else
            Buffer_word.here_is_a_symbol(word);
          end if;
          state := not_in_word;
        end if;
      end case;
    end loop;
  end loop;

  Buffer_symbol.here_is_a_symbol(eof);
  close(telegrams);
exception
  when status_error | name_error | use_error | device_error | end_error =>
  put_line("Break lines into symbols terminated due to an input error.");
  Buffer_symbol.here_is_a_symbol(eof);
  close(telegrams);

  when tasking_error =>
  put_line("Break lines into symbols terminated due to tasking_error.");
  close(telegrams);

  when others =>
  put_line("Break lines into symbols terminated due to an unknown exception.");
  Buffer_symbol.here_is_a_symbol(eof);
  close(telegrams);
end Break_lines_into_symbols;
```

```
with Text_IO; use Text_IO;
separate (analyze_telegrams_file_2)
task body Buffer_symbol is
  buffer   : array(Ø..15) of SymbolType;
  count    : Integer range Ø..buffer'length := Ø;
  next_in  : Integer range Ø..buffer'last   := Ø;
  next_out : Integer range Ø..buffer'last   := Ø;
begin
  loop
    select
      when count < buffer'length =>
      accept here_is_a_symbol(symbol : in SymbolType) do
        buffer(next_in) := symbol;
      end;
      count := count + 1;
      next_in := (next_in + 1) mod buffer'length;
    or
      when count > Ø =>
      accept give_me_a_symbol(symbol : out SymbolType) do
        symbol := buffer(next_out);
      end;
      count := count - 1;
      next_out := (next_out + 1) mod buffer'length;
    or
      accept halt;
      put_line("Buffer symbols terminated due to halt entry call.");
      exit;
    or
      terminate;
    end select;
  end loop;
end Buffer_symbol;
```

```
with increment, Text_IO; use Text_IO;
separate (analyze_telegrams_file_2)
task body Transform_symbols_into_report is
  report          : File_Type;
  symbol          : SymbolType;
  telegram_number : Natural := 0;
  word_count      : Positive;
  premature_eof   : exception;
begin
  create(report, mode => out_file, name => "TELEGRAMS_REPORT");
  put_line(report, "     TELEGRAMS REPORT     ");

  loop                                     -- This is the analysis loop.
    Buffer_symbol.give_me_a_symbol(symbol); -- Get 1st symbol of a telegram.
    case symbol is                         -- (word, zzzz, eof)
      when word =>                    -- We have another telegram.
      increment(telegram_number);     -- Compute its number, and note that
      word_count := 1;                -- we've read one word in it already.
      loop                            -- Count any more words in it.
        Buffer_symbol.give_me_a_symbol(symbol);
        case symbol is
          when word =>
          increment(word_count);

          when zzzz =>                -- Exit when end of this telegram.
          exit;

          when eof =>                 -- eof should not occur here.
          raise premature_eof;
        end case;
      end loop;
      put_line(report, "Telegram number" & Integer'image(telegram_number) &
                       " contains" & Integer'image(word_count) & " words.");

      when zzzz =>                    -- It's a null telegram.
      null;                           -- Ignore this null telegram.

      when eof =>
      exit;                           -- Exit the analysis loop.
    end case;
  end loop;

  put_line(report, "      END OF REPORT      ");
  close(report);
```

```
exception
  when name_error | use_error | device_error =>
  put_line("Transform symbols into report terminated due to output error.");
  Buffer_symbol.halt;   -- Halt this task's predecessor(s).

  when premature_eof =>
  put_line("Transform symbols into report terminated due to premature eof.");
  put_line(report, "END OF REPORT DUE TO INPUT ERROR.");
  close(report);

  when others =>
  put_line("Transform symbols into report terminated due to unknown exception.")
  if Buffer_symbol'callable then -- Be sure Buffer_symbol is still callable.
    Buffer_symbol.halt;
  end if;
  put_line(report, "END OF REPORT DUE TO UNKNOWN EXCEPTION");
  close(report);   -- Attempt to close report.
end Transform_symbols_into_report;
```

The disadvantage of this approach is that the words in the telegrams are no longer modeled. Consequently, the reporter task does not have access to this aspect of the real world. This loss of information reduces the modifiability and flexibility of the program. For example, if the user requested that the report for each telegram also contain the average length of the words in the telegram or the number of words on a list of obscene words, the program would have to be largely rewritten. The first version of the program could be easily modified to accomodate such changes.

Appendix:

Excerpts from ANSI/MIL-STD-1815A

(Reference Manual for the Ada Programming Language)

9. Tasks

The execution of a program that does not contain a task is defined in terms of a sequential execution of its actions, according to the rules described in other chapters of this manual. These actions can be considered to be executed by a single *logical processor*. 1

Tasks are entities whose executions proceed *in parallel* in the following sense. Each task can be considered to be executed by a logical processor of its own. Different tasks (different logical processors) proceed independently, except at points where they synchronize. 2

Some tasks have *entries*. An entry of a task can be *called* by other tasks. A task *accepts* a call of one of its entries by executing an accept statement for the entry. Synchronization is achieved by *rendezvous* between a task issuing an entry call and a task accepting the call. Some entries have parameters; entry calls and accept statements for such entries are the principal means of communicating values between tasks. 3

The properties of each task are defined by a corresponding *task unit* which consists of a *task specification* and a *task body*. Task units are one of the four forms of program unit of which programs can be composed. The other forms are subprograms, packages and generic units. The properties of task units, tasks, and entries, and the statements that affect the interaction between tasks (that is, entry call statements, accept statements, delay statements, select statements, and abort statements) are described in this chapter. 4

Note:

Parallel tasks (parallel logical processors) may be implemented on multicomputers, multiprocessors, or with interleaved execution on a single *physical processor*. On the other hand, whenever an implementation can detect that the same effect can be guaranteed if parts of the actions of a given task are executed by different physical processors acting in parallel, it may choose to execute them in this way; in such a case, several physical processors implement a single logical processor. 5

References: abort statement 9.10, accept statement 9.5, delay statement 9.6, entry 9.5, entry call statement 9.5, generic unit 12, package 7, parameter in an entry call 9.5, program unit 6, rendezvous 9.5, select statement 9.7, subprogram 6, task body 9.1, task specification 9.1 6

9.1 Task Specifications and Task Bodies

A task unit consists of a task specification and a task body. A task specification that starts with the reserved words **task type** declares a task type. The value of an object of a task type designates a task having the entries, if any, that are declared in the task specification; these entries are also called entries of this object. The execution of the task is defined by the corresponding task body. 1

2 A task specification without the reserved word **type** defines a *single task*. A task declaration with this form of specification is equivalent to the declaration of an anonymous task type immediately followed by the declaration of an object of the task type, and the task unit identifier names the object. In the remainder of this chapter, explanations are given in terms of task type declarations; the corresponding explanations for single task declarations follow from the stated equivalence.

3

```
task_declaration ::= task_specification;

task_specification ::=
  task [type] identifier [is
    {entry_declaration}
    {representation_clause}
  end [task_simple_name]]

task_body ::=
    task body task_simple_name is
        [ declarative_part]
    begin
          sequence_of_statements
   [ exception
          exception_handler
        { exception_handler}]
    end [task_simple_name];
```

4 The simple name at the start of a task body must repeat the task unit identifier. Similarly if a simple name appears at the end of the task specification or body, it must repeat the task unit identifier. Within a task body, the name of the corresponding task unit can also be used to refer to the task object that designates the task currently executing the body; furthermore, the use of this name as a type mark is not allowed within the task unit itself.

5 For the elaboration of a task specification, entry declarations and representation clauses, if any, are elaborated in the order given. Such representation clauses only apply to the entries declared in the task specification (see 13.5).

6 The elaboration of a task body has no other effect than to establish that the body can from then on be used for the execution of tasks designated by objects of the corresponding task type.

7 The execution of a task body is invoked by the activation of a task object of the corresponding type (see 9.3). The optional exception handlers at the end of a task body handle exceptions raised during the execution of the sequence of statements of the task body (see 11.4).

8 *Examples of specifications of task types:*

```
task type RESOURCE is
  entry SEIZE;
  entry RELEASE;
end RESOURCE;

task type KEYBOARD_DRIVER is
  entry READ (C : out  CHARACTER);
  entry WRITE(C : in   CHARACTER);
end KEYBOARD_DRIVER;
```

Examples of specifications of single tasks: 9

```
task PRODUCER_CONSUMER is
   entry READ (V  : out ITEM);
   entry WRITE(E  : in  ITEM);
end;

task CONTROLLER is
   entry REQUEST(LEVEL)(D : ITEM);   --  a family of entries
end CONTROLLER;

task USER;  --  has no entries
```

Example of task specification and corresponding body: 10

```
task PROTECTED_ARRAY is
   --  INDEX and ITEM are global types
   entry READ (N : in INDEX; V : out ITEM);
   entry WRITE(N : in INDEX; E : in  ITEM);
end;

task body PROTECTED_ARRAY is
   TABLE : array(INDEX) of ITEM := (INDEX => NULL_ITEM);
begin
   loop
      select
         accept READ (N : in INDEX; V : out ITEM) do
            V := TABLE(N);
         end READ;
      or
         accept WRITE(N : in INDEX; E : in  ITEM) do
            TABLE(N) := E;
         end WRITE;
      end select;
   end loop;
end PROTECTED_ARRAY;
```

Note:

A task specification specifies the interface of tasks of the task type with other tasks of the same or of different types, and also with the main program. 11

References: declaration 3.1, declarative part 3.9, elaboration 3.9, entry 9.5, entry declaration 9.5, exception handler 11.2, identifier 2.3, main program 10.1, object 3.2, object declaration 3.2.1, representation clause 13.1, reserved word 2.9, sequence of statements 5.1, simple name 4.1, type 3.3, type declaration 3.3.1 12

9.2 Task Types and Task Objects

A task type is a limited type (see 7.4.4). Hence neither assignment nor the predefined comparison for equality and inequality are defined for objects of task types; moreover, the mode **out** is not allowed for a formal parameter whose type is a task type. 1

2 A task object is an object whose type is a task type. The value of a task object designates a task that has the entries of the corresponding task type, and whose execution is specified by the corresponding task body. If a task object is the object, or a subcomponent of the object, declared by an object declaration, then the value of the task object is defined by the elaboration of the object declaration. If a task object is the object, or a subcomponent of the object, created by the evaluation of an allocator, then the value of the task object is defined by the evaluation of the allocator. For all parameter modes, if an actual parameter designates a task, the associated formal parameter designates the same task; the same holds for a subcomponent of an actual parameter and the corresponding subcomponent of the associated formal parameter; finally, the same holds for generic parameters.

3 *Examples:*

```
CONTROL  : RESOURCE;
TELETYPE : KEYBOARD_DRIVER;
POOL     : array(1 .. 10) of KEYBOARD_DRIVER;
-- see also examples of declarations of single tasks in 9.1
```

4 *Example of access type designating task objects:*

```
type KEYBOARD is access KEYBOARD_DRIVER;

TERMINAL : KEYBOARD := new KEYBOARD_DRIVER;
```

Notes:

5 Since a task type is a limited type, it can appear as the definition of a limited private type in a private part, and as a generic actual parameter associated with a formal parameter whose type is a limited type. On the other hand, the type of a generic formal parameter of mode **in** must not be a limited type and hence cannot be a task type.

6 Task objects behave as constants (a task object always designates the same task) since their values are implicitly defined either at declaration or allocation, or by a parameter association, and since no assignment is available. However the reserved word **constant** is not allowed in the declaration of a task object since this would require an explicit initialization. A task object that is a formal parameter of mode **in** is a constant (as is any formal parameter of this mode).

7 If an application needs to store and exchange task identities, it can do so by defining an access type designating the corresponding task objects and by using access values for identification purposes (see above example). Assignment is available for such an access type as for any access type.

8 Subtype declarations are allowed for task types as for other types, but there are no constraints applicable to task types.

9 *References:* access type 3.8, actual parameter 6.4.1, allocator 4.8, assignment 5.2, component declaration 3.7, composite type 3.3, constant 3.2.1, constant declaration 3.2.1, constraint 3.3, designate 3.8 9.1, elaboration 3.9, entry 9.5, equality operator 4.5.2, formal parameter 6.2, formal parameter mode 6.2, generic actual parameter 12.3, generic association 12.3, generic formal parameter 12.1, generic formal parameter mode 12.1.1, generic unit 12, inequality operator 4.5.2, initialization 3.2.1, limited type 7.4.4, object 3.2, object declaration 3.2.1, parameter association 6.4, private part 7.2, private type 7.4, reserved word 2.9, subcomponent 3.3, subprogram 6, subtype declaration 3.3.2, task body 9.1, type 3.3

9.3 Task Execution - Task Activation

A task body defines the execution of any task that is designated by a task object of the corresponding task type. The initial part of this execution is called the *activation* of the task object, and also that of the designated task; it consists of the elaboration of the declarative part, if any, of the task body. The execution of different tasks, in particular their activation, proceeds in parallel. 1

If an object declaration that declares a task object occurs immediately within a declarative part, then the activation of the task object starts after the elaboration of the declarative part (that is, after passing the reserved word **begin** following the declarative part); similarly if such a declaration occurs immediately within a package specification, the activation starts after the elaboration of the declarative part of the package body. The same holds for the activation of a task object that is a subcomponent of an object declared immediately within a declarative part or package specification. The first statement following the declarative part is executed only after conclusion of the activation of these task objects. 2

Should an exception be raised by the activation of one of these tasks, that task becomes a completed task (see 9.4); other tasks are not directly affected. Should one of these tasks thus become completed during its activation, the exception TASKING_ERROR is raised upon conclusion of the activation of all of these tasks (whether successfully or not); the exception is raised at a place that is immediately before the first statement following the declarative part (immediately after the reserved word **begin**). Should several of these tasks thus become completed during their activation, the exception TASKING_ERROR is raised only once. 3

Should an exception be raised by the elaboration of a declarative part or package specification, then any task that is created (directly or indirectly) by this elaboration and that is not yet activated becomes terminated and is therefore never activated (see section 9.4 for the definition of a terminated task). 4

For the above rules, in any package body without statements, a null statement is assumed. For any package without a package body, an implicit package body containing a single null statement is assumed. If a package without a package body is declared immediately within some program unit or block statement, the implicit package body occurs at the end of the declarative part of the program unit or block statement; if there are several such packages, the order of the implicit package bodies is undefined. 5

A task object that is the object, or a subcomponent of the object, created by the evaluation of an allocator is activated by this evaluation. The activation starts after any initialization for the object created by the allocator; if several subcomponents are task objects, they are activated in parallel. The access value designating such an object is returned by the allocator only after the conclusion of these activations. 6

Should an exception be raised by the activation of one of these tasks, that task becomes a completed task; other tasks are not directly affected. Should one of these tasks thus become completed during its activation, the exception TASKING_ERROR is raised upon conclusion of the activation of all of these tasks (whether successfully or not); the exception is raised at the place where the allocator is evaluated. Should several of these tasks thus become completed during their activation, the exception TASKING_ERROR is raised only once. 7

Should an exception be raised by the initialization of the object created by an allocator (hence before the start of any activation), any task designated by a subcomponent of this object becomes terminated and is therefore never activated. 8

9 *Example:*

```
procedure P is
   A, B : RESOURCE;   --  elaborate the task objects A, B
   C    : RESOURCE;   --  elaborate the task object C
begin
   --  the tasks A, B, C are activated in parallel before the first statement
   ...
end;
```

Notes:

10 An entry of a task can be called before the task has been activated. If several tasks are activated in parallel, the execution of any of these tasks need not await the end of the activation of the other tasks. A task may become completed during its activation either because of an exception or because it is aborted (see 9.10).

11 *References:* allocator 4.8, completed task 9.4, declarative part 3.9, elaboration 3.9, entry 9.5, exception 11, handling an exception 11.4, package body 7.1, parallel execution 9, statement 5, subcomponent 3.3, task body 9.1, task object 9.2, task termination 9.4, task type 9.1, tasking_error exception 11.1

9.4 Task Dependence - Termination of Tasks

1 Each task *depends* on at least one master. A *master* is a construct that is either a task, a currently executing block statement or subprogram, or a library package (a package declared within another program unit is not a master). The dependence on a master is a direct dependence in the following two cases:

2 (a) The task designated by a task object that is the object, or a subcomponent of the object, created by the evaluation of an allocator depends on the master that elaborates the corresponding access type definition.

3 (b) The task designated by any other task object depends on the master whose execution creates the task object.

4 Furthermore, if a task depends on a given master that is a block statement executed by another master, then the task depends also on this other master, in an indirect manner; the same holds if the given master is a subprogram called by another master, and if the given master is a task that depends (directly or indirectly) on another master. Dependences exist for objects of a private type whose full declaration is in terms of a task type.

5 A task is said to have *completed* its execution when it has finished the execution of the sequence of statements that appears after the reserved word **begin** in the corresponding body. Similarly a block or a subprogram is said to have completed its execution when it has finished the execution of the corresponding sequence of statements. For a block statement, the execution is also said to be completed when it reaches an exit, return, or goto statement transferring control out of the block. For a procedure, the execution is also said to be completed when a corresponding return statement is reached. For a function, the execution is also said to be completed after the evaluation of the result expression of a return statement. Finally the execution of a task, block statement, or subprogram is completed if an exception is raised by the execution of its sequence of statements and there is no corresponding handler, or, if there is one, when it has finished the execution of the corresponding handler.

If a task has no dependent task, its *termination* takes place when it has completed its execution. After its termination, a task is said to be *terminated*. If a task has dependent tasks, its termination takes place when the execution of the task is completed and all dependent tasks are terminated. A block statement or subprogram body whose execution is completed is not left until all of its dependent tasks are terminated. 6

Termination of a task otherwise takes place if and only if its execution has reached an open terminate alternative in a select statement (see 9.7.1), and the following conditions are satisfied: 7

- The task depends on some master whose execution is completed (hence not a library package). 8
- Each task that depends on the master considered is either already terminated or similarly waiting on an open terminate alternative of a select statement. 9

When both conditions are satisfied, the task considered becomes terminated, together with all tasks that depend on the master considered. 10

Example: 11

```
declare
   type GLOBAL is access RESOURCE;              --  see 9.1
   A, B  : RESOURCE;
   G     : GLOBAL;
begin
   --  activation of A and B
   declare
      type LOCAL is access RESOURCE;
      X  : GLOBAL  := new RESOURCE;  --  activation of X.all
      L  : LOCAL   := new RESOURCE;  --  activation of L.all
      C  : RESOURCE;
   begin
      --  activation of C
      G := X;  --  both G and X designate the same task object
      ...
   end;  --  await termination of C and L.all (but not X.all)
   ...
end;  --  await termination of A, B, and G.all
```

Notes:

The rules given for termination imply that all tasks that depend (directly or indirectly) on a given master and that are not already terminated, can be terminated (collectively) if and only if each of them is waiting on an open terminate alternative of a select statement and the execution of the given master is completed. 12

The usual rules apply to the main program. Consequently, termination of the main program awaits termination of any dependent task even if the corresponding task type is declared in a library package. On the other hand, termination of the main program does not await termination of tasks that depend on library packages; the language does not define whether such tasks are required to terminate. 13

For an access type derived from another access type, the corresponding access type definition is that of the parent type; the dependence is on the master that elaborates the ultimate parent access type definition. 14

15 A renaming declaration defines a new name for an existing entity and hence creates no further dependence.

16 *References:* access type 3.8, allocator 4.8, block statement 5.6, declaration 3.1, designate 3.8 9.1, exception 11, exception handler 11.2, exit statement 5.7, function 6.5, goto statement 5.9, library unit 10.1, main program 10.1, object 3.2, open alternative 9.7.1, package 7, program unit 6, renaming declaration 8.5, return statement 5.8, selective wait 9.7.1, sequence of statements 5.1, statement 5, subcomponent 3.3, subprogram body 6.3, subprogram call 6.4, task body 9.1, task object 9.2, terminate alternative 9.7.1

9.5 Entries, Entry Calls, and Accept Statements

1 Entry calls and accept statements are the primary means of synchronization of tasks, and of communicating values between tasks. An entry declaration is similar to a subprogram declaration and is only allowed in a task specification. The actions to be performed when an entry is called are specified by corresponding accept statements.

2

```
entry_declaration ::=
   entry identifier [(discrete_range)] [formal_part];

entry_call_statement ::= entry_name [actual_parameter_part];

accept_statement ::=
   accept entry_simple_name [(entry_index)] [formal_part] [do
      sequence_of_statements
   end [entry_simple_name]];

entry_index ::= expression
```

3 An entry declaration that includes a discrete range (see 3.6.1) declares a *family* of distinct entries having the same formal part (if any); that is, one such entry for each value of the discrete range. The term *single entry* is used in the definition of any rule that applies to any entry other than one of a family. The task designated by an object of a task type has (or owns) the entries declared in the specification of the task type.

4 Within the body of a task, each of its single entries or entry families can be named by the corresponding simple name. The name of an entry of a family takes the form of an indexed component, the family simple name being followed by the index in parentheses; the type of this index must be the same as that of the discrete range in the corresponding entry family declaration. Outside the body of a task an entry name has the form of a selected component, whose prefix denotes the task object, and whose selector is the simple name of one of its single entries or entry families.

5 A single entry overloads a subprogram, an enumeration literal, or another single entry if they have the same identifier. Overloading is not defined for entry families. A single entry or an entry of an entry family can be renamed as a procedure as explained in section 8.5.

6 The parameter modes defined for parameters of the formal part of an entry declaration are the same as for a subprogram declaration and have the same meaning (see 6.2). The syntax of an entry call statement is similar to that of a procedure call statement, and the rules for parameter associations are the same as for subprogram calls (see 6.4.1 and 6.4.2).

An accept statement specifies the actions to be performed at a call of a named entry (it can be an entry of a family). The formal part of an accept statement must conform to the formal part given in the declaration of the single entry or entry family named by the accept statement (see section 6.3.1 for the conformance rules). If a simple name appears at the end of an accept statement, it must repeat that given at the start. 7

An accept statement for an entry of a given task is only allowed within the corresponding task body; excluding within the body of any program unit that is, itself, inner to the task body; and excluding within another accept statement for either the same single entry or an entry of the same family. (One consequence of this rule is that a task can execute accept statements only for its own entries.) A task body can contain more than one accept statement for the same entry. 8

For the elaboration of an entry declaration, the discrete range, if any, is evaluated and the formal part, if any, is then elaborated as for a subprogram declaration. 9

Execution of an accept statement starts with the evaluation of the entry index (in the case of an entry of a family). Execution of an entry call statement starts with the evaluation of the entry name; this is followed by any evaluations required for actual parameters in the same manner as for a subprogram call (see 6.4). Further execution of an accept statement and of a corresponding entry call statement are synchronized. 10

If a given entry is called by only one task, there are two possibilities: 11

- If the calling task issues an entry call statement before a corresponding accept statement is reached by the task owning the entry, the execution of the calling task is *suspended*. 12

- If a task reaches an accept statement prior to any call of that entry, the execution of the task is suspended until such a call is received. 13

When an entry has been called and a corresponding accept statement has been reached, the sequence of statements, if any, of the accept statement is executed by the called task (while the calling task remains suspended). This interaction is called a *rendezvous*. Thereafter, the calling task and the task owning the entry continue their execution in parallel. 14

If several tasks call the same entry before a corresponding accept statement is reached, the calls are queued; there is one queue associated with each entry. Each execution of an accept statement removes one call from the queue. The calls are processed in the order of arrival. 15

An attempt to call an entry of a task that has completed its execution raises the exception TASKING_ERROR at the point of the call, in the calling task; similarly, this exception is raised at the point of the call if the called task completes its execution before accepting the call (see also 9.10 for the case when the called task becomes abnormal). The exception CONSTRAINT_ERROR is raised if the index of an entry of a family is not within the specified discrete range. 16

Examples of entry declarations: 17

```
entry READ(V : out ITEM);
entry SEIZE;
entry REQUEST(LEVEL)(D : ITEM);   --  a family of entries
```

Examples of entry calls: 18

```
CONTROL.RELEASE;                          --  see 9.2 and 9.1
PRODUCER_CONSUMER.WRITE(E);               --  see 9.1
POOL(5).READ(NEXT_CHAR);                  --  see 9.2 and 9.1
CONTROLLER.REQUEST(LOW)(SOME_ITEM);       --  see 9.1
```

19 *Examples of accept statements:*

```
accept SEIZE;

accept READ(V : out ITEM) do
  V := LOCAL_ITEM;
end READ;

accept REQUEST(LOW)(D : ITEM) do
  ...
end REQUEST;
```

Notes:

20 The formal part given in an accept statement is not elaborated; it is only used to identify the corresponding entry.

21 An accept statement can call subprograms that issue entry calls. An accept statement need not have a sequence of statements even if the corresponding entry has parameters. Equally, it can have a sequence of statements even if the corresponding entry has no parameters. The sequence of statements of an accept statement can include return statements. A task can call its own entries but it will, of course, deadlock. The language permits conditional and timed entry calls (see 9.7.2 and 9.7.3). The language rules ensure that a task can only be in one entry queue at a given time.

22 If the bounds of the discrete range of an entry family are integer literals, the index (in an entry name or accept statement) must be of the predefined type INTEGER (see 3.6.1).

23 *References:* abnormal task 9.10, actual parameter part 6.4, completed task 9.4, conditional entry call 9.7.2, conformance rules 6.3.1, constraint_error exception 11.1, designate 9.1, discrete range 3.6.1, elaboration 3.1 3.9, enumeration literal 3.5.1, evaluation 4.5, expression 4.4, formal part 6.1, identifier 2.3, indexed component 4.1.1, integer type 3.5.4, name 4.1, object 3.2, overloading 6.6 8.7, parallel execution 9, prefix 4.1, procedure 6, procedure call 6.4, renaming declaration 8.5, return statement 5.8, scope 8.2, selected component 4.1.3, selector 4.1.3, sequence of statements 5.1, simple expression 4.4, simple name 4.1, subprogram 6, subprogram body 6.3, subprogram declaration 6.1, task 9, task body 9.1, task specification 9.1, tasking_error exception 11.1, timed entry call 9.7.3

9.6 Delay Statements, Duration, and Time

1 The execution of a delay statement evaluates the simple expression, and suspends further execution of the task that executes the delay statement, for at least the duration specified by the resulting value.

2
```
delay_statement ::= delay simple_expression;
```

3 The simple expression must be of the predefined fixed point type DURATION; its value is expressed in seconds; a delay statement with a negative value is equivalent to a delay statement with a zero value.

4 Any implementation of the type DURATION must allow representation of durations (both positive and negative) up to at least 86400 seconds (one day); the smallest representable duration, DURATION'SMALL must not be greater than twenty milliseconds (whenever possible, a value not greater than fifty microseconds should be chosen). Note that DURATION'SMALL need not correspond to the basic clock cycle, the named number SYSTEM.TICK (see 13.7).

The definition of the type TIME is provided in the predefined library package CALENDAR. The function CLOCK returns the current value of TIME at the time it is called. The functions YEAR, MONTH, DAY and SECONDS return the corresponding values for a given value of the type TIME; the procedure SPLIT returns all four corresponding values. Conversely, the function TIME_OF combines a year number, a month number, a day number, and a duration, into a value of type TIME. The operators "+" and "-" for addition and subtraction of times and durations, and the relational operators for times, have the conventional meaning. 5

The exception TIME_ERROR is raised by the function TIME_OF if the actual parameters do not form a proper date. This exception is also raised by the operators "+" and "-" if, for the given operands, these operators cannot return a date whose year number is in the range of the corresponding subtype, or if the operator "-" cannot return a result that is in the range of the type DURATION. 6

7

```
package CALENDAR is
   type TIME is private;

   subtype YEAR_NUMBER    is INTEGER   range 1901 .. 2099;
   subtype MONTH_NUMBER   is INTEGER   range 1 .. 12;
   subtype DAY_NUMBER     is INTEGER   range 1 .. 31;
   subtype DAY_DURATION   is DURATION  range 0.0 .. 86_400.0;

   function CLOCK return TIME;

   function YEAR    (DATE : TIME) return YEAR_NUMBER;
   function MONTH   (DATE : TIME) return MONTH_NUMBER;
   function DAY     (DATE : TIME) return DAY_NUMBER;
   function SECONDS (DATE : TIME) return DAY_DURATION;

   procedure SPLIT  ( DATE    : in  TIME;
                      YEAR    : out YEAR_NUMBER;
                      MONTH   : out MONTH_NUMBER;
                      DAY     : out DAY_NUMBER;
                      SECONDS : out DAY_DURATION);

   function TIME_OF( YEAR    : YEAR_NUMBER;
                     MONTH   : MONTH_NUMBER;
                     DAY     : DAY_NUMBER;
                     SECONDS : DAY_DURATION := 0.0) return TIME;


   function "+"  (LEFT : TIME;      RIGHT : DURATION)  return TIME;
   function "+"  (LEFT : DURATION;  RIGHT : TIME)      return TIME;
   function "-"  (LEFT : TIME;      RIGHT : DURATION)  return TIME;
   function "-"  (LEFT : TIME;      RIGHT : TIME)      return DURATION;

   function "<"  (LEFT, RIGHT : TIME) return BOOLEAN;
   function "<=" (LEFT, RIGHT : TIME) return BOOLEAN;
   function ">"  (LEFT, RIGHT : TIME) return BOOLEAN;
   function ">=" (LEFT, RIGHT : TIME) return BOOLEAN;

   TIME_ERROR : exception;  --  can be raised by TIME_OF, "+", and "-"

private
   -- implementation-dependent
end;
```

8 *Examples:*

```
delay 3.0;  --  delay 3.0 seconds

declare
  use CALENDAR;
  -- INTERVAL is a global constant of type DURATION
  NEXT_TIME : TIME := CLOCK + INTERVAL;
begin
  loop
    delay NEXT_TIME - CLOCK;
    -- some actions
    NEXT_TIME := NEXT_TIME + INTERVAL;
  end loop;
end;
```

Notes:

9 The second example causes the loop to be repeated every INTERVAL seconds on average. This interval between two successive iterations is only approximate. However, there will be no cumulative drift as long as the duration of each iteration is (sufficiently) less than INTERVAL.

10 *References:* adding operator 4.5, duration C, fixed point type 3.5.9, function call 6.4, library unit 10.1, operator 4.5, package 7, private type 7.4, relational operator 4.5, simple expression 4.4, statement 5, task 9, type 3.3

9.7 Select Statements

1 There are three forms of select statements. One form provides a selective wait for one or more alternatives. The other two provide conditional and timed entry calls.

2
```
select_statement ::= selective_wait
  | conditional_entry_call | timed_entry_call
```

3 *References:* selective wait 9.7.1, conditional entry call 9.7.2, timed entry call 9.7.3

9.7.1 Selective Waits

1 This form of the select statement allows a combination of waiting for, and selecting from, one or more alternatives. The selection can depend on conditions associated with each alternative of the selective wait.

```
selective_wait ::=
    select
      select_alternative
   { or
      select_alternative}
   [ else
      sequence_of_statements]
    end select;

select_alternative ::=
   [ when condition =>]
      selective_wait_alternative

selective_wait_alternative ::= accept_alternative
   | delay_alternative | terminate_alternative

accept_alternative   ::= accept_statement [sequence_of_statements]

delay_alternative    ::= delay_statement  [sequence_of_statements]

terminate_alternative ::= terminate;
```

2

A selective wait must contain at least one accept alternative. In addition a selective wait can contain either a terminate alternative (only one), or one or more delay alternatives, or an else part; these three possibilities are mutually exclusive.

3

A select alternative is said to be *open* if it does not start with **when** and a condition, or if the condition is TRUE. It is said to be *closed* otherwise.

4

For the execution of a selective wait, any conditions specified after **when** are evaluated in some order that is not defined by the language; open alternatives are thus determined. For an open delay alternative, the delay expression is also evaluated. Similarly, for an open accept alternative for an entry of a family, the entry index is also evaluated. Selection and execution of one open alternative, or of the else part, then completes the execution of the selective wait; the rules for this selection are described below.

5

Open accept alternatives are first considered. Selection of one such alternative takes place immediately if a corresponding rendezvous is possible, that is, if there is a corresponding entry call issued by another task and waiting to be accepted. If several alternatives can thus be selected, one of them is selected arbitrarily (that is, the language does not define which one). When such an alternative is selected, the corresponding accept statement and possible subsequent statements are executed. If no rendezvous is immediately possible and there is no else part, the task waits until an open selective wait alternative can be selected.

6

Selection of the other forms of alternative or of an else part is performed as follows:

7

- An open delay alternative will be selected if no accept alternative can be selected before the specified delay has elapsed (immediately, for a negative or zero delay in the absence of queued entry calls); any subsequent statements of the alternative are then executed. If several delay alternatives can thus be selected (that is, if they have the same delay), one of them is selected arbitrarily.

8

- The else part is selected and its statements are executed if no accept alternative can be immediately selected, in particular, if all alternatives are closed.

9

- An open terminate alternative is selected if the conditions stated in section 9.4 are satisfied. It is a consequence of other rules that a terminate alternative cannot be selected while there is a queued entry call for any entry of the task.

10

11 The exception PROGRAM_ERROR is raised if all alternatives are closed and there is no else part.

12 *Examples of a select statement:*

```
select
   accept DRIVER_AWAKE_SIGNAL;
or
   delay 30.0*SECONDS;
   STOP_THE_TRAIN;
end select;
```

13 *Example of a task body with a select statement:*

```
task body RESOURCE is
   BUSY : BOOLEAN := FALSE;
begin
   loop
      select
         when not BUSY =>
            accept SEIZE do
               BUSY := TRUE;
            end;
      or
         accept RELEASE do
            BUSY := FALSE;
         end;
      or
         terminate;
      end select;
   end loop;
end RESOURCE;
```

Notes:

14 A selective wait is allowed to have several open delay alternatives. A selective wait is allowed to have several open accept alternatives for the same entry.

15 *References:* accept statement 9.5, condition 5.3, declaration 3.1, delay expression 9.6, delay statement 9.6, duration 9.6, entry 9.5, entry call 9.5, entry index 9.5, program_error exception 11.1, queued entry call 9.5, rendezvous 9.5, select statement 9.7, sequence of statements 5.1, task 9

9.7.2 Conditional Entry Calls

1 A conditional entry call issues an entry call that is then canceled if a rendezvous is not immediately possible.

2

```
conditional_entry_call ::=
   select
       entry_call_statement
      [ sequence_of_statements]
   else
       sequence_of_statements
   end select;
```

For the execution of a conditional entry call, the entry name is first evaluated. This is followed by any evaluations required for actual parameters as in the case of a subprogram call (see 6.4). 3

The entry call is canceled if the execution of the called task has not reached a point where it is ready to accept the call (that is, either an accept statement for the corresponding entry, or a select statement with an open accept alternative for the entry), o if there are prior queued entry calls for this entry. If the called task has reached a select statement, the entry call is canceled if an accept alternative for this entry is not selected. 4

If the entry call is canceled, the statements of the else part are executed. Otherwise, the rendezvous takes place; and the optional sequence of statements after the entry call is then executed. 5

The execution of a conditional entry call raises the exception TASKING_ERROR if the called task has already completed its execution (see also 9.10 for the case when the called task becomes abnormal). 6

Example: 7

```
procedure SPIN(R : RESOURCE) is
begin
   loop
      select
         R.SEIZE;
         return;
      else
         null;  --  busy waiting
      end select;
   end loop;
end;
```

References: abnormal task 9.10, accept statement 9.5, actual parameter part 6.4, completed task 9.4, entry call statement 9.5, entry family 9.5, entry index 9.5, evaluation 4.5, expression 4.4, open alternative 9.7.1, queued entry call 9.5, rendezvous 9.5, select statement 9.7, sequence of statements 5.1, task 9, tasking_error exception 11.1 8

9.7.3 Timed Entry Calls

A timed entry call issues an entry call that is canceled if a rendezvous is not started within a given delay. 1

```
timed_entry_call ::=
   select
       entry_call_statement
     [ sequence_of_statements]
   or
       delay_alternative
   end select;
```

2

3 For the execution of a timed entry call, the entry name is first evaluated. This is followed by any evaluations required for actual parameters as in the case of a subprogram call (see 6.4). The expression stating the delay is then evaluated, and the entry call is finally issued.

4 If a rendezvous can be started within the specified duration (or immediately, as for a conditional entry call, for a negative or zero delay), it is performed and the optional sequence of statements after the entry call is then executed. Otherwise, the entry call is canceled when the specified duration has expired, and the optional sequence of statements of the delay alternative is executed.

5 The execution of a timed entry call raises the exception TASKING_ERROR if the called task completes its execution before accepting the call (see also 9.10 for the case when the called task becomes abnormal).

6 *Example:*

```
select
   CONTROLLER.REQUEST(MEDIUM)(SOME_ITEM);
or
   delay 45.0;
   --  controller too busy, try something else
end select;
```

7 *References:* abnormal task 9.10, accept statement 9.5, actual parameter part 6.4, completed task 9.4, conditional entry call 9.7.2, delay expression 9.6, delay statement 9.6, duration 9.6, entry call statement 9.5, entry family 9.5, entry index 9.5, evaluation 4.5, expression 4.4, rendezvous 9.5, sequence of statements 5.1, task 9, tasking_error exception 11.1

9.8 Priorities

1 Each task may (but need not) have a priority, which is a value of the subtype PRIORITY (of the type INTEGER) declared in the predefined library package SYSTEM (see 13.7). A lower value indicates a lower degree of urgency; the range of priorities is implementation-defined. A priority is associated with a task if a pragma

```
pragma PRIORITY (static_expression);
```

2 appears in the corresponding task specification; the priority is given by the value of the expression. A priority is associated with the main program if such a pragma appears in its outermost declarative part. At most one such pragma can appear within a given task specification or for a subprogram that is a library unit, and these are the only allowed places for this pragma. A pragma PRIORITY has no effect if it occurs in a subprogram other than the main program.

3 The specification of a priority is an indication given to assist the implementation in the allocation of processing resources to parallel tasks when there are more tasks eligible for execution than can be supported simultaneously by the available processing resources. The effect of priorities on scheduling is defined by the following rule:

4 If two tasks with different priorities are both eligible for execution and could sensibly be executed using the same physical processors and the same other processing resources, then it cannot be the case that the task with the lower priority is executing while the task with the higher priority is not.

For tasks of the same priority, the scheduling order is not defined by the language. For tasks without explicit priority, the scheduling rules are not defined, except when such tasks are engaged in a rendezvous. If the priorities of both tasks engaged in a rendezvous are defined, the rendezvous is executed with the higher of the two priorities. If only one of the two priorities is defined, the rendezvous is executed with at least that priority. If neither is defined, the priority of the rendezvous is undefined. 5

Notes:

The priority of a task is static and therefore fixed. However, the priority during a rendezvous is not necessarily static since it also depends on the priority of the task calling the entry. Priorities should be used only to indicate relative degrees of urgency; they should not be used for task synchronization. 6

References: declarative part 3.9, entry call statement 9.5, integer type 3.5.4, main program 10.1, package system 13.7, pragma 2.8, rendezvous 9.5, static expression 4.9, subtype 3.3, task 9, task specification 9.1 7

9.9 Task and Entry Attributes

For a task object or value T the following attributes are defined: 1

T'CALLABLE — Yields the value FALSE when the execution of the task designated by T is either completed or terminated, or when the task is abnormal. Yields the value TRUE otherwise. The value of this attribute is of the predefined type BOOLEAN. 2

T'TERMINATED — Yields the value TRUE if the task designated by T is terminated. Yields the value FALSE otherwise. The value of this attribute is of the predefined type BOOLEAN. 3

In addition, the representation attributes STORAGE_SIZE, SIZE, and ADDRESS are defined for a task object T or a task type T (see 13.7.2). 4

The attribute COUNT is defined for an entry E of a task unit T. The entry can be either a single entry or an entry of a family (in either case the name of the single entry or entry family can be either a simple or an expanded name). This attribute is only allowed within the body of T, but excluding within any program unit that is, itself, inner to the body of T. 5

E'COUNT — Yields the number of entry calls presently queued on the entry E (if the attribute is evaluated by the execution of an accept statement for the entry E, the count does not include the calling task). The value of this attribute is of the type *universal_integer*. 6

Note:

Algorithms interrogating the attribute E'COUNT should take precautions to allow for the increase of the value of this attribute for incoming entry calls, and its decrease, for example with timed entry calls. 7

References: abnormal task 9.10, accept statement 9.5, attribute 4.1.4, boolean type 3.5.3, completed task 9.4, designate 9.1, entry 9.5, false boolean value 3.5.3, queue of entry calls 9.5, storage unit 13.7, task 9, task object 9.2, task type 9.1, terminated task 9.4, timed entry call 9.7.3, true boolean value 3.5.3, universal_integer type 3.5.4 8

9.10 Abort Statements

1 An abort statement causes one or more tasks to become *abnormal*, thus preventing any further rendezvous with such tasks.

2
```
abort_statement ::= abort task_name {, task_name};
```

3 The determination of the type of each task name uses the fact that the type of the name is a task type.

4 For the execution of an abort statement, the given task names are evaluated in some order that is not defined by the language. Each named task then becomes abnormal unless it is already terminated; similarly, any task that depends on a named task becomes abnormal unless it is already terminated.

5 Any abnormal task whose execution is suspended at an accept statement, a select statement, or a delay statement becomes completed; any abnormal task whose execution is suspended at an entry call, and that is not yet in a corresponding rendezvous, becomes completed and is removed from the entry queue; any abnormal task that has not yet started its activation becomes completed (and hence also terminated). This completes the execution of the abort statement.

6 The completion of any other abnormal task need not happen before completion of the abort statement. It must happen no later than when the abnormal task reaches a synchronization point that is one of the following: the end of its activation; a point where it causes the activation of another task; an entry call; the start or the end of an accept statement; a select statement; a delay statement; an exception handler; or an abort statement. If a task that calls an entry becomes abnormal while in a rendezvous, its termination does not take place before the completion of the rendezvous (see 11.5).

7 The call of an entry of an abnormal task raises the exception TASKING_ERROR at the place of the call. Similarly, the exception TASKING_ERROR is raised for any task that has called an entry of an abnormal task, if the entry call is still queued or if the rendezvous is not yet finished (whether the entry call is an entry call statement, or a conditional or timed entry call); the exception is raised no later than the completion of the abnormal task. The value of the attribute CALLABLE is FALSE for any task that is abnormal (or completed).

8 If the abnormal completion of a task takes place while the task updates a variable, then the value of this variable is undefined.

9 *Example:*

```
abort USER, TERMINAL.all, POOL(3);
```

Notes:

10 An abort statement should be used only in extremely severe situations requiring unconditional termination. A task is allowed to abort any task, including itself.

11 *References:* abnormal in rendezvous 11.5, accept statement 9.5, activation 9.3, attribute 4.1.4, callable (predefined attribute) 9.9, conditional entry call 9.7.2, delay statement 9.6, dependent task 9.4, entry call statement 9.5, evaluation of a name 4.1, exception handler 11.2, false boolean value 3.5.3, name 4.1, queue of entry calls 9.5, rendezvous 9.5, select statement 9.7, statement 5, task 9, tasking_error exception 11.1, terminated task 9.4, timed entry call 9.7.3

9.11 Shared Variables

The normal means of communicating values between tasks is by entry calls and accept statements. 1

If two tasks read or update a *shared* variable (that is, a variable accessible by both), then neither of them may assume anything about the order in which the other performs its operations, except at the points where they synchronize. Two tasks are synchronized at the start and at the end of their rendezvous. At the start and at the end of its activation, a task is synchronized with the task that causes this activation. A task that has completed its execution is synchronized with any other task. 2

For the actions performed by a program that uses shared variables, the following assumptions can always be made: 3

- If between two synchronization points of a task, this task reads a shared variable whose type is a scalar or access type, then the variable is not updated by any other task at any time between these two points. 4

- If between two synchronization points of a task, this task updates a shared variable whose type is a scalar or access type, then the variable is neither read nor updated by any other task at any time between these two points. 5

The execution of the program is erroneous if any of these assumptions is violated. 6

If a given task reads the value of a shared variable, the above assumptions allow an implementation to maintain local copies of the value (for example, in registers or in some other form of temporary storage); and for as long as the given task neither reaches a synchronization point nor updates the value of the shared variable, the above assumptions imply that, for the given task, reading a local copy is equivalent to reading the shared variable itself. 7

Similarly, if a given task updates the value of a shared variable, the above assumptions allow an implementation to maintain a local copy of the value, and to defer the effective store of the local copy into the shared variable until a synchronization point, provided that every further read or update of the variable by the given task is treated as a read or update of the local copy. On the other hand, an implementation is not allowed to introduce a store, unless this store would also be executed in the canonical order (see 11.6). 8

The pragma SHARED can be used to specify that every read or update of a variable is a synchronization point for that variable; that is, the above assumptions always hold for the given variable (but not necessarily for other variables). The form of this pragma is as follows: 9

pragma SHARED(*variable*_simple_name);

This pragma is allowed only for a variable declared by an object declaration and whose type is a scalar or access type; the variable declaration and the pragma must both occur (in this order) immediately within the same declarative part or package specification; the pragma must appear before any occurrence of the name of the variable, other than in an address clause. 10

An implementation must restrict the objects for which the pragma SHARED is allowed to objects for which each of direct reading and direct updating is implemented as an indivisible operation. 11

References: accept statement 9.5, activation 9.3, assignment 5.2, canonical order 11.6, declarative part 3.9, entry call statement 9.5, erroneous 1.6, global 8.1, package specification 7.1, pragma 2.8, read a value 6.2, rendezvous 9.5, simple name 3.1 4.1, task 9, type 3.3, update a value 6.2, variable 3.2.1 12

9.12 Example of Tasking

1 The following example defines a buffering task to smooth variations between the speed of output of a producing task and the speed of input of some consuming task. For instance, the producing task may contain the statements

2
```
loop
   --  produce the next character CHAR
   BUFFER.WRITE(CHAR);
   exit when CHAR = ASCII.EOT;
end loop;
```

3 and the consuming task may contain the statements

4
```
loop
   BUFFER.READ(CHAR);
   --  consume the character CHAR
   exit when CHAR = ASCII.EOT;
end loop;
```

5 The buffering task contains an internal pool of characters processed in a round-robin fashion. The pool has two indices, an IN_INDEX denoting the space for the next input character and an OUT_INDEX denoting the space for the next output character.

6
```
task BUFFER is
   entry READ  (C : out  CHARACTER);
   entry WRITE (C : in   CHARACTER);
end;

task body BUFFER is
   POOL_SIZE  : constant INTEGER := 100;
   POOL       : array(1 .. POOL_SIZE) of CHARACTER;
   COUNT      : INTEGER range 0 .. POOL_SIZE := 0;
   IN_INDEX, OUT_INDEX : INTEGER range 1 .. POOL_SIZE := 1;
begin
   loop
      select
         when COUNT < POOL_SIZE =>
            accept WRITE(C : in CHARACTER) do
               POOL(IN_INDEX) := C;
            end;
            IN_INDEX  := IN_INDEX mod POOL_SIZE + 1;
            COUNT     := COUNT + 1;
      or when COUNT > 0 =>
            accept READ(C : out CHARACTER) do
               C := POOL(OUT_INDEX);
            end;
            OUT_INDEX  := OUT_INDEX mod POOL_SIZE + 1;
            COUNT      := COUNT - 1;
      or
         terminate;
      end select;
   end loop;
end BUFFER;
```

11. Exceptions

This chapter defines the facilities for dealing with errors or other exceptional situations that arise during program execution. Such a situation is called an *exception*. To *raise* an exception is to abandon normal program execution so as to draw attention to the fact that the corresponding situation has arisen. Executing some actions, in response to the arising of an exception, is called *handling* the exception. 1

An exception declaration declares a name for an exception. An exception can be raised by a raise statement, or it can be raised by another statement or operation that *propagates* the exception. When an exception arises, control can be transferred to a user-provided exception handler at the end of a block statement or at the end of the body of a subprogram, package, or task unit. 2

References: block statement 5.6, error situation 1.6, exception handler 11.2, name 4.1, package body 7.1, propagation of an exception 11.4.1 11.4.2, raise statement 11.3, subprogram body 6.3, task body 9.1 3

11.1 Exception Declarations

An exception declaration declares a name for an exception. The name of an exception can only be used in raise statements, exception handlers, and renaming declarations. 1

exception_declaration ::= identifier_list : **exception**; 2

An exception declaration with several identifiers is equivalent to a sequence of single exception declarations, as explained in section 3.2. Each single exception declaration declares a name for a different exception. In particular, if a generic unit includes an exception declaration, the exception declarations implicitly generated by different instantiations of the generic unit refer to distinct exceptions (but all have the same identifier). The particular exception denoted by an exception name is determined at compilation time and is the same regardless of how many times the exception declaration is elaborated. Hence, if an exception declaration occurs in a recursive subprogram, the exception name denotes the same exception for all invocations of the recursive subprogram. 3

The following exceptions are predefined in the language; they are raised when the situations described are detected. 4

CONSTRAINT_ERROR This exception is raised in any of the following situations: upon an attempt to violate a range constraint, an index constraint, or a discriminant constraint; upon an attempt to use a record component that does not exist for the current discriminant values; and upon an attempt to use a selected component, an indexed component, a slice, or an attribute, of an object designated by an access value, if the object does not exist because the access value is null. 5

6 NUMERIC_ERROR — This exception is raised by the execution of a predefined numeric operation that cannot deliver a correct result (within the declared accuracy for real types); this includes the case where an implementation uses a predefined numeric operation for the execution, evaluation, or elaboration of some construct. The rules given in section 4.5.7 define the cases in which an implementation is not required to raise this exception when such an error situation arises; see also section 11.6.

7 PROGRAM_ERROR — This exception is raised upon an attempt to call a subprogram, to activate a task, or to elaborate a generic instantiation, if the body of the corresponding unit has not yet been elaborated. This exception is also raised if the end of a function is reached (see 6.5); or during the execution of a selective wait that has no else part, if this execution determines that all alternatives are closed (see 9.7.1). Finally, depending on the implementation, this exception may be raised upon an attempt to execute an action that is erroneous, and for incorrect order dependences (see 1.6).

8 STORAGE_ERROR — This exception is raised in any of the following situations: when the dynamic storage allocated to a task is exceeded; during the evaluation of an allocator, if the space available for the collection of allocated objects is exhausted; or during the elaboration of a declarative item, or during the execution of a subprogram call, if storage is not sufficient.

9 TASKING_ERROR — This exception is raised when exceptions arise during intertask communication (see 9 and 11.5).

Note:

10 The situations described above can arise without raising the corresponding exceptions, if the pragma SUPPRESS has been used to give permission to omit the corresponding checks (see 11.7).

11 *Examples of user-defined exception declarations:*

```
SINGULAR   : exception;
ERROR      : exception;
OVERFLOW, UNDERFLOW : exception;
```

12 *References:* access value 3.8, collection 3.8, declaration 3.1, exception 11, exception handler 11.2, generic body 12.2, generic instantiation 12.3, generic unit 12, identifier 2.3, implicit declaration 12.3, instantiation 12.3, name 4.1, object 3.2, raise statement 11.3, real type 3.5.6, record component 3.7, return statement 5.8, subprogram 6, subprogram body 6.3, task 9, task body 9.1

13 *Constraint_error exception contexts:* aggregate 4.3.1 4.3.2, allocator 4.8, assignment statement 5.2 5.2.1, constraint 3.3.2, discrete type attribute 3.5.5, discriminant constraint 3.7.2, elaboration of a generic formal parameter 12.3.1 12.3.2 12.3.4 12.3.5, entry index 9.5, exponentiating operator 4.5.6, index constraint 3.6.1, indexed component 4.1.1, logical operator 4.5.1, null access value 3.8, object declaration 3.2.1, parameter association 6.4.1, qualified expression 4.7, range constraint 3.5, selected component 4.1.3, slice 4.1.2, subtype indication 3.3.2, type conversion 4.6

14 *Numeric_error exception contexts:* discrete type attribute 3.5.5, implicit conversion 3.5.4 3.5.6 4.6, numeric operation 3.5.5 3.5.8 3.5.10, operator of a numeric type 4.5 4.5.7

15 *Program_error exception contexts:* collection 3.8, elaboration 3.9, elaboration check 3.9 7.3 9.3 12.2, erroneous 1.6, incorrect order dependence 1.6, leaving a function 6.5, selective wait 9.7.1

Storage_error exception contexts: allocator 4.8 16

Tasking error exception contexts: abort statement 9.10, entry call 9.5 9.7.2 9.7.3, exceptions during task communication 11.5, task activation 9.3 17

11.2 Exception Handlers

The response to one or more exceptions is specified by an exception handler. 1

2

```
exception_handler ::=
   when exception_choice {| exception_choice} =>
      sequence_of_statements

exception_choice ::= exception_name | others
```

An exception handler occurs in a construct that is either a block statement or the body of a subprogram, package, task unit, or generic unit. Such a construct will be called a *frame* in this chapter. In each case the syntax of a frame that has exception handlers includes the following part: 3

4

```
begin
    sequence_of_statements
exception
    exception_handler
   { exception_handler}
end
```

The exceptions denoted by the exception names given as exception choices of a frame must all be distinct. The exception choice **others** is only allowed for the last exception handler of a frame and as its only exception choice; it stands for all exceptions not listed in previous handlers of the frame, including exceptions whose names are not visible at the place of the exception handler. 5

The exception handlers of a frame handle exceptions that are raised by the execution of the sequence of statements of the frame. The exceptions handled by a given exception handler are those named by the corresponding exception choices. 6

Example: 7

```
begin
   --  sequence of statements
exception
   when SINGULAR | NUMERIC_ERROR =>
      PUT(" MATRIX IS SINGULAR ");
   when others =>
      PUT(" FATAL ERROR ");
      raise ERROR;
end;
```

Note:

The same kinds of statement are allowed in the sequence of statements of each exception handler as are allowed in the sequence of statements of the frame. For example, a return statement is allowed in a handler within a function body. 8

9 *References:* block statement 5.6, declarative part 3.9, exception 11, exception handling 11.4, function body 6.3, generic body 12.2, generic unit 12.1, name 4.1, package body 7.1, raise statement 11.3, return statement 5.8, sequence of statements 5.1, statement 5, subprogram body 6.3, task body 9.1, task unit 9 9.1, visibility 8.3

11.3 Raise Statements

1 A raise statement raises an exception.

2 raise_statement ::= **raise** [*exception*_name];

3 For the execution of a raise statement with an exception name, the named exception is raised. A raise statement without an exception name is only allowed within an exception handler (but not within the sequence of statements of a subprogram, package, task unit, or generic unit, enclosed by the handler); it raises again the exception that caused transfer to the innermost enclosing handler.

4 *Examples:*

```
raise SINGULAR;
raise NUMERIC_ERROR;    --  explicitly raising a predefined exception

raise;                  --  only within an exception handler
```

5 *References:* exception 11, generic unit 12, name 4.1, package 7, sequence of statements 5.1, subprogram 6, task unit 9

11.4 Exception Handling

1 When an exception is raised, normal program execution is abandoned and control is transferred to an exception handler. The selection of this handler depends on whether the exception is raised during the execution of statements or during the elaboration of declarations.

2 *References:* declaration 3.1, elaboration 3.1 3.9, exception 11, exception handler 11.2, raising of exceptions 11.3, statement 5

11.4.1 Exceptions Raised During the Execution of Statements

1 The handling of an exception raised by the execution of a sequence of statements depends on whether the innermost frame or accept statement that encloses the sequence of statements is a frame or an accept statement. The case where an accept statement is innermost is described in section 11.5. The case where a frame is innermost is presented here.

Different actions take place, depending on whether or not this frame has a handler for the exception, and on whether the exception is raised in the sequence of statements of the frame or in that of an exception handler. 2

If an exception is raised in the sequence of statements of a frame that has a handler for the exception, execution of the sequence of statements of the frame is abandoned and control is transferred to the exception handler. The execution of the sequence of statements of the handler completes the execution of the frame (or its elaboration if the frame is a package body). 3

If an exception is raised in the sequence of statements of a frame that does not have a handler for the exception, execution of this sequence of statements is abandoned. The next action depends on the nature of the frame: 4

(a) For a subprogram body, the same exception is raised again at the point of call of the subprogram, unless the subprogram is the main program itself, in which case execution of the main program is abandoned. 5

(b) For a block statement, the same exception is raised again immediately after the block statement (that is, within the innermost enclosing frame or accept statement). 6

(c) For a package body that is a declarative item, the same exception is raised again immediately after this declarative item (within the enclosing declarative part). If the package body is that of a subunit, the exception is raised again at the place of the corresponding body stub. If the package is a library unit, execution of the main program is abandoned. 7

(d) For a task body, the task becomes completed. 8

An exception that is raised again (as in the above cases (a), (b), and (c)) is said to be *propagated*, either by the execution of the subprogram, the execution of the block statement, or the elaboration of the package body. No propagation takes place in the case of a task body. If the frame is a subprogram or a block statement and if it has dependent tasks, the propagation of an exception takes place only after termination of the dependent tasks. 9

Finally, if an exception is raised in the sequence of statements of an exception handler, execution of this sequence of statements is abandoned. Subsequent actions (including propagation, if any) are as in the cases (a) to (d) above, depending on the nature of the frame. 10

Example: 11

```
function FACTORIAL (N : POSITIVE) return FLOAT is
begin
   if N = 1 then
      return 1.0;
   else
      return FLOAT(N) * FACTORIAL(N-1);
   end if;
exception
   when NUMERIC_ERROR => return FLOAT'SAFE_LARGE;
end FACTORIAL;
```

If the multiplication raises NUMERIC_ERROR, then FLOAT'SAFE_LARGE is returned by the handler. This value will cause further NUMERIC_ERROR exceptions to be raised by the evaluation of the expression in each of the remaining invocations of the function, so that for large values of N the function will ultimately return the value FLOAT'SAFE_LARGE. 12

13 *Example:*

```
procedure P is
   ERROR : exception;
   procedure R;

   procedure Q is
   begin
      R;
      ...                 -- error situation (2)
   exception
      ...
      when ERROR =>       -- handler E2
      ...
   end Q;

   procedure R is
   begin
      ...                 -- error situation (3)
   end R;

begin
   ...                    -- error situation (1)
   Q;
   ...
exception
   ...
   when ERROR =>          -- handler E1
   ...
end P;
```

14 The following situations can arise:

15 (1) If the exception ERROR is raised in the sequence of statements of the outer procedure P, the handler E1 provided within P is used to complete the execution of P.

16 (2) If the exception ERROR is raised in the sequence of statements of Q, the handler E2 provided within Q is used to complete the execution of Q. Control will be returned to the point of call of Q upon completion of the handler.

17 (3) If the exception ERROR is raised in the body of R, called by Q, the execution of R is abandoned and the same exception is raised in the body of Q. The handler E2 is then used to complete the execution of Q, as in situation (2).

18 Note that in the third situation, the exception raised in R results in (indirectly) transferring control to a handler that is part of Q and hence not enclosed by R. Note also that if a handler were provided within R for the exception choice **others**, situation (3) would cause execution of this handler, rather than direct termination of R.

19 Lastly, if ERROR had been declared in R, rather than in P, the handlers E1 and E2 could not provide an explicit handler for ERROR since this identifier would not be visible within the bodies of P and Q. In situation (3), the exception could however be handled in Q by providing a handler for the exception choice **others**.

Notes:

The language does not define what happens when the execution of the main program is abandoned after an unhandled exception. 20

The predefined exceptions are those that can be propagated by the basic operations and the predefined operators. 21

The case of a frame that is a generic unit is already covered by the rules for subprogram and package bodies, since the sequence of statements of such a frame is not executed but is the template for the corresponding sequences of statements of the subprograms or packages obtained by generic instantiation. 22

References: accept statement 9.5, basic operation 3.3.3, block statement 5.6, body stub 10.2, completion 9.4, declarative item 3.9, declarative part 3.9, dependent task 9.4, elaboration 3.1 3.9, exception 11, exception handler 11.2, frame 11.2, generic instantiation 12.3, generic unit 12, library unit 10.1, main program 10.1, numeric_error exception 11.1, package 7, package body 7.1, predefined operator 4.5, procedure 6.1, sequence of statements 5.1, statement 5, subprogram 6, subprogram body 6.3, subprogram call 6.4, subunit 10.2, task 9, task body 9.1 23

11.4.2 Exceptions Raised During the Elaboration of Declarations

If an exception is raised during the elaboration of the declarative part of a given frame, this elaboration is abandoned. The next action depends on the nature of the frame: 1

(a) For a subprogram body, the same exception is raised again at the point of call of the subprogram, unless the subprogram is the main program itself, in which case execution of the main program is abandoned. 2

(b) For a block statement, the same exception is raised again immediately after the block statement. 3

(c) For a package body that is a declarative item, the same exception is raised again immediately after this declarative item, in the enclosing declarative part. If the package body is that of a subunit, the exception is raised again at the place of the corresponding body stub. If the package is a library unit, execution of the main program is abandoned. 4

(d) For a task body, the task becomes completed, and the exception TASKING_ERROR is raised at the point of activation of the task, as explained in section 9.3. 5

Similarly, if an exception is raised during the elaboration of either a package declaration or a task declaration, this elaboration is abandoned; the next action depends on the nature of the declaration. 6

(e) For a package declaration or a task declaration, that is a declarative item, the exception is raised again immediately after the declarative item in the enclosing declarative part or package specification. For the declaration of a library package, the execution of the main program is abandoned. 7

An exception that is raised again (as in the above cases (a), (b), (c) and (e)) is said to be *propagated*, either by the execution of the subprogram or block statement, or by the elaboration of the package declaration, task declaration, or package body. 8

9 *Example of an exception in the declarative part of a block statement (case (b)):*

```
procedure P is
  ...
begin
  declare
    N : INTEGER := F;     --  the function F may raise ERROR
  begin
    ...
  exception
    when ERROR =>         --  handler E1
  end;
  ...
exception
  when ERROR =>           --  handler E2
end P;

--  if the exception ERROR is raised in the declaration of N, it is handled by E2
```

10 *References:* activation 9.3, block statement 5.6, body stub 10.2, completed task 9.4, declarative item 3.9, declarative part 3.9, elaboration 3.1 3.9, exception 11, frame 11.2, library unit 10.1, main program 10.1, package body 7.1, package declaration 7.1, package specification 7.1, subprogram 6, subprogram body 6.3, subprogram call 6.4, subunit 10.2, task 9, task body 9.1, task declaration 9.1, tasking_error exception 11.1

11.5 Exceptions Raised During Task Communication

1 An exception can be propagated to a task communicating, or attempting to communicate, with another task. An exception can also be propagated to a calling task if the exception is raised during a rendezvous.

2 When a task calls an entry of another task, the exception TASKING_ERROR is raised in the calling task, at the place of the call, if the called task is completed before accepting the entry call or is already completed at the time of the call.

3 A rendezvous can be completed abnormally in two cases:

4 (a) When an exception is raised within an accept statement, but not handled within an inner frame. In this case, the execution of the accept statement is abandoned and the same exception is raised again immediately after the accept statement within the called task; the exception is also propagated to the calling task at the point of the entry call.

5 (b) When the task containing the accept statement is completed abnormally as the result of an abort statement. In this case, the exception TASKING_ERROR is raised in the calling task at the point of the entry call.

6 On the other hand, if a task issuing an entry call becomes abnormal (as the result of an abort statement) no exception is raised in the called task. If the rendezvous has not yet started, the entry call is cancelled. If the rendezvous is in progress, it completes normally, and the called task is unaffected.

References: abnormal task 9.10, abort statement 9.10, accept statement 9.5, completed task 9.4, entry call 9.5, exception 11, frame 11.2, rendezvous 9.5, task 9, task termination 9.4, tasking_error exception 11.1 7

11.6 Exceptions and Optimization

The purpose of this section is to specify the conditions under which an implementation is allowed to perform certain actions either earlier or later than specified by other rules of the language. 1

In general, when the language rules specify an order for certain actions (the *canonical order*), an implementation may only use an alternative order if it can guarantee that the effect of the program is not changed by the reordering. In particular, no exception should arise for the execution of the reordered program if none arises for the execution of the program in the canonical order. When, on the other hand, the order of certain actions is not defined by the language, any order can be used by the implementation. (For example, the arguments of a predefined operator can be evaluated in any order since the rules given in section 4.5 do not require a specific order of evaluation.) 2

Additional freedom is left to an implementation for reordering actions involving predefined operations that are either predefined operators or basic operations other than assignments. This freedom is left, as defined below, even in the case where the execution of these predefined operations may propagate a (predefined) exception: 3

(a) For the purpose of establishing whether the same effect is obtained by the execution of certain actions in the canonical and in an alternative order, it can be assumed that none of the predefined operations invoked by these actions propagates a (predefined) exception, provided that the two following requirements are met by the alternative order: first, an operation must not be invoked in the alternative order if it is not invoked in the canonical order; second, for each operation, the innermost enclosing frame or accept statement must be the same in the alternative order as in the canonical order, and the same exception handlers must apply. 4

(b) Within an expression, the association of operators with operands is specified by the syntax. However, for a sequence of predefined operators of the same precedence level (and in the absence of parentheses imposing a specific association), any association of operators with operands is allowed if it satisfies the following requirement: an integer result must be equal to that given by the canonical left-to-right order; a real result must belong to the result model interval defined for the canonical left-to-right order (see 4.5.7). Such a reordering is allowed even if it may remove an exception, or introduce a further predefined exception. 5

Similarly, additional freedom is left to an implementation for the evaluation of numeric simple expressions. For the evaluation of a predefined operation, an implementation is allowed to use the operation of a type that has a range wider than that of the base type of the operands, provided that this delivers the exact result (or a result within the declared accuracy, in the case of a real type), even if some intermediate results lie outside the range of the base type. The exception NUMERIC_ERROR need not be raised in such a case. In particular, if the numeric expression is an operand of a predefined relational operator, the exception NUMERIC_ERROR need not be raised by the evaluation of the relation, provided that the correct BOOLEAN result is obtained. 6

A predefined operation need not be invoked at all, if its only possible effect is to propagate a predefined exception. Similarly, a predefined operation need not be invoked if the removal of subsequent operations by the above rule renders this invocation ineffective. 7

Notes:

8 Rule (b) applies to predefined operators but not to the short-circuit control forms.

9 The expression SPEED < 300_000.0 can be replaced by TRUE if the value 300_000.0 lies outside the base type of SPEED, even though the implicit conversion of the numeric literal would raise the exception NUMERIC_ERROR.

10 *Example:*

```
declare
   N : INTEGER;
begin
   N := 0;                      -- (1)
   for J in 1 .. 10 loop
      N := N + J**A(K);         -- A and K are global variables
   end loop;
   PUT(N);
exception
   when others => PUT("Some error arose"); PUT(N);
end;
```

11 The evaluation of A(K) may be performed before the loop, and possibly immediately before the assignment statement (1) even if this evaluation can raise an exception. Consequently, within the exception handler, the value of N is either the undefined initial value or a value later assigned. On the other hand, the evaluation of A(K) cannot be moved before **begin** since an exception would then be handled by a different handler. For this reason, the initialization of N in the declaration itself would exclude the possibility of having an undefined initial value of N in the handler.

12 *References:* accept statement 9.5, accuracy of real operations 4.5.7, assignment 5.2, base type 3.3, basic operation 3.3.3, conversion 4.6, error situation 11, exception 11, exception handler 11.2, frame 11.2, numeric_error exception 11.1, predefined operator 4.5, predefined subprogram 8.6, propagation of an exception 11.4, real type 3.5.6, undefined value 3.2.1

11.7 Suppressing Checks

1 The presence of a SUPPRESS pragma gives permission to an implementation to omit certain run-time checks. The form of this pragma is as follows:

```
pragma SUPPRESS (identifier [, [ON =>] name]);
```

2 The identifier is that of the check that can be omitted. The name (if present) must be either a simple name or an expanded name and it must denote either an object, a type or subtype, a task unit, or a generic unit; alternatively the name can be a subprogram name, in which case it can stand for several visible overloaded subprograms.

A pragma SUPPRESS is only allowed immediately within a declarative part or immediately within a package specification. In the latter case, the only allowed form is with a name that denotes an entity (or several overloaded subprograms) declared immediately within the package specification. The permission to omit the given check extends from the place of the pragma to the end of the declarative region associated with the innermost enclosing block statement or program unit. For a pragma given in a package specification, the permission extends to the end of the scope of the named entity. 3

If the pragma includes a name, the permission to omit the given check is further restricted: it is given only for operations on the named object or on all objects of the base type of a named type or subtype; for calls of a named subprogram; for activations of tasks of the named task type; or for instantiations of the given generic unit. 4

The following checks correspond to situations in which the exception CONSTRAINT_ERROR may be raised; for these checks, the name (if present) must denote either an object or a type. 5

ACCESS_CHECK — When accessing a selected component, an indexed component, a slice, or an attribute, of an object designated by an access value, check that the access value is not null. 6

DISCRIMINANT_CHECK — Check that a discriminant of a composite value has the value imposed by a discriminant constraint. Also, when accessing a record component, check that it exists for the current discriminant values. 7

INDEX_CHECK — Check that the bounds of an array value are equal to the corresponding bounds of an index constraint. Also, when accessing a component of an array object, check for each dimension that the given index value belongs to the range defined by the bounds of the array object. Also, when accessing a slice of an array object, check that the given discrete range is compatible with the range defined by the bounds of the array object. 8

LENGTH_CHECK — Check that there is a matching component for each component of an array, in the case of array assignments, type conversions, and logical operators for arrays of boolean components. 9

RANGE_CHECK — Check that a value satisfies a range constraint. Also, for the elaboration of a subtype indication, check that the constraint (if present) is compatible with the type mark. Also, for an aggregate, check that an index or discriminant value belongs to the corresponding subtype. Finally, check for any constraint checks performed by a generic instantiation. 10

The following checks correspond to situations in which the exception NUMERIC_ERROR is raised. The only allowed names in the corresponding pragmas are names of numeric types. 11

DIVISION_CHECK — Check that the second operand is not zero for the operations /, **rem** and **mod**. 12

OVERFLOW_CHECK — Check that the result of a numeric operation does not overflow. 13

The following check corresponds to situations in which the exception PROGRAM_ERROR is raised. The only allowed names in the corresponding pragmas are names denoting task units, generic units, or subprograms. 14

ELABORATION_CHECK — When either a subprogram is called, a task activation is accomplished, or a generic instantiation is elaborated, check that the body of the corresponding unit has already been elaborated. 15

16 The following check corresponds to situations in which the exception STORAGE_ERROR is raised. The only allowed names in the corresponding pragmas are names denoting access types, task units, or subprograms.

17 STORAGE_CHECK — Check that execution of an allocator does not require more space than is available for a collection. Check that the space available for a task or subprogram has not been exceeded.

18 If an error situation arises in the absence of the corresponding run-time checks, the execution of the program is erroneous (the results are not defined by the language).

19 *Examples:*

```
pragma SUPPRESS(RANGE_CHECK);
pragma SUPPRESS(INDEX_CHECK, ON => TABLE);
```

Notes:

20 For certain implementations, it may be impossible or too costly to suppress certain checks. The corresponding SUPPRESS pragma can be ignored. Hence, the occurrence of such a pragma within a given unit does not guarantee that the corresponding exception will not arise; the exceptions may also be propagated by called units.

21 *References:* access type 3.8, access value 3.8, activation 9.3, aggregate 4.3, allocator 4.8, array 3.6, attribute 4.1.4, block statement 5.6, collection 3.8, compatible 3.3.2, component of an array 3.6, component of a record 3.7, composite type 3.3, constraint 3.3, constraint_error exception 11.1, declarative part 3.9, designate 3.8, dimension 3.6, discrete range 3.6, discriminant 3.7.1, discriminant constraint 3.7.2, elaboration 3.1 3.9, erroneous 1.6, error situation 11, expanded name 4.1.3, generic body 11.1, generic instantiation 12.3, generic unit 12, identifier 2.3, index 3.6, index constraint 3.6.1, indexed component 4.1.1, null access value 3.8, numeric operation 3.5.5 3.5.8 3.5.10, numeric type 3.5, numeric_error exception 11.1, object 3.2, operation 3.3.3, package body 7.1, package specification 7.1, pragma 2.8, program_error exception 11.1, program unit 6, propagation of an exception 11.4, range constraint 3.5, record type 3.7, simple name 4.1, slice 4.1.2, subprogram 6, subprogram body 6.3, subprogram call 6.4, subtype 3.3, subunit 10.2, task 9, task body 9.1, task type 9.1, task unit 9, type 3.3, type mark 3.3.2

E. Syntax Summary

[This syntax summary is not part of the standard definition of the Ada programming language.]

2.1

```
graphic_character ::= basic_graphic_character
   | lower_case_letter | other_special_character

basic_graphic_character ::=
      upper_case_letter | digit
    | special_character | space_character

basic_character ::=
      basic_graphic_character | format_effector
```

2.3

```
identifier ::=
   letter {[underline] letter_or_digit}

letter_or_digit ::= letter | digit

letter ::= upper_case_letter | lower_case_letter
```

2.4

```
numeric_literal ::= decimal_literal | based_literal
```

2.4.1

```
decimal_literal ::= integer [.integer] [exponent]

integer ::= digit {[underline] digit}

exponent ::= E [+] integer | E - integer
```

2.4.2

```
based_literal ::=
   base # based_integer [.based_integer] # [exponent]

base ::= integer

based_integer ::=
   extended_digit {[underline] extended_digit}

extended_digit ::= digit | letter
```

2.5

```
character_literal ::= 'graphic_character'
```

2.6

```
string_literal ::= "{graphic_character}"
```

2.8

```
pragma ::=
   pragma identifier [(argument_association
                        {, argument_association})];

argument_association ::=
      [argument_identifier =>] name
    | [argument_identifier =>] expression
```

3.1

```
basic_declaration ::=
      object_declaration        | number_declaration
    | type_declaration          | subtype_declaration
    | subprogram_declaration    | package_declaration
    | task_declaration          | generic_declaration
    | exception_declaration     | generic_instantiation
    | renaming_declaration      | deferred_constant_declaration
```

3.2

```
object_declaration ::=
      identifier_list : [constant] subtype_indication [:= expression];
    | identifier_list : [constant] constrained_array_definition
                                                   [:= expression];

number_declaration ::=
      identifier_list : constant := universal_static_expression;

identifier_list ::= identifier {, identifier}
```

3.3.1

```
type_declaration ::= full_type_declaration
   | incomplete_type_declaration | private_type_declaration

full_type_declaration ::=
 type identifier [discriminant_part] is type_definition;

type_definition ::=
      enumeration_type_definition | integer_type_definition
    | real_type_definition        | array_type_definition
    | record_type_definition      | access_type_definition
    | derived_type_definition
```

3.3.2

```
subtype_declaration ::=
   subtype identifier is subtype_indication;

subtype_indication ::= type_mark [constraint]

type_mark ::= type_name | subtype_name

constraint ::=
      range_constraint       | floating_point_constraint
    | fixed_point_constraint | index_constraint
    | discriminant_constraint
```

3.4

```
derived_type_definition ::= new subtype_indication
```

3.5

```
range_constraint ::= range range

range ::= range_attribute
   | simple_expression .. simple_expression
```

3.5.1

enumeration_type_definition ::=
(enumeration_literal_specification
{, enumeration_literal_specification})

enumeration_literal_specification ::= enumeration_literal

enumeration_literal ::= identifier | character_literal

3.5.4

integer_type_definition ::= range_constraint

3.5.6

real_type_definition ::=
floating_point_constraint | fixed_point_constraint

3.5.7

floating_point_constraint ::=
floating_accuracy_definition [range_constraint]

floating_accuracy_definition ::=
digits *static*_simple_expression

3.5.9

fixed_point_constraint ::=
fixed_accuracy_definition [range_constraint]

fixed_accuracy_definition ::=
delta *static*_simple_expression

3.6

array_type_definition ::=
unconstrained_array_definition | constrained_array_definition

unconstrained_array_definition ::=
array(index_subtype_definition {, index_subtype_definition}) **of**
*component*_subtype_indication

constrained_array_definition ::=
array index_constraint **of** *component*_subtype_indication

index_subtype_definition ::= type_mark **range** <>

index_constraint ::= (discrete_range {, discrete_range})

discrete_range ::= *discrete*_subtype_indication | range

3.7

record_type_definition ::=
record
component_list
end record

component_list ::=
component_declaration {component_declaration}
| {component_declaration} variant_part
| **null**;

component_declaration ::=
identifier_list : component_subtype_definition [:= expression];

component_subtype_definition ::= subtype_indication

3.7.1

discriminant_part ::=
(discriminant_specification {; discriminant_specification})

discriminant_specification ::=
identifier_list : type_mark [:= expression]

3.7.2

discriminant_constraint ::=
(discriminant_association {, discriminant_association})

discriminant_association ::=
[*discriminant*_simple_name {| *discriminant*_simple_name} =>]
expression

3.7.3

variant_part ::=
case *discriminant*_simple_name **is**
variant
{variant}
end case;

variant ::=
when choice {| choice} =>
component_list

choice ::= simple_expression
| discrete_range | **others** | *component*_simple_name

3.8

access_type_definition ::= **access** subtype_indication

3.8.1

incomplete_type_declaration ::=
type identifier [discriminant_part];

3.9

declarative_part ::=
{basic_declarative_item} {later_declarative_item}

basic_declarative_item ::= basic_declaration
| representation_clause | use_clause

later_declarative_item ::= body
| subprogram_declaration | package_declaration
| task_declaration | generic_declaration
| use_clause | generic_instantiation

body ::= proper_body | body_stub

proper_body ::=
subprogram_body | package_body | task_body

4.1

```
name ::= simple_name
  | character_literal      | operator_symbol
  | indexed_component      | slice
  | selected_component     | attribute

simple_name ::= identifier

prefix ::= name | function_call
```

4.1.1

```
indexed_component ::= prefix(expression {, expression})
```

4.1.2

```
slice ::= prefix(discrete_range)
```

4.1.3

```
selected_component ::= prefix.selector

selector ::= simple_name
  | character_literal | operator_symbol | all
```

4.1.4

```
attribute ::= prefix'attribute_designator

attribute_designator ::=
  simple_name [(universal_static_expression)]
```

4.3

```
aggregate ::=
  (component_association {, component_association})

component_association ::=
  [choice {| choice} => ] expression
```

4.4

```
expression ::=
    relation {and relation}  | relation {and then relation}
  | relation {or relation}   | relation {or else relation}
  | relation {xor relation}

relation ::=
    simple_expression [relational_operator simple_expression]
  | simple_expression [not] in range
  | simple_expression [not] in type_mark

simple_expression ::=
  [unary_adding_operator] term {binary_adding_operator term}

term ::= factor {multiplying_operator factor}

factor ::= primary [** primary] | abs primary | not primary

primary ::=
    numeric_literal | null | aggregate | string_literal
  | name | allocator | function_call | type_conversion
  | qualified_expression | (expression)
```

4.5

```
logical_operator ::= and | or | xor

relational_operator ::= = | /= | < | <= | > | >=

binary_adding_operator ::= + | - | &

unary_adding_operator ::= + | -

multiplying_operator ::= * | / | mod | rem

highest_precedence_operator ::= ** | abs | not
```

4.6

```
type_conversion ::= type_mark(expression)
```

4.7

```
qualified_expression ::=
  type_mark'(expression) | type_mark'aggregate
```

4.8

```
allocator ::=
  new subtype_indication | new qualified_expression
```

5.1

```
sequence_of_statements ::= statement {statement}

statement ::=
  {label} simple_statement | {label} compound_statement

simple_statement ::= null_statement
  | assignment_statement   | procedure_call_statement
  | exit_statement         | return_statement
  | goto_statement         | entry_call_statement
  | delay_statement        | abort_statement
  | raise_statement        | code_statement

compound_statement ::=
    if_statement       | case_statement
  | loop_statement     | block_statement
  | accept_statement   | select_statement

label ::= <<label_simple_name>>

null_statement ::= null;
```

5.2

```
assignment_statement ::=
  variable_name := expression;
```

5.3

```
if_statement ::=
    if condition then
      sequence_of_statements
   {elsif condition then
      sequence_of_statements}
   [else
      sequence_of_statements]
    end if;

condition ::= boolean_expression
```

5.4

```
case_statement ::=
   case expression is
      case_statement_alternative
     {case_statement_alternative}
   end case;

case_statement_alternative ::=
   when choice {| choice } =>
      sequence_of_statements
```

5.5

```
loop_statement ::=
   [loop_simple_name:]
      [iteration_scheme] loop
         sequence_of_statements
      end loop [loop_simple_name];

iteration_scheme ::= while condition
   | for loop_parameter_specification

loop_parameter_specification ::=
   identifier in [reverse] discrete_range
```

5.6

```
block_statement ::=
   [block_simple_name:]
      [declare
            declarative_part]
       begin
            sequence_of_statements
      [exception
            exception_handler
           {exception_handler}]
       end [block_simple_name];
```

5.7

```
exit_statement ::=
   exit [loop_name] [when condition];
```

5.8

```
return_statement ::= return [expression];
```

5.9

```
goto_statement ::= goto label_name;
```

6.1

```
subprogram_declaration ::= subprogram_specification;

subprogram_specification ::=
      procedure identifier [formal_part]
   |  function designator [formal_part] return type_mark

designator ::= identifier | operator_symbol

operator_symbol ::= string_literal

formal_part ::=
   (parameter_specification {; parameter_specification})

parameter_specification ::=
   identifier_list : mode type_mark [:= expression]

mode ::= [in] | in out | out
```

6.3

```
subprogram_body ::=
    subprogram_specification is
        [declarative_part]
    begin
        sequence_of_statements
   [exception
        exception_handler
       {exception_handler}]
    end [designator];
```

6.4

```
procedure_call_statement ::=
   procedure_name [actual_parameter_part];

function_call ::=
   function_name [actual_parameter_part]

actual_parameter_part ::=
   (parameter_association {, parameter_association})

parameter_association ::=
   [formal_parameter =>] actual_parameter

formal_parameter ::= parameter_simple_name

actual_parameter ::=
   expression | variable_name | type_mark(variable_name)
```

7.1

```
package_declaration ::= package_specification;

package_specification ::=
    package identifier is
      {basic_declarative_item}
   [private
      {basic_declarative_item}]
    end [package_simple_name]

package_body ::=
    package body package_simple_name is
        [declarative_part]
   [begin
        sequence_of_statements
   [exception
        exception_handler
       {exception_handler}]]
    end [package_simple_name];
```

7.4

```
private_type_declaration ::=
   type identifier [discriminant_part] is [limited] private;

deferred_constant_declaration ::=
   identifier_list : constant type_mark;
```

8.4

```
use_clause ::= use package_name {, package_name};
```

8.5

```
renaming_declaration ::=
      identifier : type_mark          renames object_name;
   |  identifier : exception          renames exception_name;
   |  package identifier              renames package_name;
   |  subprogram_specification        renames
                                      subprogram_or_entry_name;
```

9.1

```
task_declaration ::= task_specification;

task_specification ::=
  task [type] identifier [is
     {entry_declaration}
     {representation_clause}
  end [task_simple_name]]

task_body ::=
   task body task_simple_name is
       [ declarative_part]
   begin
       sequence_of_statements
  [ exception
       exception_handler
      { exception_handler}]
   end [task_simple_name];
```

9.5

```
entry_declaration ::=
  entry identifier [(discrete_range)] [formal_part];

entry_call_statement ::=
  entry_name [actual_parameter_part];

accept_statement ::=
  accept entry_simple_name [(entry_index)] [formal_part] [do
     sequence_of_statements
  end [entry_simple_name]];

entry_index ::= expression
```

9.6

```
delay_statement ::= delay simple_expression;
```

9.7

```
select_statement ::= selective_wait
  | conditional_entry_call | timed_entry_call
```

9.7.1

```
selective_wait ::=
    select
      select_alternative
   { or
      select_alternative}
   [ else
      sequence_of_statements]
    end select;

select_alternative ::=
  [ when condition =>]
     selective_wait_alternative

selective_wait_alternative ::= accept_alternative
  | delay_alternative | terminate_alternative

accept_alternative ::=
  accept_statement [sequence_of_statements]

delay_alternative ::=
  delay_statement [sequence_of_statements]

terminate_alternative ::= terminate;
```

9.7.2

```
conditional_entry_call ::=
   select
      entry_call_statement
    [ sequence_of_statements]
   else
      sequence_of_statements
   end select;
```

9.7.3

```
timed_entry_call ::=
   select
      entry_call_statement
    [ sequence_of_statements]
   or
      delay_alternative
   end select;
```

9.10

```
abort_statement ::= abort task_name {, task_name};
```

10.1

```
compilation ::= {compilation_unit}

compilation_unit ::=
     context_clause library_unit
   | context_clause secondary_unit

library_unit ::=
     subprogram_declaration  | package_declaration
   | generic_declaration     | generic_instantiation
   | subprogram_body

secondary_unit ::= library_unit_body | subunit

library_unit_body ::= subprogram_body | package_body
```

10.1.1

```
context_clause ::= {with_clause {use_clause}}

with_clause ::=
  with unit_simple_name {, unit_simple_name};
```

10.2

```
body_stub ::=
     subprogram_specification is separate;
   | package body package_simple_name is separate;
   | task body task_simple_name is separate;

subunit ::= separate (parent_unit_name) proper_body
```

11.1

```
exception_declaration ::= identifier_list : exception;
```

11.2

```
exception_handler ::=
  when exception_choice {| exception_choice} =>
     sequence_of_statements

exception_choice ::= exception_name | others
```

11.3

```
raise_statement ::= raise [exception_name];
```

12.1

```
generic_declaration ::= generic_specification;

generic_specification ::=
      generic_formal_part subprogram_specification
   |  generic_formal_part package_specification

generic_formal_part ::= generic {generic_parameter_declaration}

generic_parameter_declaration ::=
      identifier_list : [in [out]] type_mark [:= expression];
   |  type identifier is generic_type_definition;
   |  private_type_declaration
   |  with subprogram_specification [is name];
   |  with subprogram_specification [is <>];

generic_type_definition ::=
      (<>) | range <> | digits <> | delta <>
   |  array_type_definition | access_type_definition
```

12.3

```
generic_instantiation ::=
      package identifier is
         new generic_package_name [generic_actual_part];
   |  procedure identifier is
         new generic_procedure_name [generic_actual_part];
   |  function designator is
         new generic_function_name [generic_actual_part];

generic_actual_part ::=
   (generic_association {, generic_association})

generic_association ::=
   [generic_formal_parameter =>] generic_actual_parameter

generic_formal_parameter ::=
   parameter_simple_name | operator_symbol

generic_actual_parameter ::= expression | variable_name
   | subprogram_name | entry_name | type_mark
```

13.1

```
representation_clause ::=
      type_representation_clause | address_clause

type_representation_clause ::= length_clause
   |  enumeration_representation_clause
   |  record_representation_clause
```

13.2

```
length_clause ::= for attribute use simple_expression;
```

13.3

```
enumeration_representation_clause ::=
   for type_simple_name use aggregate;
```

13.4

```
record_representation_clause ::=
   for type_simple_name use
      record [alignment_clause]
         {component_clause}
      end record;

alignment_clause ::= at mod static_simple_expression;

component_clause ::=
   component_name at static_simple_expression
                  range static_range;
```

13.5

```
address_clause ::=
   for simple_name use at simple_expression;
```

13.8

```
code_statement ::= type_mark'record_aggregate;
```

Syntax Cross Reference

In the list given below each syntactic category is followed by the section number where it is defined. For example:

adding_operator 4.5

In addition, each syntactic category is followed by the names of other categories in whose definition it appears. For example, adding_operator appears in the definition of simple_expression:

adding_operator 4.5
  simple_expression 4.4

An ellipsis (...) is used when the syntactic category is not defined by a syntax rule. For example:

lower_case_letter ...

All uses of parentheses are combined in the term "()". The italicized prefixes used with some terms have been deleted here.

abort ...
  abort_statement 9.10

abort_statement 9.10
  simple_statement 5.1

abs ...
  factor 4.4
  highest_precedence_operator 4.5

accept ...
  accept_statement 9.5

accept_alternative 9.7.1
  selective_wait_alternative 9.7.1

accept_statement 9.5
  accept_alternative 9.7.1
  compound_statement 5.1

access ...
  access_type_definition 3.8

access_type_definition 3.8
  generic_type_definition 12.1
  type_definition 3.3.1

actual_parameter 6.4
  parameter_association 6.4

actual_parameter_part 6.4
  entry_call_statement 9.5
  function_call 6.4
  procedure_call_statement 6.4

address_clause 13.5
  representation_clause 13.1

aggregate 4.3
  code_statement 13.8
  enumeration_representation_clause 13.3
  primary 4.4
  qualified_expression 4.7

alignment_clause 13.4
  record_representation_clause 13.4

all ...
  selector 4.1.3

allocator 4.8
  primary 4.4

Index